ALL ABOUT
EARNINGS

Also by The Profit Advisors, Inc.:

The Profit Game: How to Play–How to Win
100 Ways to Win the Profit Game

All About Earnings

100 Ways to Profit in the New Economy

By Barry R. Schimel, CPA

Gary R. Kravitz and

Barry J. Friedman, CPA

CAPITAL
BOOKS, INC.

Sterling, Virginia

Published by
Capital Books, Inc.
P.O. Box 605,
Herndon, Virginia 20172-0605

ISBN 1-892123-48-7

Schimel, Barry R., 1941-
  All about earnings : 1000 ways to profit in the new economy / Barry R. Schimel, Gary R. Kravitz, and Barry J. Friedman.
    p. cm.
  ISBN 1-892123-48-7
    1. Business enterprises–Finance. 2. Strategic planning. 3. Management. I. Kravitz, Gary R. II. Friedman, Barry J. III. Title.

HG4026 .S2985 2001
658.15'5–dc21   2001025546

Printed in the United States of America on acid-free paper that meets the American National Standards Institute Z39-48 Standard.

First Edition

10 9 8 7 6 5 4 3 2 1

CONTENTS

*To all those who are passionate about making
a positive difference for their organizations.*

*This book is written to assist you in your quest to be
a winner in business, where the goal is "All About Earnings."*

ALL ABOUT EARNINGS

Whether the economy is good, bad, or indifferent, New or Old—the game of business is still "all about earnings." Why? Because the value of most companies is still based on earnings. Earnings are a significant component in determining the value of a closely held business when it is bought and sold. On Wall Street, earnings determine stock values (price earnings ratios)—especially when they go down or up. Nothing can bring a stock price down faster than when earnings go down, although for quite some time the market was very patient with bright new high techs and dot.coms with no earnings. Now that has changed dramatically.

After the greatest economic expansion in modern history, the year 2000 was the worst in NASDAQ history. Punished most severely were the investors and shareholders in companies with disappointing earnings or no earnings at all.

People who started out in business during this period had never experienced an economic downturn—until recently. For these people, the economic climate of the new millennium will bring some surprises. For those of us who have been in business for a long time, we know—it's always about earnings.

At the beginning of the new century, Montgomery Ward was forced to close 250 stores as well as ten distribution centers. Its 128-year-plus existence, one of the retail industry's longest, came to an end. Why? Because Ward's was not able to generate earnings. Hard to believe that this retailer whose sales were in excess of $2 billion had to lay off its 28,000 person workforce!

Sears & Roebuck was forced to close stores because they were not profitable.

Chrysler once earned more profit per vehicle than any other U.S. automobile manufacturer. It has now restructured its financial arrangements with dealers, closed factories, and terminated more than 20,000 employees. Why? Because of the profit drain on Daimler-Chrysler

More sales do not create profits—only more profitable sales. A client once said, "Sales feed egos and profits feed families." Where is the focus of your company?

When the economy is booming, the seeds of destruction could be sprouting, ready to burst into bloom. When the economy slows down markets shrink, and the margin for error becomes that much narrower. Planning for profit helps keep earnings up even when the economy turns down.

To achieve greater profitability, every employee in the organization must have, what we call, profit*ability*. As you'll read in Chapter 2, we define profit*ability* as the skills necessary to identify financial opportunities and the ability to turn the ideas into bottom line results. Do your employees go to work daily armed with the skills necessary to make a positive difference to your company's bottom line? Our experience is that all too often employees view their job as a function, not part of the bigger picture and not how they can help grow the bottom line.

As profit coaches, our job is to help proactive CEOs discover and achieve their companys' profit potential. We know that most owners and managers live in constant fear of what tomorrow will bring. What if your new product is so successful you can't produce enough of them? What if consumers stop buying?

What if someone sues your socks off? What if the plant equipment fails? What if you can't get the financing you need to continue to grow? What will a downturn in the economy do to your business? These are all real concerns.

In fact, what assurance do you ever have that your business will succeed? The answer is none unless you have a system in place, a plan, for generating continued profits, and employees who understand what business is about: profits.

That is why we developed the Profit Enhancement Process (PEP)—a revolutionary system for generating ideas for new profit from everyone in the organization and shaping, focusing, and implementing them to potentially add millions to your earnings.

We know this system works because it has already produced enormous bottom line results for hundreds of businesses in more than 70 different industries and not-for-profit organizations. Now it is your turn.

In Part I of this book, we introduce the basics of the Profit Enhancement Process (PEP). The mission of this revolutionary process is to dig out employees' and managers' new ideas for profit and to put them into a plan that the entire organization is committed to and will implement to meet your profit goals. We guarantee that it will change your thinking and the profitability of your entire organization.

In Part II of this book, we present you with our playbook of the best 100 profit-generating ideas we've developed with our business clients over the last twenty years. Use them with your management-turned-profit team to start the new profit ideas flowing. These profit strategies will increase sales and profit margins, reduce your overhead, attract new customers, improve cash flow, marshal the creative forces of your entire company to keep you improving and growing with the demands of the times, while adding hundreds of thousands, potentially millions to your bottom line.

There's no magic elixir that will maintain the health of a company forever, but there are strategies that businesses can use to remain competitive for sustained periods of time. And those companies that develop and execute a profit plan, as outlined in this book, will be able to take advantage of the surprises and beat their competition. Good, sound profit strategies work equally well in good times or bad.

The material in the second section of this book was originally published in Barry's book, *100 Ways to Prosper in Today's Economy* (Acropolis, 1994), updated in *100 Ways to Win The Profit Game*, and updated again here. These are battle-tested strategies for business success that work in any economy.

Read through the 100 ways, share them with your team, then identify those that will work for your organization. To make your work a little easier, there's a mini-action plan at the end of each of the 100 ways with space for you to jot down ideas that are generated as you read. These mini-plans also call for you to assign a priority or relative importance (1 to 3) for each profit strategy, designate an individual in your organization with a passion for implementing the recommendation (a profit champion), establish a date for action, and project a potential bottom line dollar effect for your organization.

At the end of the book you'll find The Profit Advisors' Master Plan. In the spaces provided, put in each of the strategies you identified earlier as you went through the book. When you've completed it, you'll have your own profit plan ready to bring hundreds of thousands, even millions, to your company's bottom line—not just this fiscal year, but for years to come, season after season. After all, it's "all about earnings."

So, start improving your profits right now. This book is only the beginning.

—The Profit Advisors, Inc.
Barry R. Schimel, CPA, Gary R. Kravitz, and Barry J. Friedman, CPA

Part I: The Profit Game
How to Play—How to Win

Business is the game.
The objective is to score profits.

In sports, players understand the rules for playing the game, know what's expected of them as team members, are coached and practice their skills, know how to score. Plus every successful sports team has strategies for winning, and everyone on the team learns what those strategies are. Players strive to reach their potential. Team members strive to maximize the score. They like playing because competing is exciting and it is fun to win.

In business, although people go to work every day, do they understand the big picture, its rules, or how to improve the score? Are they coached to maximize their skills and understand their role as a team member? Do they know the score, or even if their team is winning or losing? Have the players and profits reached their potential?

On Wall Street earnings are the greatest force that influence stock prices. The Year 2000 reminded us of this basic investment principle.

Part I is about playing the game of business—scoring profits for the benefit of everyone in the company as well as investors. It teaches how to score, be a winner, and develop greater profit*ability.*

Introduction

THE PROFIT OPTION

"Our goal is to make our company the most valuable and respected business on earth."

—Steve Case, chairman, AOL-Time Warner

When we first open a dialogue with business leaders, it's amazing how many of them tell us: "I really don't think there is anything more we could do to increase profits. We're doing everything we can, I'm sure."

Yet we know that owners and managers live in constant fear of what tomorrow will bring. What if your new product is so successful you can't produce enough of them? What's going to happen next to knock you off your perch? What if you lose customers? What if the plant equipment fails? What if someone sues your socks off? What if in ten or fifteen years you want to sell your firm and get your money out of it, and you don't have anyone who can operate at the same level you do? If the company has to "downsize," where will you be? What assurance do you have of continued—or any—success?

Without a system for generating continued profits, the answer to the last and most important question is...none.

Fortunately, many business owners have been savvy enough to find out more about the Profit Enhancement Process and have been willing to let us help them discover and achieve their unrealized profit potential. It's these partnerships that have turned into our most gratifying testimonials. This one is from Gilbert Carpel, CEO of Washington Express:

"I must admit that my personal expectations were not very high since we have, for three years, been aggressively and continuously seeking ways to improve our bottom line. I was, therefore, quite surprised that we were able to identify an additional $500,000 per year in unrealized profits."

We all know that profit is the fuel that powers a business. Profit fuels growth, rewards your shareholders and stakeholders, and ultimately determines the success or failure of your enterprise. Peter Lynch, the former all-star manager of Fidelity's Magellan Fund, has often proclaimed that earnings are the single most important factor in determining a stock's value and price. Profit is what gives a business opportunities, choices, and options. It's what provides funds for new acquisitions and for research and development of new products and services to add value to your business. It's what provides the cash for increasing salaries, bonuses and benefits; for training; for new technology and equipment; for reducing debt; for more effective marketing and promotion; and for enhancing working conditions. At the same time, it's what provides personal security. A company that is reaching for its profit potential is an exciting place to work. Everyone likes to be associated with a winner.

And when a company does reach its profit potential, everyone involved feels a sense of accomplishment, enhanced egos, heightened self-esteem, and a chance for personal gain. Owners get a greater return on their investment and reap the cash benefits from their financial risk-taking and hard work.

We all know it takes continued profits to build longevity into a business. Without a process for generating recurring profits, any business won't be around long. Even the healthiest firms go through difficult financial periods. Many fail. Forty-six percent of the companies that made the Fortune 500 in 1981 were gone from the list by 1991.

Employees at all levels share top management's fear. Tough economic times mean they could lose their jobs. They can't plan for the future. A company on shaky financial footing means everyone's focus becomes short-term survival rather than capturing long-term opportunities. We spend at least one third of our adult life working. This time can be enjoyable. But it takes sustainable profits.

Having established that a never-ending profit generating machine is imperative for your business's survival. Here's a question for you! Do you have a plan for a profit in place?

You've probably got a decent business plan. You certainly have a good marketing plan. You may even have a solid "exit plan." But, do you have an astute "profit maximizing plan"—a plan that locks in the extra money you should be making from your business?

How important is a Profit Plan? It's vital. In today's highly competitive environment, all companies are looking for ways to improve their processes and increase their profitability. Wall Street demands increased profitability continuously—or else stock prices tumble. That generally means taking a step back to make an honest appraisal of where you stand. That's why you need a Profit Plan. It's like the game plan for winning the Super Bowl. It's a plan that focuses everyone in the business on the bottom line—no matter what their job is. It's a plan for realizing the profit potential your business is capable of generating. In business, it's "The Plan" that assists you in winning the Profit Game.

In this book you're going to learn how to develop a realistic Profit Plan for your business and put it to work. You're going to discover how to...

- Provide a forum for generating exciting new profit ideas from your managers and employees all down the line;

- Put the best of these ideas into a Profit Plan the entire company is committed to;

- Put that "game plan" to work generating immediate and longer-term bottom-line results—all in harmony with your company's strategic goals and objectives;

- And, best of all, keep the profits rolling in— during good times and bad.

We're going to reveal to you the profit management system that has already produced enormous profit results for already profitable businesses—literally hundreds of them in more than 40 different industries so far, plus not-for-profit organizations. It's a system that has discovered hundreds of millions of dollars of previously unrealized profits for the companies that have implemented their Profit Plan, and it never stops generating new profit ideas that fuel their next level of business development. It's a system that delivers never-ending profits to those who manage it effectively.

We call this system the Profit Enhancement Process, PEP for short. And we liken it to the process that a great football team goes through to compete in and win the Super Bowl. We believe winning in the business world is just like winning on the football field. To win the Super Bowl, you need a great head coach—a motivator with a vision of what the entire team is capable of accomplishing. You need excellent, motivated assistant coaches who are experts in their areas and know the strengths and weaknesses of the competition and their players. You need an excellent team with a goal in sight, conditioned to produce maximum results and motivated to win. And you need a well-thought-out game plan everyone understands and is committed to.

Like the best coaches, you'll learn how to...

- Share responsibility for profitability with your management team (soon to be a Profit Team);
- Identify financial strategies which will increase sales, maximize profit margins, and control expenses;
- Establish measurable financial goals that will enhance profitability;
- Install a system of accountability and responsibility that produces positive financial performance;
- Implement practical and logical business strategies that will turn ideas into bottom-line results.

PEP is really quite simple as compared to other popular management systems like Reengineering and Total Quality Management. They can be likened to the movie, *Field of Dreams.* In that film the Kevin Costner character stands in the cornfield listening to the voice that says, "Build it and they will come." If you launch a complex organization-wide endeavor that touches many people and processes and gets them working in sync, profits *may* come. Unfortunately, many companies have discovered that this isn't necessarily so. Some businesses now believe that TQM stands for Too Quirky to Manage and have employed the Profit Enhancement Process because of its practicality and sustainable results.

Without a system to discover ideas that were previously unimaginable and that measure progress, profits may not come.

That's why PEP emphasizes and supports the implementation process with as much rigor as the initial gathering of ideas and building of teams to carry them out.

This book will also give you some proven ideas to start generating greater profitability in your business, even if you never implement our entire system. Enhanced profitability is exciting, exhilarating, euphoric and an endless journey. This book is not about cost-cutting. Your company is in business to generate profits, not to cut costs. That is what this book is about.

We are called The Profit Advisors, and we're so convinced that PEP works that we'll reimburse you for the cost of the "basic training" you'll receive in this book (its purchase price) —if, after reading it, you can't turn your new knowledge into new profits. And if, and when, you would like help taking your new Profit Plan to the next level, contact us or one of almost 100 leading edge members of The Institute of Profit Advisors in the United States, an organization we co-founded along with Practice Development Institute, LLC (PDI). Our system is also being utilized in the United Kingdom by their Association of Profit Advisors, of which Barry Schimel (co-author of this book) is an honorary member.

Start improving your profits right now, in harmony with your company's goals and objectives. This book will turn you into the head coach and your managers into the assistant coaches who will lead your team into the Super Profit Bowl and win, season after season. Let's start training.

Remember, your goal is to make your business the most valuable business it can be!

Chapter 1

Profit Training For Coaches

We, as entrepreneurs, are always miles ahead in our vision from the realities of the present. We tend to focus on growth at the expense of profit, knowing that it is only a matter of time before the profits come. What we tend to forget is that the company's culture will tend to generate more growth at the expense of profit.

—Mark Salman, CEO of La Parisienne Bakery

One of our more seasoned clients is a wholesale bakery. For the past two years, CEO Mark Salman has committed his company to the Profit Enhancement Process (PEP) to ensure that he and his employees are focused on profits as the business grows. He knows how easy it is for an owner to focus on growth (more sales, a bigger plant, more customers, more employees, bigger budgets) at the expense of that all-important bottom line. This CEO agrees with the client who informed us that sales feed one's ego and profit feeds one's family. The right question is: Where is your focus?

In profit management, making short-term goals is
as important as attaining long-term goals.

La Parisienne Bakery has completed two Profit Super Bowls, or profit management retreats. This is the stage of our profit management system during which the Chief Executive Officer, managers and department heads create their Profit Plan for the coming business season. During the initial profit planning session, the department heads and managers analyzed the cost-effectiveness of their production and delivery schedules among other issues partially identified by "Coach" Salman. They discovered that they were not maximizing sales from customers who sell breakfast bakery products because they were not focused on delivering bagels and breakfast rolls before the morning rush. A Profit Champion and Profit Team were assigned the task of revising the production and delivery times to meet the retail store's schedule. Delivery of bakery products by 6 a.m. brought the company increased customer satisfaction and sales. A simple operational change meant big profits.

Before the second Profit Super Bowl, Mark met with his managers to congratulate them. He posted a chart demonstrating the growth in profits from the previous year. He reviewed each manager's successful profit projects. Then with a flourish, he opened his briefcase and handed each of them a bonus—a "token" of his appreciation for their good work. Do you think those managers went into their second Profit Super Bowl with high enthusiasm that year? You bet.

One of the issues identified that year was the company's need to improve its sanitation and equipment maintenance efforts. A Profit Team member came up with the brilliant idea of creating an "Adopt a Bakery Area" program, similar to the "Adopt a Highway" campaign. The management team devised a plan in which employees would volunteer to be responsible for a section of the bakery or a piece of equipment. Employees were to keep their "adopted" areas or equipment safe and clean, and make sure that regular maintenance was performed. To recognize employees for their efforts, the company placed signs in the adopted areas similar to the "Adopt a Highway" program, announcing the employees' roles in keeping the bakery safe, clean and operational. The results were reduced equipment and repair costs, improved bakery-goods production, and reduced worker's compensation claims because there were fewer accidents.

We'll watch the scoreboard with Mark for this company's third winning "season." This bakery now knows how to make dough rise!

Half of the word "profit" is "pro." Is the profitability of your business PROfessionally managed?

Your employees are your most valued players. Hidden in their minds are ideas for adding hundreds of thousands of dollars—maybe even millions—to your company's bottom line. They deal with your customers and your vendors and your production processes every day. They know where the problems and the opportunities are, but they may not know how to communicate them to you. The vital skill all players must have to score profits for your business—their "profit*ability*"—is undeveloped.

Some people are born with "profit*ability*." It's like athletic ability. For them it's a natural talent that enables them to find profit wherever it's hidden. But most people, like most athletes, must be coached on playing for profit, and everyone needs training (and that means coaching and practice) before they can hone these skills.

Look at the word "profit." Divide it into two syllables. The "pro" stands for *professional*, a person who has as much experience in the business world as a star athlete does on the field. And "fit" takes training, stamina and commitment to maintain peak performance. So what is "profit*ability*"? It's the skill necessary to look objectively at your entire business or a single department, determine what more can be done to add value to the bottom line, and the *ability* to turn ideas into financial results.

If you are an entrepreneur, you probably have natural "profit*ability*" or you wouldn't be where you are today. How many of your managers have this ability? And how about your employees? We are convinced that every employee knows where there is real money to be made in the minutiae of everyday business activity. The receptionist may have one suggestion, so might Joe from accounting. The trouble is, no one ever asks them to share their profit-generating ideas. In fact, employees don't even realize it's their job to do so, and there is no forum for it to happen.

For whatever reason, a lot of companies have no mechanism to promote profit-generating ideas to senior management. Part of the problem is that most employees, while they care about the company's success, feel that they were hired to do a job, perform a function, and nothing else. They think that little will change for them whether profits go up or down. It's the job of the head coach to change their perception, to make each and every one into a Profit Enhancement Officer or PEO. Winning the Profit Super Bowl will mean super benefits for the entire team.

Playing for profit means a new way of analyzing your team's performance.

The CEO of a trash removal company tried the Profit Enhancement Process. This particular firm has a fleet of trucks, and services businesses and residences in the suburbs of a large metropolitan area. During the Profit Super Bowl, the group identified one of their largest expenses as landfill charges. While empty, all of their trucks were weighed to establish a base weight. Each truck was certified with its exact weight empty. After a pickup route was completed, the truck went to the land-fill to deposit its load. It was driven onto a scale, and the weight of the empty truck was subtracted, leaving the weight of the trash that was assessed at the appropriate landfill.

At first glance, this sounds like a pretty routine transaction. No room for extra profit here. But in reality, $78,000 per year of profit waste was discovered by one of the managers. It seems like a small detail, but she discovered that when the truck was driven onto the scale and weighed, the 150 to 200 pound driver and helper were still sitting in it. The trash truck driver and helper didn't even think about it, and neither did their supervisor. But when you consider the number of truck loads per day times the number of days in a year, an insignificant weight becomes very meaningful. Then further, multiply that by the number of trucks in the entire fleet.

TIMES x TIMES x TIMES =
Endless Profit Opportunities

The Profit Team immediately decreed that the trash collectors must get off their truck while it's being weighed. Out goes the truck driver and helper and in comes an extra $78,000 a year to this company's bottom line—in perfect harmony with the company's strategic goals and objectives.

Admit it. You're really in business to make
profits—no matter what you make or do.
It's okay to use the "P" word—Profits!

During our years as Profit Advisors, we've been astounded at how many companies know how to produce their product or sell their service, but don't realize the importance of profits. It's always the means to the end in business. Without it, financial dreams will never materialize.

When we review the clients' business goals with them, it's often like pulling teeth to get the owner to admit that his primary goal is to make his business more profit*able* so that the organization and everyone in the company has more options and choices. His initial focus is usually on growth in new business. His management team may be frustrated because they have concentrated their efforts on sales, but the company's bottom line has not dramatically improved.

As we work with clients like this, their perspective of the company begins to change. When the owner, finally, after much deliberation, answers, "To make more profit so that we have greater opportunities, options, and choices," everyone seems relieved. It's almost as if profit is a dirty word that is rarely mentioned.

When the words, "I'm in business to make a profit," come out of a CEO's mouth, it's like "Eureka, we've got it!" Everyone on the management team becomes very excited. Their enthusiasm has been dulled for so long while the business wanders aimlessly. Now a bright, new vision appears. It is often the beginning of the solution that will improve a company's financial performance because now everyone will focus on what needs to be done to improve profit*ability*. They know that everyone is the beneficiary when the organization reaches its profit potential.

Develop your bottom-line vision.
You must first see it to capture it.

Reflect on all the time you spend in meetings. How many have dealt exclusively with ideas to improve profits? Do any of your various manuals, i.e., operations, personnel, and so forth, even mention the word *profit*? Do you have a bottom-line vision, a profit management system that clearly focuses your business on how to attain its primary goal—profit, the fuel necessary to power your business?

We assure you that if your business does not have a profit management system in place, it is probably not a fun place to work. It's like going to a football game where there is no scoreboard. Imagine the effort to advance a football 100 yards and neither players nor fans know if their team is winning or losing. Boring!

Are profits everybody's job? They certainly are! Why should your business pay salaries to employees who don't feel responsible or even know that their job is improving the bottom line? Managerial positions are often established to oversee functional processes within organizations, but who is responsible for bottom-line results?

The most successful leaders are those whose
people state, "We did it ourselves,"
when the work is completed.

A manufacturing business called us in. The owner was frustrated. He knew that his business had greater profit potential than was being realized. His instinct told him that the company's bottom line was under performing, but he didn't know how to get a commitment from his management team to focus on improving the company's bottom line. He did not know how to involve his management team in the process of profit improvement. We got him a front row seat at a Profit Super Bowl.

At that time the business had experienced a previous year's loss of $200,000. His management team was comprised of the owner and 15 departmental managers. This group had two members who were identified as potential problems. One manager clearly lacked the commitment to make the business successful and was just marking time until retirement. In fact, she had already retired, but failed to inform the rest of the company. The other manager, who had been there a number of years, appeared to have a good attitude, yet the owner was convinced that this individual had done a poor job in communicating effectively with other members of the management team.

As the profit management process progressed, the management team became more and more excited and enthusiastic about improving the bottom line. They pulled together, perhaps for the first time in years, to help this business maximize its financial success. One of the problem individuals (the one who had already "retired," but hadn't "told" her employer) showed no concern for the business's profits and was unwilling to change her behavior. The other "problem" individual who had difficulty in communicating became a significant contributor of profit ideas because the Profit Super Bowl provided a process in which he could participate in a nonthreatening environment.

Most members of the profit management team bonded together in a way the CEO had never experienced in the history of this company. What was the result? The person who was uncommitted to profit*ability* left within a few months. The commitment of the CEO to make profits flushed this unsupportive manager out of the company. The other potential problem manager learned to communicate his ideas and to be an effective manager. This business, with the efforts of its management team, turned the corner. It went from a $200,000 loss to a $300,000 profit in 12 months—a $500,000 positive change.

Why did this happen? It happened because the owner and managers became a Profit Team willing to change their attitudes and their ways of doing business. This company has been involved in the Profit Enhancement Process for seven years. Here are the results: substantial profits in each of the years they held a Profit Super Bowl and losses in the two years in which they weren't involved in the profit process. They have now learned that PEP has a significant bottom-line effect on their business. It works! They now have the profit*ability* to continue producing greater financial results, limited only by their new ideas.

Here are a few examples of the kinds of profit ideas these profit*able* people come up with now. The Profit Team, in analyzing purchasing practices, realized the company needed a qualified purchasing manager whose job was to contain costs. They hired such a person, and one of her first ideas was to go to the source to buy raw materials instead of paying a middle- man. The company actually bought the mineral rights to aggregate fields. The result: $300,000 in potential profits annually.

There was no sales manager. The Profit Team came up with the idea of semi-monthly sales meetings with the CEO (who is acting as the sales manager of this company). Without any additional expense, they were able to generate new sales leads and discuss current prospects and accounts. They established benchmarks for their sales team, each one setting six goals for themselves that had to be specific, measurable and challenging. Incentives were put into place to "super charge" everyone. They met their goals. Regular sales meetings produced sales goals that generated an extra $120,000 in profits that year.

The Profit Team looked into their inventory control. Excess inventory was costing them about two percent a month, a huge cost. They decided to hold an inventory close-out sale, and even contacted their suppliers who added consigned merchandise of their own to the sale. The company cleared out its unwanted inventory and generated an extra $60,000. The excess inventory that didn't sell was donated to charity. Because the fair market value was greater than cost, they received a nice tax deduction of cost plus 50 percent of the difference between fair market value and what they paid for the donated inventory, as permitted under tax law.

One of the Profit Team's most creative ideas was to develop the "24-Hour Customer Response Program." The team realized that they were losing market share because they weren't providing what we call "World Class Service"— doing whatever you do so well that whoever you do it for, asks for more. This "24 Hour" campaign gave customers just what they wanted. The company ordered brightly colored pins with "24" imprinted on top of their logo and gave one to every employee. They were requested to wear it daily. When a customer asked, "What does that mean?" the employee proudly replied, "It means that within 24 hours our company will take care of whatever you request from us courteously, efficiently, and accurately." This campaign built the company's reputation for being extremely attentive to their customers' requests. Can you imagine everyone in your organization repeating several times a day, "Within 24 hours our company will take care of whatever you request from us courteously, efficiently, and accurately?" It will change the culture of your business as it did this client's.

The Profit Team analyzed the company's discount policy. In fact, they found that there was no uniform discount policy. No one followed up on whether those businesses that were granted an extra discount actually increased their business activity from the company afterwards. Discounts were tightened and controls put in place. The result: more realized profits!

The Profit Team eliminated the company's practice of permitting contractors to go into their "self-service" yard and pick up their own merchandise. This effort alone generated an extra $75,000 by reducing inventory shortages. This is just one success story. You can create one, too. You *can* achieve greater financial success for your business.

Transform your management team into
a powerhouse Profit Team.

For your business to change, three things must happen.

1—You, as head coach, owner, top financial officer, department or division head, must recognize that your company has not reached its true profit potential.

2—You must accept the fact that old ways of looking at ideas won't uncover new profit possibilities.

3—You must transform your management team into a powerhouse Profit Team.

Everyone in your business must become a possibility thinker. Change is a critical element in every business. Patience is a modern day excuse for not performing at higher levels. If you are patiently awaiting future events before initiating changes, you are harming your company by not capitalizing on tomorrow's opportunities today. It was Yogi Berra who said that "if you always do what you have always done, you'll always get what you've already got."

Take the ball and create new profit opportunities,
become profit possibility thinkers, execute well, and
score in the profit zone. Remember,
if you don't know where you are going,
it doesn't matter which direction you travel.

Just think about the profit possibilities you'll unleash when you create a profit culture within your company. Think about the possibilities of pooling all the great new profit ideas your team will begin to generate into a comprehensive, new Profit Plan for action. Think of all the profit projects your team will carry out. Think of all the profit possibilities and don't stop until you've got at least *100 Ways to Prosper in Today's Economy* (Barry Schimel's first book).

Here are some more examples of profit initiatives other clients have put in place. . .

■ A manufacturer changed the composition of a portion of its sales force from commissioned sales to merchandising specialists. These specialists created better point-of-purchase displays which increased their customers' sales. Also, profits increased because the sales force focused on new business development rather than maintaining existing accounts. This resulted in $250,000 annually in potential recurring profits from additional sales.

■ An automobile dealership developed a reactivation program to re-establish relationships with service department customers who hadn't used their services for a year. This resulted in $725,000 in profit potential.

■ A nonprofit association reduced the paper size used for their national publication by 1/8 of an inch and "found" an extra $18,000 in recurring annual profit. (By cutting 1/8 inch, the publication could be printed on an economical standard-size paper instead of the expensive special-order paper.)

■ A manufacturer installed a process to eliminate billing omissions on last-minute orders. These rush orders were usually handwritten and were not always entered into the computerized accounts receivable system. The estimated profit potential from this initiative? $180,000.

■ A retail tire company established a "Red Carpet Service" to provide pick up and delivery service for people who could not take the time to get away from their office to purchase tires. Estimated recurring annual profit potential: $100,000.

PEP is the profit-making process for the future.
Financial statements only report the scores from
last season—they represent the present
value of the past, not the future value
of tomorrow's profit opportunities.

How can your company get this kind of profit*ability*? How can you turn people from task-oriented to profit-oriented—for the good of everyone in the business or organization? How do you get them to give you the new ideas that will add to the company's bottom line? And how do you accomplish those ideas so they make money for your business?

Over a decade ago, when the economy was not healthy, we had the chance to sit around a table with a group of top CEOs. We asked them what they expected from their CPA firms, their business advisors. Were we ever surprised! Almost every one of these top executives complained that their CPA firms, for the most part, did little more than fill out tax forms and prepare financial statements. They performed mostly compliance services. They reported past transgressions, alerting them about what they had done wrong in the past (you've seen this in the management letter you receive from your accounting firm), but did not offer them ideas for being more financially successful in the future. Their advisors were stuck back in history, looking at their past scoreboard—without really appreciating what could be done to make the plays of the future. Of course, much of what accountants do is mandated by regulatory authorities and their profession. But these top entrepreneurs wanted more. They wanted new ideas. We learned from them that the loneliest place in any organization is at the top. There is no one to turn to.

The Bear Market of 2000 was caused to a great degree by a drop in earnings—and in the case of dot.coms an absence of earnings—making bottom line growth even more critical.

We decided then and there to change the way clients are served. At the same time, we set out to change the hearts and minds of their advisors. That's the moment the Institute of Profit Advisors was born. Barry gave up a successful accounting practice to devote full time to uncovering ingenious methods of finding hidden profits in businesses of all kinds. Now approximately 100 change-ready business advisory firms are trained and licensed through the Institute of Profit Advisors to coach clients to new profit heights through the Profit Enhancement Process. Their coaching adds value to their client's business and focuses the entire organization right on the bottom line. Businesses throughout the U.S., as well as the U.K., are the beneficiaries. These firms have made the quantum leap from keeping score to making the plays.

Take the profit pledge.

Before we start, let's make sure your company is change-ready. Take a moment to answer these questions. This is a quiz that helps us determine whether prospective clients will be successful with the Profit Enhancement Process. Now you take it. It will provide you with your first hints about areas for discovering unrealized bottom line potential in your organization.

The *Are-You-Ready-for-Greater-Profitability* Quiz

1. Where is your profit on a scale of 1 to 10 (1 is lowest and 10 is highest)? (Describe your thoughts.)

_____

_____

_____

Many businesses start out below 5. That leaves a lot of unrealized bottom line potential—the difference between the profit you are now achieving and what your business can achieve.

2. Does your company have a Profit Plan? (This is different from a business plan, you'll find.) (Describe your thoughts.)

_____

_____

_____

Don't worry, few do. But think what having a Profit Plan might mean to your business. Present it to a banker or investor and it can mean all the difference between receiving funding for your business or being strapped for cash. If you are planning to sell out in a few years, every "extra dollar of profit" you earn may add five to even ten dollars of market value to your company.

3. Does your firm set sales targets that include gross profit objectives? (Describe your thoughts.)

_____

_____

_____

Many businesses set sales targets, but fail to understand the real costs for achieving them.

4. Does your business take its long-term objectives into account in its hiring process? (Describe your thoughts.)

_____

_____

_____

Often companies hire reactively rather than objectively. Now you'll need to hire "possibility thinkers" who become part of the Profit Enhancement Process.

5. Are the people on your staff willing to accept change? (Describe your thoughts.)

_____

_____

_____

Are your employees too busy working to make profits? Is your organization set in rigid patterns that don't invite new ideas and their implementation? How many new ideas from your employees are waiting on your desk right now for your consideration? Do your employee manuals even mention the word profit?

6. What is the culture of your organization? (Describe your thoughts.)

_____

_____

_____

Do you know that you know all there is to know about running your business profitably? Do you know that you don't know everything? Or do you not know that you don't know everything about reaching your profit potential? Are you open to new ways of doing business, new ways of thinking, new strategies for facing the challenges of the future?

7. Do you realize that your employees are your business's most valuable asset? (Describe your thoughts.)

_____

_____

_____

Your carefully scouted employees should be your most valuable players. They have the ideas for adding hundreds of thousands of dollars—maybe even millions—to your company's bottom line if you unleash their profitability. These people deal with your cus-

tomers and your vendors and your production processes every day. They know where the problems and the opportunities are, but they may not know how to tell you what they are. Are you willing to provide a nonthreatening forum for offering new ideas? Are you willing to reward your employees who put their most significant profit initiatives into action? Are you willing to get rid of your organization's sacred cows?

8. Has your organization determined how the demand for your products or services may change based on the economy, competition and customer needs?
(Describe your thoughts.)

_____

_____

_____

The Profit Enhancement Process will help you get these answers by communicating effectively with your customers and vendors.

9. Does your management team receive bonuses and/or incentives based on their performance, as well as their department's and the financial success of your business? Are there *consequences* for not meeting performance objectives?
(Describe your thoughts.)

_____

_____

_____

It's difficult to change. The Profit Enhancement Process requires everyone to work smarter, be more innovative and be absolutely committed to making your Profit Plan work. Bonuses and/or incentives (and they don't always have to be monetary) are absolutely essential to inspire this kind of commitment. If you aren't willing to compensate your employees, the process will not succeed in your company.

10. Is customer service in need of improvement? Is the "bragability index" of your company higher than your competition's? Does your organization assess customer/client product and service expectations and satisfaction levels?
(Describe your thoughts.)

_____

_____

_____

Providing World Class Service—doing things so well that customers can't help asking for more—is essential for a successful company. It always needs improving.

11. Does your organization work as a cohesive Profit Team?
(Describe your thoughts.)

_____

_____

_____

If not, PEP will inspire management teams and employee teams by pulling them together in the challenge to identify and realize profit goals. Only with every member of a company knowing what their "real" job is—enhancing the company's bottom line profits—can it reach full potential.

12. Do you believe there is opportunity to improve the profit management of your business? (Describe your thoughts.)

_____

_____

_____

The Profit Enhancement Process transforms management teams into Profit Teams. Your managers must be ready to re-focus their attention from performing tasks to assisting your business in reaching its profit potential.

13. Is your Profit Team committed to your organization's success? (Describe your thoughts.)

_____

_____

_____

This is very important. If everyone is not committed to the financial strategies developed during the Profit Enhancement Process, it won't work.

14. Does your firm determine its unrealized bottom line potential by putting a dollar value on profit projects that your organization commits to undertake? (Describe your thoughts.)

_____
_____
_____

If you can't measure it, you can't manage it. You're sure to have sales goals, but these may not be as profitable as you think. This book will teach you how to compute your unrealized bottom line potential—possibly hundreds of thousands or millions of dollars.

15. Is there a written Profit Plan in place to achieve your organization's profit objectives?
(Describe your thoughts.)

_____
_____
_____

If not, the Profit Enhancement Process will show you how.

16. Are you committed to implementing new ideas if they have measurable bottom line value to your business and are in harmony with your strategic goals and objectives?
If yes, sign your name here, and let's get started. . .

❏ Yes, I'm ready to put the Profit Enhancement Process to work in my business.

Your signature here_____

Instant Replays

In profit management, making short-term goals is as important as attaining long-term goals.

Half of the word "profit" is "pro." Is the profitability of your business PROfessionally managed?

Playing for profit means a new way of analyzing your team's performance.

TIMES x TIMES x TIMES = Endless Profit Opportunities

Admit it. You're really in business to make profits —no matter what you make or do. It's okay to use the "P" word—Profits!

Develop your bottom-line vision. You must first see it to capture it.

The most successful leaders are those whose people state, "We did it ourselves," when the work is completed.

Transform your management team into a powerhouse Profit Team.

Take the ball and create new profit opportunities, become profit possibility thinkers, execute well, and score in the profit zone. Remember, if you don't know where you are going, it doesn't matter which direction you travel.

PEP is the profit-making process for the future. Financial statements only report the scores from last season—they represent the present value of the past, not the future value of tomorrow's profit opportunities.

Take the profit pledge.

Chapter 2

UNDERSTANDING THE GAME

> We know that we have employees who are highly skilled and experienced and who could contribute a great deal to our bottom line profitability—if they would work with us as a team. However, to get them to work with us as members of a team focusing on the broader success of the company, we knew we had to persuade them that we are committed to the success of the company and that we are open to hearing their criticism and concerns. We had to be open to the negative to draw out the positivity and creativity of our employees.
>
> – Robert Funk, President/CEO, EKA Health & Mobility Systems

This thought expresses one of the major issues clients ask us to help them with—how do you get your employees to feel such a part of the team that they offer their ideas freely and work their hardest to help you succeed? And how do you transform managers into leaders capable of coaching their own particular group or team of players?

Again, we turn to football for the answer. Our good friend, Larry Pecattiello, former Defensive Coordinator for the Washington Redskins, would make a great CEO. He's brought out the best in his players, and he knew that is how to win the game.

It was Larry who gave us the idea for the model to start new ideas flowing in any organization. He was telling us one day about a typical pre-game coaches' meeting when he was an assistant coach with the Washington Redskins under the great Joe Gibbs. Larry says that Joe encouraged all the coaches to offer their ideas and play strategies during discussions, based on their knowledge of the strengths and weaknesses of the players in their area of expertise—whether offense, defense, or special teams. They reviewed films of the competition and of their own team, and built the game plan together. Joe Gibbs listened to all their ideas and was always the master facilitator and final arbitrator. And no matter how heated the discussions during the session, by the end of meeting, all the coaches were committed to the game plan and ready to introduce it to the players. They were united.

This seemed like a ready-made model for the business world, where employees are the most-valued players and the best managers are the coaches who can inspire them to give their best ideas and their best hours to "winning" profits for the success of the business. So with football as our model, we developed the Profit Enhancement Process. Here's how it will work for your business.

Profit is always a journey; it's never a destination.

We all know how many financial reports we receive. They pile up at the end of every month waiting for interpretation. We attend meetings with *this* department and *that* project team. Financial and industry publications arrive on our desks by the score. What does it all mean? And how can this information be useful in our own business or organization? We all know that we can't manage it unless we can measure it. (Actually we can't manage it unless we DO manage it!)

We developed the Profit Enhacement Process so businesses will capture previously unrealized profits through an identification process and then teamwork. The process is an organized system for focusing Profit Team members in the organization on ways to turn their ideas and inside knowledge into improved financial results. It breaks the entire process into controlled, measurable profit projects that add an element of fun and excitement to the organization as each project's goal is achieved or, in many cases, surpassed. In other words, PEP is a way to identify and capture your organization's previously unrecognized and *unrealized bottom line potential.*

The Profit Enhancement Process measures the only things that can be measured in the business world:

(1) Revenues,
(2) Costs,
(3) Quality,
(4) Quantity, and
(5) Time.

These areas must be measured and measured and measured to discover hidden profits and develop a Profit Plan for transforming profit ideas into bottom line results.

Here are the five steps that will help your entire organization become profit-focused for the future so that everyone in the company benefits.

Step #1 in the Profit Enhancement Process is
to create a culture where profit will thrive.

You've begun the work on this step by picking up this book! A shrewd head football coach knows that if his team is not winning or attaining its goals, something needs to change. He will look at his most important asset—his coaches and players— and analyze what his competition is doing, then change. Best of all, he will ask his coaches and players what they can be doing better. He will begin to share some of the heavy responsibility for winning with the whole team.

Ask yourself what's impossible to do in
your business today that will make
your business more profitable tomorrow?

This may be the most important question you ever ask in your business life.

There are three classical phases of growth in business. Phase One is an emerging business, struggling to be profitable. Everyone is working as hard as they can, but profits stagnate because many other things are necessary to make it successful. The business is experimenting with the products or services it can sell best and the marketing strategies necessary to generate those sales. This company either succeeds or goes out of business. Its key strength is the energy and entrepreneurial spirit of its founders.

Phase Two, companies exist only if they survive Phase One. They concentrate on efforts to repeat successful sales and new marketing strategies. Rapid growth occurs by developing niches and finding market opportunities that accelerate sales. Establishing sales processes and support systems are a substantial part of the second phase of growth. Profits are necessary to develop the support systems required to move the company towards its next phase.

Eventually, a business grows as much as it can by using its previous success models. Profits flatten and revenue growth becomes stagnant. New opportunities must be created to improve the bottom line and increase market share. This triggers the third phase of growth.

Look at IBM and Apple. Both companies were able to change their profit culture and find new ways to compete in the business. IBM was able to change, Apple is trying hard. Think about the American automobile business over the last decade. For the most part, it has been able to adapt to many markets, not just the big gas-guzzling American market of the past. There have been disasters in the automobile industry as well, as recently as the demise of Oldsmobile. They were not able to keep up with their competition. Most manufacturers have pared down their expensive labor costs and moved their plants to less expensive areas of the country or the world, introduced new technology, and adapted model designs to the needs of their customers in each market segment. They've adapted to a changed marketplace and saved the American automobile industry. They heeded what Henry Ford once said, "Failure is only the opportunity to begin again, more intelligently."

Changing its ways from the way a company has done business in the past is vital for remaining financially competitive. PEP helps CEOs and managers analyze what changes are necessary to get those profits and sales to reach their potential and continue into the future. PEP will help you redesign the way you do business when the old models and methods are not producing the improved financial results you know are possible.

Most successful companies go through the first two phases, then commit to change when moving into Phase Three. This phase is most challenging because it gives entrepreneurs the opportunity to reinvent their business and maximize their sales and profit*ability*. They must be successful in this phase or else the business will continue to lose its forward motion.

No matter what phase your business is in, PEP is valuable, but particularly in Phase Two. This is the stage where change is very important. A football team's coaches don't decide on a new game plan when there are only two minutes left to go in the game. By Phase Three, a business has often lost its momentum, and its ability to change is far more difficult to achieve. It's at that moment that change is mandatory and when profit coaching is most needed. There is no luxury of time, just a sense of urgency.

There are a lot of businesses with profits of two to three percent of sales, but very few that reach 10 percent. What if a stagnant business were able to engage and empower all its employees to come up with ideas and initiatives that would reduce costs by just 10 percent? That business could almost double its profits. Do the math yourself. Let's say your revenues are one million dollars, your costs are $900,000 and you're earning a nice $100,000 a year profit. What if you were able, with attention and intention, to cut your costs by just 10 percent? You would add $90,000 to your bottom line! In other words, your profits would nearly double (hypothetically speaking) with less effort than nearly doubling your sales.

Many businesses leave considerable profits on the table, because the management team is not focused on identifying exploitable profit opportunities and just hasn't been coached to improve financial performance. How many businesses in America send their managers to courses on generating greater profit*ability*? How many managers read books on profits? Just because a company knows how to make bricks, doesn't mean it knows how to make bricks for profit. Just because a law firm knows how to service its clients' legal problems, doesn't mean it knows how to boost its bottom line. The technical work of the business is just the beginning.

As a good profit coach, like a good football coach, you can provide the forum for your employees to discover the unrealized profit opportunities in their own departments and the organization. So, Step #1 is to change your focus to the bottom line and share the responsibility for profit*ability* with your Profit Team. They'll help you come up with great new profit-enhancing ideas as soon as they begin to understand the almost limitless bottom line possibilities. One good idea will lead to another, then another, then another when they learn that profit achievements are more important than traditional responsibilities.

Profit Team leaders and members know that their
job is to identify financial opportunities
and be responsible for turning their ideas
into bottom line results.

A hospital outpatient clinic found it was running out of space and was about to invest in a brand new and costly physical therapy facility and hire additional physical therapists for its growing number of patients needing these services. They were experiencing increased demand for more patient appointments, but were limited by treatment rooms and available staff. During the Profit Super Bowl, it was discovered that the hospital had an appointment scheduling problem. There were a lot of cancellations and fluctuations in scheduling.

The Profit Team leader given the responsibility for studying this problem discovered that most cancellations occurred during certain predictable times of the day, week, and year, including holidays. The outpatient clinic adopted a booking plan similar to the one used by airlines. They began to overbook appointments based on the statistical trends of no-shows. The result was that more patients could be accommodated, and there was no need to either increase staff or add facilities. Rather than building a new facility to handle the overflow times, they learned to schedule the appointments more systematically—and saved the hospital millions in capital expenditures on a new facility with minimal increases in personnel expenses. The interesting point is that the scheduling data was available all along, but no one had thought to use it. It took the Profit Super Bowl to provide the nonthreatening forum where the problem (an opportunity turned inside out) was identified. A manager was appointed to solve it and devise a strategy for a profit*able* solution.

Fleeing fortunes are the result of years of denial
of significant profit opportunities.

Read this sentence again and tell us how many letter f's you see. Most people, even our editor, see only four; but there are really seven! The reason is that people have been conditioned to read the word *of* as if the f were a v. We have difficulty seeing the f's. This process will teach you to see every "f" in your business. It's missing the little things and doing the little things right that make all the difference.

Step #2 is to conduct a Profit Audit
of your business.

Like a good coach, your next step is to analyze where your business stands today and develop priorities based on what you find. You need to do a complete *Profit Audit* of your business. This audit should delve into all aspects of your business with a focus on five key areas:

(1) Employees,
(2) Organizational Structure,
(3) Sales and Marketing,
(4) Operations, and
(5) Financial Management.

Businesses are drowning in information
but are thirsty for knowledge.

Start with a review of your financial statements and corporate records, such as tax returns, mission/vision statements, annual reports, organizational chart, personnel manuals, operations and procedures manuals, and promotional and marketing materials. Ask yourself questions about the opportunities and challenges you discover there.

Then start asking your managers and other key employees the probing questions about your business that you know need answers and solutions. We've found that 70 percent of the issues uncovered in a Profit Audit come from employees. In other words, if you've got 100 employees, about 70 are consultants just waiting to be asked. The answer is the right question. This is such a vital step in the auditing process that we've developed an employee survey of carefully selected questions which we adapt to each client's requirements. You'll find a sample of that survey in Chapter 3. In our survey, employees are asked to rank the company on a scale of 1 to 10 (10 being the highest) on a variety of issues, such as:

- Do you understand our firm's profit strategy? Can you describe it?

- What do you think the company's maximum profit potential is this year?

- Do you know the company's mission/vision? Does what you do on the job support this mission?

- Do you understand the opportunities you have to increase our firm's bottom line?

- Do you think the company identifies and eliminates redundancies in tasks?

- Do you think potential customers are aware of our products and services?

- Do you catch mistakes before they impact customers and profits?

■ Can you describe the relationship of your work to the company's bottom line?

These are contemplative questions. It is vital that respondents feel free to answer the survey without repercussions. And, of course, most employees typically only know the true rank of their own areas of expertise. But their perceptions are very important to your understanding of the profit*ability* of your company. Just as the linebacker might not know how to defend every type of offense, he will appreciate the job the coaches perform—determining the likelihood of certain plays occurring and what the opposition's game plan might be.

Average your employees' rankings on these important issues and analyze just where they think your business ranks today in relationship to where it could be.

Another thing you should consider is to survey select customers to determine the "Bragability Index" of your company. This is how your customers rank your business today. We are successful in obtaining a response rate of over 70 percent for our clients who ask us for help with this survey. A comprehensive survey includes questions on the organization's administration, communications, products/services and sales/marketing. Each category offers a series of detailed questions and statements that provide in-depth information about how your customers view your firm and your products or services. A sample of these questions follows:

1. *On an overall basis, how satisfied are you with our company?*

2. *Would you purchase products or services from our company again?*

3. *Would you recommend our company to other prospective customers?*

4. *How satisfied are you in your dealings with our company as a business partner?*

5. *How satisfied are you with our company's overall communication efforts?*

6. *When you think of quality products and services, do you think of our company first?*

7. *How satisfied are you with the delivery of our products and services?*

8. *Do our sales representatives keep you well-informed about our new products or services?*

9. *Do you have to buy from other sources because we don't offer the products you need?*

10. *How satisfied are you with the warranties we provide for our products?*

11. *Do our sales representatives thoroughly know and understand our products and services?*

12. *Do our sales representatives suggest solutions to improve your business?*

13. *How satisfied are you with the personal commitment of our sales representatives?*

14. *How satisfied are you with the commitment of our company's management to assist you?*

15. *Can you always promptly contact someone in our company who will make decisions that affect you?*

The results of these customer surveys, impartially analyzed, will help you identify a list of profit issues you will want addressed right away and others to be addressed over time.

"Traditional budgeting is a waste of time!"
–Former Accountant turned Profit Advisor

Traditionally, budgeted profit is computed by subtracting budgeted overhead expenses and budgeted cost of sales from budgeted sales. More often than not, those figures are based on historic information without the insights gained through profit*ability*. By conducting a Profit Audit, potential profit will be revealed in a more realistic and meaningful way and quantified into a profit*ability* budget.

■ Sales projections will be based on the number of customers, the frequency of customer transactions, and how much customers are willing to pay for each transaction.

■ Selling price will be based upon customers' perceptions of value as well as eliminating preconceived, market-defined price barriers. In part, the value customers perceive will be based on the support and world-class service they feel they receive. Customers will happily pay greater prices for *value* when they feel your product or service has equaled or exceeded their expectations.

The customer never says your prices are too high.
They say the value of what they received
is too low.

Previously, you may have increased revenues by selling more and raising prices. Today, the greater your price—unless value is given—the more reason you give your customers to look for alternative suppliers. Your customers actually set your sales prices based on their perception of how valuable they believe your products and services to be.

When you create greater perceived value, you have the opportunity to raise your prices (within limits, of course).

Costs that are necessary to enhance perceived value are essential and include costs of goods sold, assuming your customers perceive value in what you produce. Overhead is not valued by your customers unless they understand it and get value from the service and function it provides; i.e., timely billing, timely response, clean and exceptional facility, and so on. Overhead expenses—such as insurance, office supplies, permits and licenses, and accounting departments—do not have perceived value to your customers, but you can't operate without them. So make sure your customers understand how valuable what you sell is to them and that includes the "whole" business.

Consider not only the well-executed plays,
but also the profit "fumbles."

Ah, yes, you must consider the negatives or profit "fumbles." Did your survey indicate your employees don't understand the Big Picture, and that they lack knowledge and training on how to make the business more successful? Did your customers say their orders were completed without mistakes? Did the majority of your employees say that they don't understand the company's mission and where they fit into it? Did they say they need further training to do their jobs with more profit*ability*? These are all fumbled plays. We call them "profit fumbles." They cause lower profits, but they can be identified. They can be measured, and they can be eliminated, reduced or improved via the Profit Enhancement Process.

Try to assign a negative dollar figure to these trouble areas. Quantify, quantify, quantify. Know the numbers. It's the language of business! Here's how:

(1) Assign a negative value to each of the "fumbles" you know have a negative impact on your profit*ability*. Think of these fumbles as all the words that start with *mis, re,* and *un.* Here is a list of the kinds of "fumbles" that could be keeping your team out of the profit zone.

Mis	**Re**	**Un**
Misunderstood	Restock	Unclear
Mistakes	Retrain	Undone

Missed deadlines	Redo	Unkept promise
Mismanaged	Redeliver	Unnecessary
Misplaced	Reposition	Unfocused

It's these kinds of issues that send customers away in a huff, cost the company unplanned-for expenses in having to redo or remake, and result in a warehouse full of unsold inventory.

Profit fumbles are costly problems. Detecting problems means identifying and measuring recurring expenses. Preventing problems equals recurring profits. The choice is yours. These are the costly issues, the challenges, that your Profit Audit will identify. Once you have recognized them, it is possible, in many cases, to eliminate them through the Profit Enhancement Process.

(2) Now look at your Income Statement in a new way:

OLD Traditional Presentation		NEW Non-traditional Profit Fumbler Presentation	
Sales	XXX	Sales	XXX
Less Costs of Sales	<XXX>	Less Costs of Sales	<XXX>
Gross Profit	XXX	Gross Profit	XXX
Less Overhead	<XXX>	Less Overhead	<XXX>
	< N/A >[1]	Less; Profit Fumbles	<XXX>[2]
Net Profits	XXX	Net Profits	XXX

[1] *Unidentified and unmeasured profit fumbles are buried in lower sales and inflated cost of sales and overhead.*
[2] *Profit fumbles are identified and measured and available for instant replay to allow the coach and the Profit Team to improve the system and/or the process towards constant and never-ending improvement.*

As you can see, this is a meaningful way to identify your profit potential opportunities. It helps you understand the toll those negative "profit fumbles" take on your bottom line.

We agree with the assessment of Jack Welch, legendary CEO of American giant General Electric, on the budgeting process:

The budget is the bane of corporate America. It never should have existed. A budget is this: if you make it, you generally get a pat on the back and a few bucks. If you miss it, you get a stick in the eye —or worse. Making a budget is an exercise in minimalization. You're always trying to get the lowest out of people, because everyone is negotiating to get the lowest number.

The Profit Enhancement Process creates predictable bottom line results that look toward the future. Standard budgeting produces probable results based on the past. And the past does not equal the future of a profit*able* business.

Profit fumbles are really opportunities to score...
in disguise.

Put the fumbles together with the opportunities you've uncovered and your Profit Audit will offer you a real menu of options and issues to be addressed. It will give you the opportunity to see the letter f's that were previously hidden to you, and a checklist of actions you consider most important for the future of your company—not just some projected figures based on the past.

Now prioritize the issues in your Profit Audit, identifying six to ten of the best that you would like to tackle first. These are the issues you will want to bring to what we call the Profit Super Bowl.

Step #3 is to hold a profit management retreat—
a Profit Super Bowl—where managers and
employees become your powerhouse Profit Team.

Just as the head coach calls his assistant coaches together to analyze the previous season and to formulate a game plan for the future, your next step in the Profit Enhancement Process is to call your Profit Team together. Now it's time to share the most important ideas from the Profit Audit with your team, to get their consensus, and to begin devising strategies to address these opportunities and challenges. In football, the coaches look at films and statistics from past games and begin analyzing information. They learn what they and their opponents did right and wrong, analyze patterns of play, and begin to anticipate what they might expect next season. They begin to revise the "playbook" and devise game plans for the future. As head coach for your business, it's time for you to do the same.

The Profit Super Bowl turns department managers
into team players.

The Profit Super Bowl is a profit management brainstorming/planning session rolled into one: it is your coaches' meeting. So select your "assistant coaches" well, at least one from each department, or from each region if yours is a larger company. Try to limit the number to no more than about 20. More than this makes the meeting too unwieldy. Make sure the people you invite are willing to put forth the effort to make a profit difference for your company. Make sure they really want to coach and have the ability to do so.

During this retreat, the goal is to convert your Company Team into a Profit Team. How do you do this? Provide a free forum of ideas, away from the office, with no complaints, no criticisms, no hashing over old times. This game is not about the past, it's about the future that begins right now. This is a meeting where the backed-up dam of ideas locked in each team player's head is released, considered, quantified, and put into place in the new Profit Plan if warranted.

When we hold such Profit Super Bowls for our clients, the length of time is tailored to our client's need list. Our role is multifaceted. We act as the facilitators. The CEO's role is to listen intently and yet participate as freely as his team players. One or two days seems the right amount of time necessary to facilitate an in-depth discussion of top issues. This also allows time for bringing out additional issues for group discussion.

Now is when you'll get the group's consensus for implementing profit strategies. It is important that the Profit Plan be developed with the consensus of the Profit Team. People do not resist their own ideas, but they may resent and then resist other people's ideas that are imposed upon them.

You must demonstrate support for the Profit Team members in their efforts to improve the company's bottom line. Above all, you must create an atmosphere where real problems can be discussed without fear of retribution. Profit Team members should realize their value to the business and learn that each and every one of them is in charge of profit. As profit strategies are discussed, the Profit Team must reach a consensus on which are to be accepted for the Profit Plan. For each accepted strategy, a team leader (or Profit Champion) should be appointed with responsibility for "carrying the ball" for that strategy and mastering the play that will take it over the goal line. If it's everyone's job, it's no one's job, and the project will fumble. But with one staunch champion to run with it, the play could lead to a profit touchdown!

Suddenly, you'll all see the Profit Plan begin to unfold before you. A real sense of Profit Team cohesion will be developing. There will be excitement in the air.

Step #4 is to take all those good ideas and build the Profit Plan—your company's game plan for winning big over the next season.

Besides building profit*ability*, the Profit Super Bowl is the time when your company's plan for profit will emerge. As the attendees define specific profit initiatives—some for eliminating profit fumbles, others for implementing new strategies—Profit Team members are coached to quantify a dollar amount that could be added to the company's bottom line with completion of each profit strategy. Why spend $1,000,000 to make $100,000? Why not spend $100,000 to make $1,000,000? This computation involves enumerating the financial assumptions upon which that estimate is based—the projected income less the costs associated with the profit initiative. This is difficult for Profit Team members to comprehend, but it is essential because it helps the Profit Team understand the financial implications of a profit generating idea. This estimate may then be tweaked some by the Profit Team to make it more conservative, thus more credible as it is internalized by the team.

Step #4 takes place when these financial strategies are totaled and the actual unrealized bottom line potential of the business is revealed. Each strategy has a financial goal. Without financial goals, profits will not occur. Expectations create results. This figure can be hundreds of thousands to millions of dollars. The unrealized bottom line potential is much more meaningful than a budget. In fact, businesses need to revise their budgets when they determine their unrealized bottom line potential. This is where your Profit Plan is transformed into a quantitative goal for "Super Bowl" profits. The unrealized bottom line potential is activity-based and results-driven. Its financial goals are based on future opportunities. It is very different from a budget which is based on past performance. Now you will have a never-before-realized confidence in your company's profit*ability*.

Accountability and responsibility will create greater profit*ability* and prevent early retirement.

With your Profit Plan in writing and accountability assigned for its many profit projects, everyone has a sense of what they can do to enhance the bottom line. As a former player said when he played for the San Francisco 49ers in their glory days:

> Each year, the 49ers believe they're going to the Super Bowl. It doesn't matter who's wearing the uniforms. There's a level that's expected of you, and if you don't reach it, they'll find someone else. That's the attitude we need around here—the attitude that says, "We're going to win every game." If I can help the guys here get that attitude, I will have accomplished something.

That's the kind of attitude you should expect from your Profit Super Bowl, and what you want to hear from every one of your new Profit Champions or project leaders.

Your next step is to appoint your top "assistant coach" to work most closely with the team during the profit process. This Profit Activities Leader or PAL could be the COO, CFO or senior vice president of your company, someone who shares your vision for the company, understands the big financial picture, and will help you guide the entire process over the financial goal line. Your Profit Activities Leader should also be a good coach who is skilled in helping each individual team member "play" his or her best to reach their genuine profit*ability* level.

Characteristics of a Profit Activities Leader:

■ Develops self-motivating Profit Team leaders.

■ Gets Profit Team leaders to carry out their own ideas for greater profit*ability*.

■ Creates Profit Teams that manage the bottom line.

■ Encourages Profit Team members, working effectively with other departments, to advance the bottom line of the entire organization.

■ Instills "World-Class Service." This creates change that enhances the bottom line and advances the mission of the organization.

Step #5 is to play the Profit Game to win.

The world is full of great ideas that never went anywhere because they were not implemented well. In football, the players and coaches refer to the playbook constantly. The coaches introduce new plays during verbal presentations, in visual presentations on film and overheads, and in written form, constantly seeking player feedback for buy-in and improvement. They revise the playbook based on past experience, and an analysis of all the coaches' feedback about their competitors' winning moves. Players come to understand the reasons and strategies behind each new play and how it fits into the game plan and the team's goals for the season. Then practice begins.

During the PEP, Profit Champions form additional Profit Teams to implement their assigned profit projects. The Profit Activities Leader meets with them regularly to assess how they are doing and to hold them accountable. The job of the PAL is to make the company successful by giving Profit Champions the resources they need. Do they need more time allotted to complete the project, more staff support, assistance from other departments? Are there additional profit opportunities that have become apparent as a result of working on the projects? Is there a better idea to attain that goal? Should a project be modified to better accomplish it?

Our experience has taught us that the main reasons for the failure to implement ideas are:

- No one individual is responsible;

- Deadlines are not set, adhered to, or focused on;

- No means of measuring progress exists;

- Priorities have not been established;

- Those responsible for implementation aren't rewarded if successful or do not suffer consequences if they are not successful;

- People haven't been trained to implement profit projects; and

- Consensus was not strong enough at the start.

During the all-important implementation segment of the profit process, your Profit Activities Leader must have the authority to give Profit Champions and their committees the time and resources necessary to accomplish the profit projects. If no one is responsible for monitoring progress, it is likely deadlines will be missed. People do properly what is inspected—not just expected. Without accountability, projects will keep slipping until everyone forgets them. The PAL must be someone your team respects and who is empowered by the CEO to ensure that ideas identified by the Profit Team are carried out. Profit strategies need the unequivocal backing of the CEO. The CEO has the right to veto any initiative, but from our experience he or she rarely does. If Profit Teams are developing strategies to make a business more successful, there is little reason to exercise the veto power. However, remember the Golden Rule of the late Jack Kent Cooke, owner of the Washington Redskins:

"The man with the gold, rules."

Initiate rewards for success and enforce consequences for not living up to the commitments, and your implementation process is destined to win. Super profits are the trophy.

As Profit Advisors, we meet regularly with our client's Profit Activities Leader to share the responsibility with him or her and to help work through the issues. There's only one way to eat an elephant: one bite at a time. We also prepare a monthly progress report to the CEO which measures, among other things, the percentage of completion for each profit project.

These are the steps in the Profit Enhancement Process. If you believe that you are already accomplishing them, try this test.

1. List five people who report to you.

2. Beside each name write five proactive profit projects that person has suggested to you in the last six months.

3. Record the date when each initiative was or will be completed, who is responsible for doing the work, and the amount of profit each will add to your bottom line.

A TEST OF YOUR COMPANY'S CURRENT PROFIT*ABILITY*

Employees Who Report to You	Suggested Profit Projects (5 for each reports to you)	Expected Completion Date	Profit Champion	$ Profit Expected
1._____				
_____				
_____				
_____				
_____				
2._____				
_____				
_____				
_____				
_____				
3._____				
_____				
_____				
_____				
_____				
4._____				
_____				
_____				
_____				
_____				
5._____				
_____				
_____				
_____				
_____				

If your worksheet is full of ideas that are consistently being implemented, congratulations. You are successfully following a Profit Enhancement Process of your own. If you were unable to complete this test—most business owners and managers can't—read on.

Instant Replays

Profit is always a journey; it's never a destination.

Step #1 in the Profit Enhancement Process is to create a culture where profit will thrive.

Ask yourself what's impossible to do in your business today that will make your business more profitable tomorrow?

Profit Team leaders and members know that their job is to identify financial opportunities and be responsible for turning their ideas into bottom line results.

Fleeing fortunes are the result of years of denial of significant profit opportunities.

 Step #2 is to conduct a Profit Audit of your business.

Businesses are drowning in information, but are thirsty for knowledge.

"Traditional budgeting is a waste of time!"
                    —Former Accountant turned Profit Advisor

The customer never says your prices are too high. They say the value of what they received is too low.

Consider not only the well-executed plays, but also the profit "fumbles."

Profit fumbles are really opportunities to score…in disguise.

The Profit Super Bowl turns department managers into team players.

Step #3 is to hold a profit management retreat—a Profit Super Bowl—where managers and employees become your powerhouse Profit Team.

The Profit Super Bowl turns department managers into team players

Step #4 is to take all those good ideas and build the Profit Plan—your company's game plan for winning big over the next season.

Accountability and responsibility will create greater profitability and prevent early retirement.

Step #5 is to play the Profit Game to win.

Chapter 3

PRE-SEASON TRAINING:
Identifying Your Profit Audit
Opportunities

> By making each person involved in the program...we were able to come up with our own ideas. Ideas to save money, work smarter, and make our company a better place to work for our employees, and a better environment for our valued customers.
>
> – Carlos B. Hart, President, Hart Motor Company, Inc.

You can't tackle problems unless you know what they are. You can't leap into profit opportunities until you have identified them.

A great football coach spends the first weeks after the season is over reviewing and revising the team's playbook— its record of every possible play the team has ever used that works. He reviews films of the winning teams' games, analyzing their formations, the areas of the field where they are effective making plays, and what they did during the first down, the second, and that crucial third. He analyzes their patterns of play and how his team might utilize some of their most successful opponents' strategies to play ever better and beat them at their own game during the next season.

Great profit coaches spend 33% of their time on product service and idea development, 33% on coaching, and 34% on implementing the new Profit Plan.

In the same way, a great CEO must start with what we call a Profit Audit—taking complete stock of the business, identifying new opportunities and old challenges. How do you do this? One way is by asking questions. Ask yourself, your customers, and your employees. The goal is to identify meaningful profit opportunities.

The Profit Audit is designed to be a systematic assessment of where the business can improve. It should delve into five key areas of every business:

(1) Employees
(2) Organizational Structure
(3) Sales and Marketing
(4) Operations
(5) Financial Management

Keep each of these areas in mind as you conduct your Profit Audit. You can get some ideas from your financial information. But these, after all, are simply scoreboards. They tell you the score at the end of the game, not how you got there, or where to go next. The most significant opportunities are locked up in the minds of those you work with.

Never, never, never stop asking questions.

This is a chapter full of questions, the kind of questions we ask when we work with a client. Questions are what help us help our clients identify the hidden profit opportunities that have made thousands, if not millions, of dollars of difference to their bottom lines. And questions are what will help you do the same.

After all our years in business, we can now drive into the parking lot of any business or organization, park, go into the reception area, walk around the office or plant, stroll through the warehouse, talk to a few employees, drive away and suggest three or four profit opportunities that weren't previously apparent to their business. Much of it is common sense and much of it is learning how to identity it. That has to come from years of experience. That's what this chapter will share with you.

Start your Profit Audit with a profit*ability* tour
of your business.

Drive into your own parking lot. What do you see? Is it well maintained, no potholes, few empty spaces? But maybe there are no expensive cars parked there, and no prestige signage on buildings.

What about the reception area? Is it nice, neat and clean? Are there recent magazines available? How well is the receptionist fielding calls? Does she answer the phone abruptly? Does she sound more like a machine instead of a customer goodwill ambassador? Is she getting a predictable result from her mannerisms, ways and words? Does she seem to be referring sales inquiries to the person who can answer them and turn them into an order? What signs of smooth operations can be seen by watching the receptionist do her job? When calls are transferred, are they promptly answered or is the customer left dangling, or worse, lost in the shuffle?

When you stroll through any part of the organization, do you observe the simple clues that give you an indication of how well the company is doing?

When talking to employees, do they seem upbeat? Are they supportive of the company's policies and procedures? Do they know the company's policies and procedures? Taking an unofficial trip (with attention and intention) around any company is a real eye-opener.

We once walked into the reception area of a client who had hired us to help the company reach its profit potential. We took one look at their huge underutilized space, and came up with an idea that saved the company thousands of dollars. You guessed it. Why not rent out the part they weren't using, and use the money to improve the bottom line? Simple, yes! Profit*able*, yes! But the CEO couldn't see the obvious. He wasn't using his profit*ability*.

As a profit coach, you must be a bloodhound honing in on hidden profit opportunities.

If we were to walk into your office right now and throw a million one-dollar bills on the floor, what would you do? You'd stoop right over and pick them up, right?

In a way, that is what we are doing when we ask clients these questions. The answer to any one of them will be the creative spark for finding hidden profits.

So start your Profit Audit by asking yourself these primary questions:

(1)   Are you currently selling to enough customers?

(2)   Are you selling enough to your current customers?

(3)   Are your customers bragging about doing business with you?

(4)   What can you do to increase the number of current customers?

(5)   What can you do to increase the transaction value of each customer?

(6)   What can you do to keep your customers coming back more often?

(7)   What conflicts between departments influence customer satisfaction, timeliness, and/or quality?

(8)   What redundancies occur within tasks?

(9)   Do you have long-term, motivated, loyal employees?

(10) How can you increase the perceived value of your products and services so that your customers will be willing to pay you more?

(11) What are your customers' expectations of your business, products and services?

(12) What can be done to improve the process of all of the above in each departmentment and in the company as a whole?

If you can answer these questions, you will be a long way towards identifying where your real profit opportunities are hiding. This is the essence of the Profit Audit. It's significantly more involved than these key questions, but we believe that if every business knew the answers to these basic questions, they would be ready to win the Profit Game today.

> The Profit Audit provides you with a scouting report of profit possibilities—not answers.

Your audit should consist of every question you'd like answered about how your business is organized and how it operates, about those who work there, those who buy your products or services, and about the state of your finances. But all these questions, answered by you, your employees, and even your customers, won't provide you with a plan of action, a game plan. The opportunities and problems discussed during the Profit Audit are like the football coach's "scouting report"—a list of profit issues you will wish to address in your game plan for the season. The Profit Audit will make you aware of all the challenges and opportunities that your business can pursue, a menu of options, choices you never knew existed for your business. It doesn't come right out and tell you how to be more financially successful. It's your play book of possible plays. You must then decide which ones will produce the biggest payoff.

You'll need to introduce the plays to your Profit Team, toss the ball around with them, see which ones work best for your team and its players, perfect your plays with them, then you'll be ready to play ball. Just as in football, it's up to you and your managers to choose the issues you feel are most important. In order to choose the right strategies for your team and implement their ideas, you'll need to put your Profit Team to work.

> Financial statements are the scoreboard from last season. Ask yourself: What can we do better next season?

In most cases, financial reports, your balance sheet and income statement, represent the present value of your company's past performances. They are a report card that reaffirms which strategies work and illustrates when your business is not living up to expectations. They are important, there is no doubt about that; but keep in mind the fact that there are many more clues to profit*ability* than financial information provides.

For instance, consult your trade association or franchise organization. They are in business to help you be successful, and consider themselves to be the advocate for your business. They will supply you with industry statistics and trends, access to their library of information, and invitations to their activities intended to offer opportunities for networking with others who will have profit ideas to share with you.

But, of course, for your Profit Audit you should review the following documents (always keeping the five key areas of your business in mind) and ask yourself questions like these:

#1 - Employees
Personnel Manual

- Are employees required to sign a statement acknowledging that they have received the personnel manual and understand that the rules specified govern their employment?

- Are regular employee evaluations performed to correct inappropriate behavior and to reinforce good performance?

- Are there coaching sessions between evaluations?

- Has your company protected itself from unfounded employee claims and lawsuits?

- Are you satisfied with your employee retention rate?

- Do job descriptions exist so that employees know what is expected of them?

#2 - Organizational Structure
Succession Plan

■ If something happened to the owners of the business, is there a written succession plan?

■ Key employees can be the lifeblood of your business. Are there contingency plans for filling the void if they are unable to work or were to leave the company?

Organization Chart

■ Is your organization chart complete and up-to-date?

■ A person can be effective in directly managing only a limited number of people.
Do any department heads have too many people directly reporting to them? Which department heads are constantly in demand and have little time to finish projects or supervise others?

■ Does a logical chain of command exist?

#3 - Sales & Marketing
Marketing Plan

■ Many companies have not identified potential customers for their products and services. Have you developed customer profiles for your products and services? What are you doing to create interest in your products or services with these potential customers?

■ It is much easier to sell more to existing customers than to find new ones. Are your customers aware of the products and services that are appropriate for their needs?

■ Is your mission statement visible for customers and employees to see? Do they understand it?

■ Has your mission statement been recently reviewed and is it in sync with your existing goals?

#4 - Operations
Business Plan

■ Does a business plan exist?

■ Are the long-term goals of your business identified, and are there action plans in place to realize them?

■ Do your employees understand what your company is trying to achieve?

Policies and Procedures Manual

■ Do you have guidelines in place to ensure production and performance standards in all areas of your business?

■ Are your procedures spelled out clearly and precisely so that different people doing the same job have similar performance standards?

■ Have you documented relevant policies and procedures so that there is a map for others to follow?

#5 - Financial Management
Financial Statements

■ Can you explain what caused favorable results? Can you cause them to be repeated predictably?

- Can you explain unfavorable results? Can you cause them NOT to be repeated?

- In any income or expense category, can you explain why there are differences between current and prior periods? What can be done to change the results during the next period?

- Have you developed benchmarks from past financial information that will be useful in determining if you are improving in certain areas or getting worse? Are you using those benchmarks?

Business Tax Returns

- Have you optimized federal tax savings at the expense of state taxes?

- Have you optimized tax deductions and credits for income tax purposes?

- In a "C" corporation, donating excess inventory to certain charities can create a tax deduction greater than what you paid for the inventory. Would such a donation help this year's bottom line?

- There are tax credits available that produce significantly greater tax benefits than tax deductions. Each dollar of tax credit can save up to a dollar of tax. These credits are available for expenditures in research and development, hiring certain economically disadvantaged individuals, and various other areas. Have you pursued the significant opportunities available to you by capturing these lucrative tax credits?

Shareholders' Tax Returns

■ Have you established medical reimbursement plans to cover expenses not covered by your traditional health plans?

■ Review the interest rates you are paying on your personal residence and other loans. Can the loans be restructured to give you lower interest rates and greater tax deductions?

Compensation Plans

■ Do your employees understand your compensation plan?

■ Does your compensation plan motivate the type of behavior you want from employees that will result in financial gain for your company?

If you do not have the answers to these questions, you have work to do. Consider adding their development to your Profit Action Plan.

Remember that the financial information sources you use are scoreboards from previous periods. They show you where your business stands, but they don't tell you how you got there or the game plan necessary to improve the score. Suppose you have a bad quarter, and your financial statement shows a decrease in profits. Traditional financial reporting states it happened, but does not answer the most important question: Why?

There are a number of potential reasons to explain the decline. For example, your product may no longer be competitive in the marketplace, or deficiencies in customer service have alienated potential and existing customers. Late deliveries may have caused customers to seek more reliable alternative sources of supply, or your sales people may have been ineffective in their job and are either not finding new opportunities or are unable to convert existing ones into sales. Perhaps you are burdened by excessive interest, inadequate gross margin, inadequate expense control or excessive carrying costs. These are a few of the many causes of decline in profits.

When you review your financial statements, you may learn that costs have risen. In some cases, trends will be recognized and costs contained in selected areas. Most of our clients are mature and stable companies who are already doing a proficient job at cost control. In many cases, they are operating within industry-accepted norms.

So what less-obvious situations may be causing a rise in costs that are not revealed in traditional financial reports? Perhaps, equipment is outmoded and frequently breaks down. This increases labor costs, because employees can't work up to their capacity. Perhaps there are redundancies in your order fulfillment department. This increases the time and expense of getting products to your customers. Perhaps your costs are rising because certain departments are not effective. Perhaps, as happened in the late 1990s, a tight labor market may have caused labor costs to increase. Someone or some process that worked in an earlier phase of your business is no longer in sync with your present organizational goals. Employee turnover is also a major cause of increased costs and decreased sales. Besides the expense and inconvenience of finding new people, disruption in operations has a ripple effect in many other areas.

When your company has plateaued and is not making the gains you feel are possible, what do you do? Traditional financial information is the basis from which to begin asking many of the tough questions. However, this is extremely complex and difficult for someone to do who is too close to the business or industry. The longer you are with a company, the less ability you have to identify the possibilities. You can no longer see the letter "f's".

Ask your employees!
They know 70 percent of the answers.

While performing Profit Audits for our clients, we invite department heads, managers, up-and-coming all-stars, and others who have a sense of what's going on in the organization to fill out a survey specifically designed for the needs of our clients, but similar to the sample below. Employees are assured that their personal answers will not be shared with others. It is important to have honest answers, untainted by what employees think the company wants to hear. They must reflect what they really believe. Perceptions are real! When we work with a client on a Profit Audit engagement, we often have employees send their surveys directly to us to ensure confidentiality.

Here are a few sample questions from a questionnaire we use. Adapt it to your company's needs.

The Profit Audit Questionnaire

Name of Company_____

Employee's Name_____ (*you can make this optional*)

Department_____Date:_____

Instructions: *This questionnaire focuses on the five integral parts of a successful organization. Its purpose is to illustrate your organization's unrealized profit opportunities. For each issue, select a number between 1 and 10 that best ranks your organization's standing. One is the least and ten is the greatest. Select N/A for those questions that you think are not relevant. Base your answers on your impression of your company, and not just your department. Your answers should reflect the way things are, not the way they should be! Your answers will be kept confidential.*

Overall Perspective:

On a scale of 1 to 10, with 10 being your company's maximum profit potential, how do you rate your company this year?
(Circle your answer.)

1   2   3   4   5   6   7   8   9   10

What would moving several notches mean to your company's profit*ability*?
Your estimate in dollars of Profit Potential: $_____.

EMPLOYEES: Section #1

On a scale of 1 to 10, rate your company's standing with your employees in these areas:

Issue	*Score*
Our employees are focused on generating profits and have a plan to follow.	_____
We have thorough orientation and initial training programs.	_____
Our evaluation process lets people know where they stand throughout the year.	_____
We have the right people in the right jobs at the right wage.	_____
Our employees know our firm's mission and vision, and their activities support its realization.	_____

ORGANIZATIONAL STRUCTURE :Section #2

On a scale of 1 to 10, with 10 being the best, rate your company's organizational structure in these areas:

Issue	*Score*
We are effective in implementing projects.	_____
Up-to-date job descriptions exist and guide employees' activities.	_____
We continually fix the causes of problems, instead of fighting the same fires.	_____
We leverage decisions to lower staff, to free time and to maximize resources.	_____
Employees put the welfare of our company ahead of their department.	_____

SALES & MARKETING: Section #3

On a scale of 1 to 10, with 10 being the best, rate your company's sales & marketing in these areas:

Issue	Score
Potential customers are aware of our products and services.	_____
We set sales targets with gross profit objectives.	_____
We maximize sales from our complete product line to existing customers.	_____
Our customers are easily able to obtain reliable information about their order.	_____
Strong two-way communications occur between sales and other departments.	_____

OPERATIONS: Section #4

On a scale of 1 to 10, with 10 being the best, rate your company's operations in these areas:

Issue:	Score
We meet our customers' delivery requirements.	_____
Our procedures provide maximum efficiency and minimum waste.	_____
We catch mistakes before they impact customers and profits.	_____
A problem with our product/service is quickly and satisfactorily resolved.	_____
We know our customers' expectations and satisfaction levels.	_____

FINANCIAL MANAGEMENT: Section #5

On a scale of 1 to 10, with 10 being the best, rate your company's financial management in these areas:

Issue	*Score*
Cash flow is good. We collect receivables and pay bills on time.	_____
Our pricing strategies are based on market value.	_____
We measure labor-and-equipment productivity and use the data in decision-making.	_____
Flash reports of key business indicators are distributed and used on a timely basis.	_____
Our inventory control achieves maximum turns and is equal to industry norms.	_____

When you look at the results, you'll see a pretty clear picture of how your business, or any business, measures up.

When a company scores 6 or higher in all sections, the business is well-balanced and profit*able*, but hasn't started to exploit its profit potential. Unless the business scored 8 or higher in every section, our experience suggests that there is always room to improve—and additional profit to generate.

When we perform a Profit Audit for clients, we also conduct personal interviews with management and selected employees. This might be hard for you to do because employees may feel awkward revealing their feelings to their boss. We are able to ask the Barbara Walters' type questions, the ones that cut to the chase. We assure them we will keep their individual answers confidential so they don't feel threatened. We abide by this promise because we want their message heard and don't want the messenger destroyed.

Through these questions our goal is to find out for clients further information on why their employees think as they do. We ask each employee for the reasons they gave particularly low or high scores. We listen carefully for issues each person thinks are most important. We reinforce the promise that top management is eager to hear their ideas for increasing sales and margins, improving processes, controlling costs and increasing customer satisfaction.

Our questions always begin with: "What do you think your company is trying to accomplish?" The answers are amazing. What we're looking for here is their ideas about where the company may be missing some profit opportunities, and whenever an issue is stated, we ask for examples.

Our next question always is: "What is holding your company back from getting to the next profit plateau?"

After exploring the answer to this vital question, we continue with questions like:

- Why did you join the company, and what has influenced you to stay?

- What would you identify as your organization's greatest strengths?

- What additional strengths do you think your company must develop to remain competitive?

- What would you identify as your organization's greatest weaknesses?

- How do you think you could eliminate these weaknesses to remain competitive?

- What does your company do better than any other?

- What unique value do you provide to customers?

- How can you increase that value next year?

- What new markets could you explore?

- Which current products or services do you think should be eliminated and why?

- Do you know what your competition does better than you?

- Who do you think your competitors will be in the future?

- Does your department have all the resources it needs to be successful?

- What business issues do you think management should concentrate on?

You may be able to gain enough knowledge of what your employees are thinking from the written survey. If not, try some of these personal interviews. It's not easy, especially if there is some distance between management and employees. You may need to assign these interviews to another level of management or to the Profit Advisor.

Create a profit opportunities checklist of the issues you've discovered and pick the top ten. These are the first plays your Profit Team should consider practicing.

Once you've gathered this information, make a list of all the profit opportunities and challenges you've discovered. Don't stop asking questions. Challenge yourself to consider all sorts of issues that could optimize your company's profit potential. But start by selecting the top ten profit opportunities based on what you think should be done first. Once these have been addressed, another ten or so can be tackled by your Profit Teams.

After we perform a Profit Audit for a client, we offer a comprehensive list of possible "options" or profit plays which the CEO has not been able to see. We put this list into the Profit Opportunities Report. These plays hold the keys to moving the company forward toward the profit zone.

In our Profit Opportunities Reports, we raise profit-probing issues. A brief sample follows:

Revenue

Have you considered training your customer service employees to sell all the company's products or services, not just those from their own department?

Are your sales people using low prices as the main tool to maintain customer loyalty?

Should you initiate a process to identify customers' expectations and the types of services necessary to satisfy them?

Should you have a lead-generation system?

Do you think your prices match the value your customers believe they are worth?

Gross Margins

Can selected prices be raised now?

Do you have mechanisms in place to regularly evaluate pricing levels and make appropriate changes?

Have you considered announcing future price increases to create additional sales in the current period?

Can you unbundle your products and services and charge more in total?

What is your criterion for accepting low or unprofit*able* sales? Should they be eliminated?

Have you determined which sales are unprofit*able*, and what should be done to make them more profit*able* or eliminate them altogether?

Operating Expenses

Are you spending enough on sales and marketing? Reduced sales may be a result of not committing reasonable resources to advertising and marketing.

Should the procurement of supplies for all locations be consolidated to get better prices and terms?

Are vendors asked for ideas to help control expenses, services or supply alternatives?

Can maintenance contracts be renegotiated and/or eliminated?

Employee Issues

Is overtime being controlled? When is it approved?
Are bonuses based on incentives? Are bonuses subjective or objective?

Have you considered varying the deductible amount from compensation for health insurance, based on employee compensation?

Have you considered upward evaluations of management?

Inventory

Is your management of inventory as effective as it should be?

Do you have a regular system for eliminating slow moving inventory? The average monthly cost of carrying inventory is two percent.

Fixed Assets

Have you considered a process to regularly measure the sensibility of keeping old equipment vs. acquiring new?

Notes Payable

Instead of receiving interest income from the bank, have you thought about paying down your line of credit since this more than doubles your yield?

Corporate Tax Matters

Have you considered investing in domestic dividend-paying companies and/or mutual funds? "C" corporations are entitled to a 70-percent dividend exclusion.

Personal Tax Matters

Have you named your estate, rather than individuals, as beneficiary to your retirement plans? If you have, you have accidentally accelerated your tax liability when you die.

Management Issues

Does management interact regularly with employees and make them feel like part of the success of your business? Are your employees coached to fix a problem when they make a mistake?

Have you considered a monthly report of unkept promises to customers, prepared by each office or location? This will help focus everyone on attentive customer service and taking care of your customers' needs in a timely fashion.

Organizational Issues

Is there a process in place to fully evaluate how new ideas for the growth of your business are implemented? Here is a samle list of questions you might ask:

Is the idea financially viable?

Is there a strategy for the allocation of resources?

Do you have personnel with proper skills available to increase the sales and deliver the product? If not, is adequate training provided?

Will your focus be pulled from other critical functions?

Will the idea be completed on time and be fully functional?

Are there too many uncompleted projects?

How are employees prioritizing their activities?

Has management helped them establish priorities?

Are goals clearly communicated to the appropriate people?

Is there a system in place to keep management aware of the status of all projects?

How does accountability break down?

Is the idea part of your core business?

Are all people who contribute valuable insight into the evaluation process included in the decision to move forward?

Are contingencies in place to deal with negative results? Do employees understand what your company does?

Do employees understand the rationale for change?

How do you eat an elephant? One bite at a time.

These are only a small sample of the kinds of questions that help uncover opportunities. You'll have many more when you've assessed your financial information, reviewed corporate documents and surveyed your key employees.

How do you eat an elephant? One bite at a time. You can't tackle all the issues at once. Take your top ten into your Profit Super Bowl and ask everyone to take a bite. This is the last step you'll have to perform alone during the Profit Enhancement Process.

Now let's learn how the Profit Enhancement Process shares the responsibility for profit-making.

Instant Replays

You can't tackle problems unless you know what they are. You can't leap into profit opportunities until you have identified them.

Great profit coaches spend 33% of their time on product service and idea development, 33% on coaching, and 34% on implementing the new Profit Plan.

Never, never, never stop asking questions.

Start your Profit Audit with a profitability tour of your business.

The Profit Audit provides you with a scouting report of profit possibilities—not answers.

Financial statements are the scoreboard from last season. Ask yourself: what should we do better next season?

Ask your employees! They know 70 percent of the answers.

Create a profit opportunities checklist of the issues you've discovered and pick the top ten. These are the first plays your Profit Team should consider practicing.

How do you eat an elephant? One bite at a time.

Chapter 4

TEAM PRACTICE:
Building a Winning Profit Game Team

This was the first seminar where we rose above personalities and finger pointing and focused entirely on the issues. We also brought to the table those "sacred cows," which are always there but no one talks about. We discussed these openly and discovered ways of disposing of all of them.

– Ronald P. Ruchalski, President, East End Moving & Storage, Inc.

Again you wowed us at our recent Profit Enhancement seminar. Thank you. You have brought me back into the flock of the faithful and showed me how good I really have it, not how tough the road is that I walk as a small business CEO. You truly are a friend and I appreciate you, Barry, both as friend and consultant. My Dad told me that it would be lonely at the top, however, with friends like you my loneliness is shared.

–Philip N. Potvin, President, Western Concrete Products Co.

In this chapter you are invited to participate in a profit management retreat. We call it the Profit Super Bowl because it's the time when your top team, your starters, pull together to create the game plan to win. It's the time when your star performers get an opportunity to take the company to the top. Those chosen to participate should be experienced players, trained in the company's strategies and goals, and dedicated to winning.

During the Profit Super Bowl the starting team works together to develop a Profit Plan for your business. They work through a process of discovering previously unrealized profit possibilities and identifying strategies for adding them to the bottom line.

Here, it is everyone's job, as members of your starting

Profit Team, to share ideas that will make the organization more successful. We've already discussed how most employees do work that is functional, but it may not add real value to the company. This session will define activities that will change the way people work—from just completing tasks that satisfy their department's functions to participating in the development of a truly profitable business whose success benefits—and depends upon—everyone in the business.

"I can is more important than I.Q."
—Clark A. Johnson, Chairman of the Board, Pier 1

In this chapter you will participate in a "virtual" Profit Super Bowl, where you will learn how the responsibility for profit*ability* is shared among management. You'll see managers coming up with great new profit-enhancing ideas because they are really going to begin to understand the bottom line possibilities...the big picture. One good idea will lead to another as they learn that profit achievements are more important than completed tasks. You'll see managers discovering that their job is to identify financial opportunities and be responsible for turning ideas into dollars in addition to their other assignments.

In this chapter we are the outside Profit Advisors who will facilitate the group through various Profit Team building exercises, focusing on improving the organization's bottom line. During this session, managers will discover and identify areas that will make the business more profitable, in total harmony with the goals and objectives of the business. Then they will organize profit project committees that define the company's profit goals, and develop strategies to achieve them.

Soon you'll understand how effective it is for the group to discuss the financial ideas suggested by individual members and how they should be implemented. Together we will set financial goals for each profit project which are specific and measurable, and fix accountability and responsibility for each. We know that without quantifiable financial goals, profits will not occur. What you can measure, you can manage. Profit goals should be motivational. Remember, profit results are the name of the game. Without a map you get lost, or worse, you may never get there at all. Financial goals should be in total harmony with the business's goals and objectives.

The focus of this Profit Super Bowl is to maximize the organization's bottom line. We encourage our clients to focus first on "quick fix" and easily attainable goals that can be realistically attained over a a short period of time. This gives them the confidence necessary to pursue more difficult opportunities later on. The Profit Plan developed during this workshop will inventory resources, labor dollars, and goals and describe how they will be used most effectively to reach the ultimate goals of the company. We believe that business profit planning is really the act of matching available information and resources with educated estimates to project bottom line possibilities.

Your goal—a Profit Plan that is a bottom line, logical strategy for finding profits in a whole new way.

What exactly is a Profit Plan—as opposed to a budget or business plan? A Profit Plan is a bottom line-oriented, logical strategy. It takes into account literally dozens of ways you are letting money slip through your fingers. It's a shift in corporate culture, implemented by management, but carried out by every employee in your firm. A Profit Plan forces you, and everyone in your organization, to look for profits in a whole new way, and in so many fresh new areas that you'll be amazed at its leverage ability.

Some profit strategies will be obvious. You may already be practicing them to a lesser degree. But the Profit Super Bowl is a time for pulling them out and looking at everything your business does today that it could be doing better, including strategies you haven't tried yet.

The Profit Super Bowl is being held right here in this book. Dress is casual. Your ideas are very important to us. Your attendance is absolutely necessary for the entire session. You may find that one retreat is all you need, but most of our clients find that regularly scheduled Profit Team meetings keep the fires burning year after year.

Your guest list should include everyone you think has the best ideas for your company and who will put forth the effort to turn ideas into bottom line results.

Just as in those first important scrimmages the team plays before the season begins, you'll want to chose your best players for this management retreat—those who are ready for action.

Every great coach knows you can't win by yourself. So a profit coach can't improve profit*ability* by working in a vacuum. The real reason for holding the Profit Super Bowl is that it's difficult for any one individual to see the whole picture, but everyone can see part of it. The retreat is an opportunity for the starting team—representing each major department—to come together with their own ideas and be prepared to listen to others. The profit retreat shifts the sole burden for making profits from the CEO to a shared responsibility with the Profit Team. It transforms team members into leaders of the profit ideas they generate and teams they develop. So identify and make the guest list carefully. Each is invited to join this group because he or she has the following personal characteristics:

■ A thorough understanding of their function in the business;

■ The ability to comprehend the big picture, not merely one aspect of it;

■ The willingness to search for better ways of doing things;

■ The willingness to change;

The most expensive cost in a business is the cost of a closed mind.

- A passion for helping the company be successful and a high energy level;

- The ability to work effectively with other members of the Profit Team in a peer-group environment;

- The commitment and authority to make the time to devote to profit projects;

- The belief that being selected by the company to serve as a Profit Team member is an honor; and

- A positive profit attitude and commitment to serve as an effective member of the Profit Team.

Each manager will receive an invitation and a challenge similar to the one we've made to you as the profit coach.

> It's difficult for any one individual to see the whole picture, but everyone can see part of it.

Nearly every person who works in a business has ideas, but most businesses have no forum for communicating those ideas. How much effort is spent trying to encourage ideas? For years a major U.S. car manufacturer had problems with the quality of their paint. They hired expensive consultants. No one could help. One day a supervisor went down and asked people in the paint shop if they had ideas to improve the quality of paint on the vehicles. One bright line worker responded to this question with, "Yes, I thought you'd never ask." She had the solution and was glad to share it.

Most organizations have a CEO, a CFO, and even a COO; but how many have"PEOs"? A PEO is a Profit Enhancement Officer, charged with developing and implementing good, new profit ideas. Who should be this PEO? *Everyone* in your organization.

At the start of our profit brainstorming session we'll appoint all the participants as "PEOs" to get them thinking about those ideas. And when it's over you'll want to make everyone in your organization into a PEO, too.

Some businesses like to play it too safe. They set the bar for performance too low. But if that bar is raised by the Profit Team, and you are successful as a group, the organization will jump even higher.

The Profit Super Bowl must be a nonthreatening forum for sharing ideas. It is also the time to transform management teams that manage the affairs of their department into Profit Teams focused on the bottom line of the company as a whole. Most people in an organization don't know how high to jump. It's never been communicated to them. The Profit Super Bowl allows everyone to realize the potential of the company and their contribution to it. Some businesses like to play it safe, the bar for performance is set too low. If that bar is raised by the Profit Team, and you are successful as a group, the organization will jump even higher. Henry Ford once said, "If you think you can or you think you can't, you're probably right."

Expectations create results. You get what you expect—NOT what you want.

The Profit Super Bowl delegates the responsibility for improving the bottom line to all Profit Team members. It transforms them into profit leaders for the future. It emphasizes the impact they as individuals have on the bottom line. Team members get excited and accept challenges. That's why this retreat needs the starting team from each department. However, there has to be an attendee limit. Keep the group to 20 or fewer per session. The retreat for a large corporation might involve various divisional Profit Super Bowls that lead to an "All-Star" game with the best from each team invited to attend.

The first Profit Super Bowl should be an "away" game where no one from the home office will interrupt.

We recommend that the CEO appoint a meeting coordinator to make all the arrangements for the Profit Super Bowl. Hold it away from the office. A nearby hotel meeting room is best so that there is complete focus on the meeting without the traditional office interruptions. In the meeting room, tables and chairs should be set up in the shape of a horseshoe to allow all participants to feel equal and to see each other. The room should be equipped with all the audio-visual equipment you feel is necessary.

The meeting coordinator should make sure the room is a comfortable temperature, that there is adequate lighting, and enough space for everyone to work comfortably. The more natural sunlight, the more energy participants will feel.

Each participant should receive updated financial information. If you feel it is necessary, delete selected information you are uncomfortable sharing with the group.

When we facilitate a Profit Super Bowl, we ask the coordinator to arrange for rewards: $250 worth of two dollar bills! Why? Because two dollar bills are unusual. A two dollar bill signifies that unusual dollars are rewarded for unusual ideas and efforts. Award the two-dollar bills, or other rewards as you choose, to participants who provide valuable ideas during the session. On the back of the two-dollar bill is a picture of the Continental Congress working on the Declaration of Independence. Could we say this was America's first Profit Super Bowl?

"People like to be rewarded for their efforts," says Larry Pecattiello, our football coach friend. Some teams reward their players during the team meeting after each game. "Some of these players are making millions of dollars a year, but you should see how proud they are when we hand them a $100 bill in front of their peers. We give a $100 bill to the player who made the best sack, the best hit, the most decisive third down; and we reward the guy who tried hardest."

Coaching is motivating team members to try harder. Larry never criticizes a player for a bad move in front of the rest of the team. "If you want to motivate someone," he says, "only motivate in a praiseworthy way in front of his peers."

At the beginning of the meeting, appoint one person as note taker, responsible for capturing all agreed-upon profit strategies. This person is the football team's equivalent of the team statistician. Be sure to emphasize how important this job is. When we facilitate the Profit Super Bowl, we provide a specially formatted Excel spreadsheet for the "team statistician" to record ideas and assignments for each profit project.

The Profit Super Bowl is played strictly by the rules. Strict guidelines ensure that the Profit Plan will emerge strong, focused, and with motivating concensus.

The Profit Super Bowl is a nonthreatening forum, an opportunity to talk about the tough issues in a friendly way.

No one should get personal. We encourage talk about issues, not people. We challenge participants to discuss what can work—not what hasn't.

The rules for the Profit Super Bowl must be as follows:

1. *Listen with attention.*

2. *Stay focused with intention.*

3. *No sacred cows. Say what needs to be said. Speak the unspeakable.*

4. *Don't attack people. Attack business concepts.*

5. *No "cheap shots."*

6. *Respect differences of opinion rather than placing the blame.*

7. *Focus on solving problems.*

8. *Only new information will be discussed.*

9. *Keep it positive. Help others develop their ideas. No negative statements are allowed at this meeting. Thus none of the following foul language:*
   "Don't be ridiculous."
   "Let's shelve it for right now."
   "We're not ready for that."
   "It won't work here."
   "Our business is different."
   "Let's think about it some more."
   "We did all right without it."
   "It's too radical a change."
   "Management won't like it."
   "Where did you dig up that idea?"
   "It's not practical."
   "We've never done it before."
   "I have something better."
   "It's too risky."
   "Let's be sensible."
   "We can't afford that."
   "We'll never get it approved."
   "It's good, but. . ."
   "Let's check on it later."
   "Too much work."
   "Let's get back to reality."
   "That's been tried before."
   "You can't be serious."

These are the kinds of remarks that hold back any discussion, but particularly our nonthreatening forum where ideas are supposed to flow freely. Keep it positive!

10. Only one discussion at a time.

11. Look at your business through the eyes of a Profit Enhancement Officer.

12. Represent the company, not your department or function.

You as profit coach are not exempt from the rules. You are a participant, too, not the big boss. You retain the veto power, but are urged to use it sparingly. In fact, the less the CEO says and the more he or she listens, the more successful the retreat. A client once informed us that God gave us two ears and one mouth so that we can listen twice as much as we talk. This should be your rule for the Profit Super Bowl, and the words you do speak should be of encouragement, support, acknowledgment, and recognition.

Keep the group on target for achieving the goals of the retreat. Keep pushing for action when the discussion gets bogged down. Move the agenda when appropriate. Monitor the rules and provide a framework for each issue, broadening it when it seems to represent a larger issue than is generally perceived by members of the Profit Team. When and if they get personal, focus on what's good for the company and keep the human element out of the discussions.

In too many businesses, profit happens randomly.
The employees are like players playing without a
scoreboard. They need to know if they are
winning or losing to be effective team players
in the Profit Game.

You're all gathered around the room, comfortable and eager to begin. Your first goal is to transform this room full of managers and employees into a Profit Team.

Start with a PEP talk. Tell the group why you are gathered and what your expectations are for this particular session and for the process as a whole. Use this opportunity to inspire your team. Suggest that rewards may be offered in the future—both cash and non-cash—for coming up with new ideas, when they add value to the company's bottom line. Describe how they will be rewarded for putting forth the effort to turn those ideas into bottom line results. If the company is more successful, those who make it happen will be also.

Then ask the group to identify their goals for the session and write these on a flip chart. As an example, one of our clients, a firm of professionals, offered these expectations:

1. Create new ways for increasing the inventory of services we have to offer clients at higher billing rates;

2. Provide the groundwork for billing 20 percent additional revenues over the next 12 months;

3. Change the culture to make the practice more fun and more profitable;

4. Open lines of communication;

5. Come up with a plan for profit project implementation;

6. Create greater perception of value to our clients for services which will generate more profit for the firm;

7. Increase client satisfaction with the firm;

8. Gain new outlook on client relationships;

9. Feel better about what we do with our own careers because of the way clients feel about our firm;

10. Promote teamwork in our firm by sharing client projects.

This list is displayed during the entire Profit Super Bowl, so that you and your group will be reminded of your goals.

Begin the Profit Game by transforming your
managers into a powerhouse Profit Team. Then
make everyone in the organization
a PEO (Profit Enhancement Officer).

Now you must get your team ready to play—to change
the way they think, view the world, and act. Unlike traditional
management teams, you want your group to feel a greater
degree of ownership and commitment to financially quantified
profit projects.

■ Management teams advance the cause of their
department, while Profit Teams advance the
cause of their organization's bottom line.

■ Managers focus on yesterday. Profit Team
members focus on tomorrow.

■ Managers accept responsibility for the business
issues associated with their department.

■ Profit Teams identify financial strategies that
enhance the bottom line of the organization, designate Profit Champions to be responsible for
each profit project, establish quantifiable financial goals, set meaningful completion dates and
determine their relative importance, and are
responsible for turning profit ideas into bottom
line results.

We find that once people develop profit*ability*, they alter
their viewpoint and realize the possibilities open to them as
they help the business become more profitable, excitement
glows and commitment grows. The immediate challenge is to
transmit this excitement not only to this all-important starting
team but throughout the organization. The breakthrough
occurs when this diverse group of people work together to create a Profit Plan with identified strategies they agree are vital,
then carry their enthusiasm back to the rest of the team. Once
the paradigm has shifted, ideas flow.

Assign each player a "position," a role in
your emerging Profit Plan.

Now that each participant's focus is profit, how are they going to help generate it? We go around the room asking each person such questions as:

- Describe the company's profit strategy.

- Justify why you have a job with this firm.

- Describe the connection between the work you do and how it benefits the bottom line.

- What are your primary responsibilities?

- How is what you are doing today going to make the company more successful in the future?

Openly discuss each participant's role in the company. Often other participants will add comments about what that person has said about his or her job because they contribute to the company in ways that they don't recognize themselves. This helps the group understand the basic responsibilities of everyone and appreciate their place in the organization.

At the end of this discussion we praise anyone who mentioned the essentials of successful businesses:

- Profit generation so that the company has more choices and options available.

- Fulfilling the mission/vision of the company.

- Providing world-class customer service for customers.

Your organization must have PRIDE (Personal Responsibility In Delivering Excellence).

As we know from previous chapters, it's rare for an employee to link his or her job into the bigger picture. So here you can begin to explore the company's mission and vision and relate each person's job and responsibility for adding value to it. The goals of Profit Teams are defined as enhancing prof-it*ability* while providing "world-class customer service" (doing things so well that whomever you do it for, asks for more) and accomplishing the mission of the business, getting there because of a vision. A great quarterback's "mission" is to beat the other team; his "vision" is to throw the ball to where he thinks the receiver will be. In football you need a well-balanced team composed of offense, defense and special teams. In business, there must be a balance among profit, world-class service, and mission/vision to have a profit*able*, well-run company. Further, the business must achieve the goal of satisfied long-term employees. You can't have the first three without this fourth element.

Define your goal: To have everyone in the organization working towards realizing its bottom line potential, in harmony with the company's strategic goals and objectives.

This leads naturally into an introduction of the concept of unrealized bottom line potential. You can't realize your bottom line potential unless you discover your unrealized profit potential. Focus on the five engines that drive a successful business:

<u>The Five Engines that Drive A Successful Business</u>
 Employees
 Organizational Structure
 Sales and Marketing
 Operations
 Financial Management

As you focus on each of these five areas, tell the team what was uncovered in that area through the employee and customer surveys and the Profit Audit. Show the group how the company was ranked in these five areas. Show them on the scale of 1 to 10 the potential for profit that exists between the way the company operates today and what could be achieved in the future. Our experience is that most businesses fall below six in two to five of the engine categories, leaving 40 percent of the capacity unutilized. How effective is a team operating at 60 percent of profit capacity? Once the starting team accepts the fact that there is substantial unrealized profit for them to go after, they'll begin to examine the essential aspects, ideas, and processes of the organization with growing enthusiasm.

> Before the group recognizes new profit strategies, they have to deal with the challenges. What is preventing the organization from achieving its full profit potential?

A great football coach can tell you what caused the "fumbles" in each important game. You've performed your Profit Audit and now know what's causing those "profit fumbles" in your business. Help your team identify these profit fumbles as well as their causes. Ask what is holding the company back financially, and what each manager can be doing that he or she is not doing today to realize more profits for the company? Let employees know it's their job to add value to the bottom line. Involve them in identifying profit strategies, so those profit fumbles won't keep the company from making that all-important third down. Explore how profit fumbles have a negative effect on the final score. Profit equals income minus expenses including those profit fumbles. They are similar to sales returns—you earned it, and now you have to give it back. They minimize the bottom line. Profit is what's left at the end of the day. Have the group identify the profit fumbles that are keeping your business from winning and beating your competition.

> Profit fumbles are really opportunities to score in disguise.

Now introduce some of your priority profit opportunity issues for general discussion. Help your team discover them for themselves.

For instance, if you identified sales and marketing as a weak area, have the group discuss ways to increase sales for the company:

■ Increase the number of customers,

■ Sell more to each customer, and

■ Increase the value of each sales transaction.

Pricing is another important issue identified in most Profit Audits. The selling price of goods and services is perhaps one of the most central business decisions an organization must make. Profits begin with the sale, in concert with the proper selling price. If products and services are not priced effectively, profits will be sacrificed needlessly. Focus on pricing strategies that fit into your customer profiles.

Introduce your Profit Team to the way to play and win the game—The Profit Enhancement Process.

The Profit Enhancement Process is in no way just cutting expenses. No business can cost-cut its way to prosperity. The key to financial success involves creating a profit culture along with effective cost controls and innovative ways of increasing sales and profit margins. Generating profits requires a process just like every other normal business activity.

As members of the Profit Team, the group is charged with:

■ Sharing responsibility for profitability;

■ Establishing financial strategies that will improve profitability;

■ Setting meaningful, measurable financial goals

■ Fixing accountability so that certain people are responsible for getting each profit project accomplished;

■ Implementing and coordinating profit
   activities so that profitable ideas turn into
   financial successes.

Imagine the power of this starting team when it begins working closely with the soon-to-be-appointed Profit Activity Leader (PAL) to carry out the new profit initiatives defined during your Profit Super Bowl! You will be there to support their efforts with extra resources and time to ensure that the profit projects stay on track. You will see to it that their activities will be measured, monitored, and nurtured towards enhanced financial results.

Profit Teams implement change most effectively. Properly coached, they make informed bottom line improvement decisions, rather than just decisions. They are closer to the reality of what's going on in the organization than owners, because of their personal involvement and experiences. Coaching the implementation of profit projects is as important as deciding which activities should be tackled to begin with. Profit Teams take ownership of financial opportunities because they are part of the process that identifies them. Thus, they willingly accept responsibility for implementation. Proactivity is foremost on their agenda.

Profit Teams do much more than just manage rank-and-file employees. Typically, managers accept responsibility for the business issues associated with their department. Profit Teams identify financial strategies that enhance the bottom line of their organization in harmony with strategic goals and objectives, designate Profit Champions to be responsible for each profit project, establish quantifiable financial goals, set meaningful completion dates and are responsible for turning profit ideas into bottom line results.

Put your Profit Team onto the field to practice their
new plays, and let the good ideas flow.

The Profit Team is now ready to practice their own ideas for improving the company's bottom line. Break the Profit Team down into smaller groups, each charged with developing five profit-enhancing strategies.

Each idea must be completed with:

■ Action date—when will the business begin to realize a financial benefit;

■ Profit Champion—the individual responsible for managing the project;

■ Degree of Difficulty—whether the project has a high, low, or medium degree of difficulty to accomplish it;

■ Priority—how important is the idea—whether the project has a high, medium or low priority;

■ Unrealized bottom line potential—quantified in dollars;

■ Realized bottom line potential—filled in later as the actual financial results are achieved;

■ Financial assumptions—notes on how unrealized bottom potential was computed.

This is the first real quantification of the value the project will add to the company's bottom line. It must be based on an educated estimate of gross income less related expenses. For example, if the profit idea increases sales, estimate the additional profit margin on one sale. Multiply that amount by the projected number of units that will be sold to determine the gross profit. Then subtract additional expenses incurred as a result of the idea. The goal is to determine the realistic bottom line potential for each profit project that has yet to be realized—the unrealized bottom line potential.

Turn short-yardage plays into big gains.

As head profit coach, meet briefly with each group. Remember, you are the only one who knows your top profit priorities. Make sure that each of these priorities becomes a profit strategy in at least one of the Profit Team huddles. Never insist that the group implement it; just ask if they believe it to be a worthy project, and see if they take it from there. Also expand each suggested issue so that it becomes a bigger one, more global than local. For instance, someone may suggest that customer service operators are sometimes rude to customers. Your job as coach is to help the team discover why. Are customer service operators overworked? Do they know everything about the products so they don't have to run around asking other busy people questions? Are they properly trained? Are certain issues that affect one department more global than the group realizes? Do they actually affect various other departments as well?

> The real power of the Profit Super Bowl is the creation of a culture that brings employees into the profit process and assists them in taking ownership of profit strategies that enhance the bottom line.

Without profit coaching, your starting team will never get to the Profit Super Bowl. Help your team generate ideas. Broaden them, and expand your starters' perspectives.

> Select plays from your new playbook and turn them into a full-blown game plan.
> Put the Profit Plan together.

Once the groups have formulated their ideas, gather again to discuss them as a group. Start recording profit strategies on large sheets of paper taped around the room so everyone can watch the plan unfold. We have created attention-grabbing software templates which systematically record the Profit Plan. It is projected, using an LCD, for the group to observe. It is exhilarating for the team to see their ideas entered into our software, with the focus on the dollars of unrealized bottom line potential each profit project will generate. Without this software, be sure you record the following:

1. Each profit project idea

2. Its action date

3. Who is responsible for its implementation

4. Whose idea it is

5. Degree of difficulty

6. Priority (the relative importance of the issue to your company)

7. Quantified, unrealized bottom line potential in dollars

8. Financial assumptions used to determine the unrealized bottom line potential

The Profit Advisors' proprietary software template actually adds up the unrealized bottom line potential so that after each profit idea and at the end of the session, the group looks with amazement at the possibility dollars they have discovered. A Profit Champion (or project leader) for each strategy should be selected along with profit project committee members. After the Profit Super Bowl, each responsible manager, or Profit Champion, will select a committee, if needed, from the rest of the company's employees to carry out their profit initiative. They will then lay out the process to turn the idea into financial results.

■ Each profit strategy requires identifying, step-by-step and task-by-task, what is required to accomplish it. Remember, there is only one way to eat an elephant, one bite at a time. The goal is to break a big idea into comprehensible and manageable tasks.

■ Review with attention and intention the financial assumptions for each strategy. If the idea is successfully carried out, what will it contribute to the bottom line? It is critical that these estimates be extremely conservative so that expectations will be met with realistic support and be credible. The goal is to under-promise and over-deliver. Later, the Profit Teams will define additional tasks as they develop their own project.

■ The "Action Date" is when the company will begin to benefit financially from each strategy. This is the date when all preparations are completed and you are ready to begin playing the Profit Game. After the retreat, additional dates will be assigned for each specific task.

■ To keep enthusiasm high and good ideas flowing, give out the two-dollar bills or other rewards to every person who originated a profit-generating idea, as well as to those Profit Champions who will be carrying them out. The starting team congratulates one another for each strategy with growing gusto, and begins to compete for additional rewards themselves. This is what you want to continue happening in a more meaningful way when you get back to day-to-day reality. During the Profit Super Bowl, each special team offers its most significant issues. Often there is overlap, but you as profit coach can encourage each team to suggest at least one profit strategy, and be rewarded for it.

■ Most importantly, there must be a consensus that to tackle an idea, if accepted, will be for the good of the organization. Remember, you have veto authority at this point ("the man with the gold, rules"). Our experience is that this is rarely done. You'll wind up with a profit fumble if you do.

■ Make sure each strategy is thoroughly reviewed and analyzed, depending upon its significance to the company. Our football coach and friend, Larry Pecattiello, said players are presented with each new play verbally, visually through films of past games, and in a written form. Then they practice it. This way team members have an opportunity to hear it, see it, then practice it.

Let's look at the worksheet (opposite page) we use to help clients manage their Profit Plan. The following is a sample Profit Project Worksheet for a Profit Plan which we create on our template as we coach the client's starting team.(Names and dates have been changed.)

Once information is agreed upon by the Profit Team and recorded in the worksheet, only negotiations between each Profit Champion and the Profit Activities Leader will alter it.

At the end of the session, add up all the unrealized bottom line potential, and voila! The Profit Plan—complete with strategies, accountability, financial measures, and supporting information—is ready to put into action.

To sum up our session, the group now reviews the list of expectations they developed at the beginning of the Profit Super Bowl. We review each item to ensure expectations have been exceeded. They always are, because the Profit Team is proudly part of the process.

As a concluding exercise, each member of the Profit Team summarizes their commitment and evaluates the benefits of the retreat. We ask them to look at this exercise from the following three perspectives:

■ Themselves (the participant)

■ The group (the Profit Team as an entity)

■ The company (the organization)

A Profit-Focused Company's Profit Plan-Project Worksheet

Profit Project	Action date	Profit Plan Champion	Profit Plan Idea Generator	Priority (1 high 2 med 3 low)	Degree of Difficulty (1 high 2 med 3 low)	Unrealized Bottom Line Potential**	Realized Bottom Line Profit*
1- Maximize delivery loads from factory to stores.	1/1/99	Joe	Sam	2	3	$100,000	
2 - Improve sales process in the followng areas: Incoming telephone inquiries, Cross-selling, Developing sales database	2/1/00	Carl	Webb	1	2	$565,000	
3 - Establish acceptable moisture contents for raw materials.	2/1/99	Larry	Laura	2	1	$100,000	
4 - Repair broken pallets rather than buy new ones, & evaluate their size in relationship to what they hold.	2/1/99	Ray	Chuck	2	3	$ 80,000	
5 - Recycle shipping materials that are used on incoming deliveries.	2/1/99	Sue	Curtis	3	3	$18,000	
6 - Determine the causes of manufacturing products that do not meet our quality standards. Establish a process to minimize the cost of waste in production by not doing things right the first time.	2/1/00	Bruce	David	1	1	$220,000	
7 - Establish a close-out procedure for excess inventory.	6/1/99	Dina	Allan	2	3	$180,000	
8 - Develop and implement a preventative maintenance plan for equipment, so that the manufacturing process doesn't stop when machinery breaks down.	1/1/00	Steve	Todd	1	2	$259,00	

*The "realized" column will not be completed until results have occurred.
** The financial assumptions used to quantify the unrealized bottom line potential are recorded on other worksheets for subsequent review.

Totals $1,522,000   *

Most of these evaluations are very positive. After a Profit Super Bowl coached by one of our Florida members of the Institute of Profit Advisors, a participant praised:

> The Enhancement program helped me make the decision to stay. . . even though yesterday I received an unsolicited employment opportunity with another company, with a larger salary; 100% paid health insurance; 4 weeks paid vacation; 4 weeks paid sick leave, hours of 6:30 a.m. to 2:30 p.m. I believe in the goals of this seminar and decided I would much prefer to be a part of the team implementing these programs.

Other successful Profit Super Bowls we've facilitated have elicited such glowing participant remarks as:

> "From your initial presentation of the Profit Enhancement Process, I was captivated by the idea, and excited by the potential for both increased profitability and enhanced teamwork; now, upon completion of the entire process, I remain captivated and excited."

■

> "I increased my overall knowledge of the company...I am beginning to experience the feeling of belonging and not as an outsider."

■

> "I'm refocused, renewed and have further built my belief that this company can and will be even more successful. Energized. It helped me see some of the problems others are having as well as the incredible opportunities."

■

> "My pledge for the next 21 days will be to make a commitment to excellence every day."

During the Profit Game—always monitor progress,
cheer along the sidelines, and consult
with assistant coaches and players.

Finally, review the implementation system that is discussed in the next chapter. Each Profit Champion completes a report of how they will implement their profit project. It is vital that the Profit Activities Leader continue the enthusiasm, excitement and momentum that was created by the Super Bowl.

The day after a banking client's Profit Super Bowl that we facilitated with a Pennsylvania member of the Institute of Profit Advisors, we met with the Profit Champions to discuss their implementation plans. One Champion came in weeping. Her immediate boss had already tried to force her to fumble her profit project. He had participated in the Profit Super Bowl, and agreed to accept her profit project then. Why was he being so uncooperative now? We talked with the president of the bank and urged him to prevent a profit fumble before the profit project could roll away. The president was determined that the Profit Enhancement Process succeed. He gave our Profit Champion's supervisor a choice: either do what the Profit Team had agreed upon during the Profit Super Bowl, or leave the company. The choice wasn't pleasant for him. It showed the president was committed. The profit fumble was recovered and the supervisor began applauding the employee's work on her profit project!

Instant Replays

"I can is more important than I.Q."
　　—Clark A. Johnson, Chairman of the Board, Pier 1

Your goal—a profit plan that is a bottom line, logical strategy for finding profits in a whole new way.

Your guest list should include everyone you think has the best ideas for your company and who will put forth the effort to turn ideas into bottom line results.

The most expensive cost in a business is the cost of a closed mind.

It's difficult for any one individual to see the whole picture, but everyone can see part of it.

Some businesses like to play it too safe. They set the bar for performance too low. But if that bar is raised by the Profit Team, and you are successful as a group, the organization will jump even higher.

Expectations create results. You get what you expect —NOT what you want.

The first Profit Game should be an "away" game where no one from the home office will interrupt.

The Profit Super Bowl is played strictly by the rules. Strict guidelines ensure that the Profit Plan will emerge strong, focused, and with motivating concensus.

In too many businesses, profit happens randomly. The employees are like players playing without a scoreboard. They need to know if they are winning or losing to be effective team players in the Profit Game.

Begin the Profit Game by transforming your managers into a powerhouse Profit Team. Then make everyone in the organization a PEO (Profit Enhancement Officer).

Assign each player a "position," a role in your emerging Profit Plan.

Define your goal: To have everyone in the organization working towards realizing its bottom line potential, in harmony with the company's strategic goals and objectives.

Before the group recognizes new profit strategies, they have to deal with the challenges. What is preventing the organization from achieving its full profit potential?

Profit fumbles are really opportunities to score in disguise.

Introduce your Profit Team to the way to play and win the game—The Profit Enhancement Process.

Put your Profit Team onto the field to practice their new plays, and let the good ideas flow.

Turn short-yardage plays into big gains.

The real power of the Profit Super Bowl is the creation of a culture that brings employees into the profit process and assists them in taking ownership of profit strategies that enhance the bottom line.

Select plays from your new playbook and turn them into a full-blown game plan. Put the Profit Plan together.

During the Profit Game—always monitor progress, cheer along the sidelines, and consult assistant coaches and players.

Chapter 5

WINNING THE SUPER BOWL
Implementing Your Profit Plan

We currently have between 6 and 10 projects underway; each being managed by separate teams, each with its own unique profit opportunity. At the same time we have already implemented some of our programs and are beginning to enjoy returns from the energy and the initiatives that you helped us create.

—Barry P. Foreman, President, CEO, Forman Brothers Inc.
Owned by National Distributing Company, Inc.

I must tell you that, while the workshop itself was worth the investment many times over, some of the most exciting times in our organization have come from helping the management staff achieve their ways and tasks.

—Michael C. Martin, President, Dudley Martin Chevrolet

The more you get people to write down their commitments, the better chance you will have to win the Profit Game.

Implementation is the most important step in the entire Profit Enhancement Process. It is where the rubber hits the road because effective implementation means good ideas go somewhere—to your bottom line.

The implementation process *is* the Super Bowl of business—the time when your profit teams really show their worth and score—right to your bottom line. The more you encourage people to write down their commitments, the better chance you will have for profit success. Expectations create results.

So before we even begin this chapter, read and sign this pledge. (We want to make sure you are convinced and commited.)

The CEO's Pledge

Profit is a journey that never ends. It is the result of a series of small steps that, added together, will dramatically improve the performance of our company. Our company has been in business for ___ years. Practices which have been in effect for years cannot be changed overnight. I recognize that there are no quick fixes in this world. Improvements to our bottom line will take time and hard work. I understand that the following rules will hasten profit improvement for our firm. Also, I recognize that their violation will handicap the realization of our profit goals.

As part of our Profit Enhancement Process, an inventory of profit initiatives will be identified and a commitment made to successfully implement them. Profit Teams will be created to work on these projects. Each profit project will have one employee who is responsible for its implementation. There will be specific time designated for completion of each project. The unrealized bottom line potential for each profit project will be computed.

I agree to follow these rules to ensure the success of our Profit Enhancement Process:

1. If a person on the profit project team is not capable or unwilling to do the necessary work, they will be replaced with another employee. For each project team, one person will be designated as Profit Champion, and they will be responsible for implementation.

2. Consequences will be established for non-completion of a profit project.

3. As additional profits are earned, rewards will be provided to Profit Team members whose efforts contribute to our company's success.

4. I will communicate the importance of completing profit projects. I expect Profit Team members to regularly allocate a portion of their work week to the profit projects they are responsible for. The Project Champions will report their progress regularly. I recognize that normal daily interruptions will occur, but I will not accept continued excuses that people are too busy.

5. Initially, the goals of each project will be clearly defined. When the projects are assigned, each Project Champion will prepare an outline of their activities within one week.

6. The ability to obtain "buy in" by members of my management team and employees who are affected by projects will ensure successful implementation.

7. Benchmarks will be set for each project in order to gauge success.

8. I understand that the completion of project tasks will not necessarily lead to immediate profit. It may take months for the results to be realized.

9. I will continually communicate the importance of incorporating a profit culture in my company and stress the sense of urgency to completing the assigned profit-generating tasks.

10. Some projects may require the investment of resources. These requests will be fairly evaluated and quickly resolved.

11. I will continue the quest for profit improvement by encouraging my team to identify and implement additional profit-generating initiatives.

12. When a project is completed, we will institutionalize the required ongoing activities to ensure the realization of the desired profits. As our company embarks on the Profit Enhancement Process, I understand that successful implementation is contingent upon these rules being followed.

[To be signed by CEO]

■

Are you ready to sign this pledge? Then let's go on!

After a Profit Super Bowl, your Profit Team members will be all fired up and ready to begin work on their profit ideas. By the end of the session, the group will have completed the following steps:

■ Prioritized profit projects

■ Assigned accountability for each task

■ Clearly defined profit projects and the steps needed to complete them

■ Assigned accountability for each sub-task

■ Established benchmarks and measurement processes

■ Defined time limits and completion commitments for each task.

Now, let's examine how to control the energy that has been let loose.

Project implementation is the key component of maximizing profit.

We have all seen this scenario occur: a great idea develops, and everyone agrees that it would be worthwhile for the organization. Enthusiastically, people want to start to make it happen, but over time the project just withers and dies. Why does this happen?

Project implementation is a key component of maximizing corporate profit in the Profit Enhancement Process. We don't believe in starting something we can't finish, and we don't let our clients do so either.

To win the game, a successful football team executes a number of specific activities—the right combination of running, blocking, passing, receiving, tackling, and kicking. They complete their downs, execute punts and kick-offs effectively, and then score more touchdowns than the opponents. What happens when a team is not having a winning season? The coaches help players refocus on the fundamentals of the game, and adopt and adapt to new ideas, plans, plays and processes.

In business, the fundamentals of success are sales and marketing, organizational structure, people, operations and financial management. When your company lags behind in any one of these areas, new ideas must be generated to take care of the short fall. We've seen how the Profit Enhancement Process provides a forum for generating these new ideas, for capturing hidden profit strategies from your starting team, and creates a structure to turn them into completed tasks with measurable financial benefits. We've learned the plays, we've done some practicing during the Profit Super Bowl, and now we are ready to play the Profit Game.

We're out on the field, the fans are cheering in the stands, the referee tosses the coin. Then reality sets in. People get back to their offices and face the pile of work awaiting them. You must focus on possible obstacles first, before they do, to be sure these "reasons" do not destroy your implementation process. You are the master implementer.

Here is a list of typical "reasons" that prevent profit projects from succeeding.

- Pressing daily issues
- People are not sold on the idea
- No buy-in from top management
- Too many issues to deal with
- Project is not clearly defined

- New obstacles arise
- Issue is too big for allocated solution resources
- Lack of consistent motivation
- No clear-cut demonstrable reward system
- Poor communication channels
- Issue develops in another department's domain
- Lack of necessary skills
- Environmental changes occur
- No sense of urgency from participants because target dates weren't set
- No system was established for measuring results
- Unrealistic expectations were set for results
- No consequences were set for failure to accomplish an initiative.

These are big road blocks to success. As profit coach, you've pledged not to let these kinds of fumbles interfere with your Super Bowl win. Now it is your job as profit coach to help your Profit Team Champions and their committees overcome these challenges.

Clearly define each project and the steps
needed to complete it.

During the Profit Super Bowl, the starting team was encouraged to clearly define each issue and pertinent variables by discussing how each profit project might be completed. Profit Champions for every project were selected and the group was committed to it.

This is a good beginning, but let's face it, no matter how important they are when profit projects compete with daily responsibilities, require more financial and/or human resources than originally committed, or need assistance from individuals who are not completely sold on the idea, implementation could be derailed or at least delayed.

To prevent this from happening, consider incorporating the following thoughts into your implementation plan:

- All of the people who will be affected by the idea and are instrumental in its success or failure must be brought in at the beginning.

- There must be an uncompromising and clear-cut commitment from the top that change is good for the organization. There must be a commitment behind the completion of profit projects that allows the appropriate staff to have time to work on their projects. In some cases, this might require that existing duties be prioritized and those of lesser importance delegated, postponed or eliminated.

- Finally, you must inform the entire organization that there is one individual who has the authority to be the "overall champion" for all profit ideas that are in the works. This is the Profit Activities Leader (we call him or her a PAL) who was selected at the Profit Super Bowl. This responsible and respected person provides regular assistance, encouragement and a focal point of accountability for the Profit Team Champions charged with each project. In a nutshell, the PAL's job is to make the Profit Teams successful. He or she is your assistant coach.

Every Profit Champion needs support and the opportunity to consult with their PAL.

In our system, no one stands alone. Profit project leaders regularly meet with the PAL to review their profit projects. Together they may revise the projects and devise new strategies or in some cases even scrap a project altogether. You can become the PAL if your company is small enough, but in most cases it is the next in charge, perhaps your COO, Executive Vice President or General Manager. Whomever you appoint, it is vital that you hold him or her responsible for the successful implementation of the various profit projects and grant the authority to carry them out.

At the beginning of the implementation process, meet with your Profit Activities Leader and consider the following:

1. Among the profit projects included in the Profit Plan, which are the most important? Alter any you think were incorrectly prioritized.

2. Do you have the right person assigned as Profit Champion for each profit project? Have the best team members been selected for each project?

3. Are the issues and initiatives clearly defined and are they understood?

4. What are the obstacles, from an organizational perspective, that you anticipate?

5. What will be accomplished at your meetings with Project Champions?

6. How will momentum be maintained?

7. What will be the short-and long-term rewards?

When you have determined the answers to these questions, the PAL will be ready to begin meeting regularly with Profit Champions.

As profit coach you'll want to meet frequently with your PAL to assess progress, consult, and act as the reality check to keep the entire process on track.

When you've got this system in place, other causes of profit project breakdown are resolvable. Without this support, it is very difficult, if not impossible, to achieve the hundreds of thousands of dollars envisioned during the Profit Super Bowl.

Each Profit Team is responsible for planning
their own profit project.

Profit project Champions are the next in the chain of command. Your PAL should help them get started with their planning. Each Champion should write a short paragraph describing their vision for their project and what they will accomplish. Then they should list the assumptions the starting team made in adding this project to the Profit Plan, listing the benefits they want to achieve and the obstacles they will face.

We recommend breaking each project into sub-tasks. Remember the adage about eating the elephant one bite at a time. Profit Champions should assign deadlines for each task. Next they should make an initial to-do list for the first task. Then they are ready to meet with their profit project committees.

No one, no matter how capable, will be able to implement profit strategies without the help of others in the organization.

Profit Teams must work together to implement profit strategies. No one, no matter how capable, will be able to implement profit strategies without the help of others in their organization. To begin the implementation process, each Profit Team should be assembled with their Champion and begin brainstorming how they will develop their project. We created the following acronym to help Profit Teams think through what process is necessary to accomplish their assignments.

I is for IDENTIFY THE STUMBLING BLOCKS.
What are the problems you are likely to encounter?

M is for MANAGE AND MOTIVATE.
How can you manage this profit project and motivate others to buy into it?

P is for PLAN.
Lay out the "big picture" so that others understand just what's involved. Develop a plan to make the ideas happen—one step, one task at a time. Also, work on alternative plans if the original strategy isn't going as planned.

L is for LEARN.

Gather information necessary to ensure success. Seek out every source possible. Libraries and books (of course), consultants, the Internet, professional and trade associations, and seminars are just a few sources that will help you learn.

E is for EXPERIMENT.

Test your plan, step by step. Don't change everything at one time unless you are satisfied things are working to your satisfaction.

M is for MEASURE RESULTS.

If you can't measure the results, you won't really know if your project will improve profitability. What are you going to measure? What benchmarks must be developed to ascertain if progress is being realized?

E is for EXPEDITE.

If your experiment is successful, what can be done to expedite this strategy so that profit benefits are accelerated?

N is for NEEDS.

Perform a needs analysis to make sure you have the people, technology, know-how, and capital to make this profit strategy successful.

T is for TENACITY.

How tenacious is your Profit Team going to be in turning this profit strategy into bottom line results? What commitment is going to be expected?

Each team should build a consensus on how they
want to work and what they plan to do,
step by step, task by task.

Brainstorming about each of these items, as it relates to their profit project, helps everyone understand and develop the necessary steps to follow in the process to accomplish it.

Each team should build a consensus on how they want to work and what they plan to do, step by step, task by task. This plan should be formalized by putting it into writing and distributing it to each Profit Champion and to the PAL. It becomes a map as well as a benchmark for progress. Make sure that all the Profit Champions are aware of potential profit fumbles. These could upset their carefully laid out plan, unless they address such concerns in the plan itself. During the PAL's meetings with Champions, the plan is reviewed, progress noted, subsequent deadlines defined, and a summary report prepared for the profit coach each month.

Motivate your Profit Teams with a well-touted
and fully-understood reward program.

Just as the starting team enjoyed the two-dollar bill rewards during their retreat, and football players are often motivated by $100 bills after each game, your employees must know what rewards they can expect from successful completion of their projects. When all employees of a company participate in the Profit Enhancement Process, they are each making a personal investment in the business — of their time, talents, and experience. They each then deserve a portion of the profits their hard work generates (cash and non-cash rewards, including, most importantly, acknowledgment and appreciation).

You and your PAL must make everyone aware that increased profits benefit the entire company. When Profit Champions and their teams prove successful, reward them. If your company has a great year, reward the employees who worked hard to make it happen. If your year wasn't as profitable as you expected, do not penalize your employees who tried to increase profits because without them things would have been worse. Reward them. Incentive compensation helps kindle the flames of employee motivation.

Profit Team members and Champions need to be recognized for their efforts. When they effectively perform work which improves the profitability of their organization, they deserve an addition to their bottom line as well. Demonstrating employee appreciation by sharing profits will generate new ideas for profit projects that are never-ending.

And remember, most people don't just work for profit — they work for the benefits that come from profits. Profit provides opportunities and choices. It is the fuel that powers every successful business. That is the real benefit!

Bottom up—rather than top down—implementation is the key to winning the Profit Super Bowl.

The Profit Enhancement Process trains Profit Teams to become effective problem-solving, opportunity-creating units. Unthinkable ideas are brought up for discussion, discussed in a nonthreatening environment, consensus built, and a plan for implementation enacted. People who are involved "buy into" concepts, add their creative touches and actively work for completion. This is far different than in companies where issues are swept under the rug because they are difficult and cause discomfort. Problems are created in companies when reality is avoided. The best run companies discuss tough topics.

Greater profit*ability* comes when players know they are accountable, responsible, and will reap rewards for scoring profits or be penalized if they consistently fail to make it to the profit zone.

People do better what is inspected rather than expected. Monitor, evaluate, and acknowledge each task's accomplishment or fumble. PEP provides a well-defined system for implementation.

First, let's pretend you are the Profit Activities Leader. Use the following to guide you as you plan how you will manage the Profit Enhancement Project effectively:

1. Determine the most important projects, and if necessary alter previously established priorities. Doing first things first will propel your project

onto the best course. By now you will have had an opportunity to review the profit projects and, with time, have determined that one or more of them aren't feasible or need to be altered in some way. You may also have seen that some are really more important than their original priority ranking. This is the time to make appropriate alterations to the plan.

2. Do you have the right person assigned as Profit Champion for each project? Do you have the right team members? As head coach, you probably have better insight into how various people work together. You may determine that some of the assigned champions or committees have personality differences or can use a more-qualified Champion. Move with caution and gain consensus to accomplish each project.

3. Review each project and make sure that the issue is clear. This is very important. If the issue is not clear, it will be difficult to establish the steps to achieve it.

4. What are the obstacles, from an organizational perspective, that you anticipate? How are you going to deal with them? Get your strategy in place for each obstacle. Many of these obstacles were brought up at the Profit Super Bowl, but you may discover more and they should be noted at this time.

5. What should you accomplish at the meetings with the Profit Champions? This is your all-important planning function. Understanding the strengths and weaknesses of each Champion as well as each project will help you plan how to effectively manage them. Set agendas for your

meetings. Be open-minded and sensitive, but also firm on the important issues.

6. How will momentum be maintained? What goals, objectives, and deadlines will you set? What incentives will you be able to offer? How will you keep everyone excited and motivated?

7. What will be your short- and long-term rewards? This is a further refinement of number 6.

Now you are ready to begin your meetings with Profit Team Champions. Here is a suggested format for helping each champion focus on his or her project:

Profit Team Champion's Project Instructions

1. Write a short paragraph describing the vision of your project and the desired results.

_____

_____

_____

_____

_____

2. List the assumptions that were made in determining the profit potential of your project.

A._____

B._____

C._____

D._____

3. List the benefits to your company and its employees for pursuing the project.

A._____

B._____

C._____

D._____

4. List project obstacles to overcome. (Obstacles are opportunities in disguise.)

A._____

B._____

C._____

D._____

5. List the members of your Profit Team. Note possible causes for assignments to go off track, and record suggestions to stay on track.

Team Members	Causes for Assignment to Go Off Track	Suggestions for Staying on Track
_____	_____	_____
_____	_____	_____
_____	_____	_____
_____	_____	_____
_____	_____	_____
_____	_____	_____
_____	_____	_____

6. What resources will be required to complete your project?

_____

_____

_____

_____

_____

7. How will results be measured?

_____

_____

_____

_____

_____

8. Break the profit project into its most important sub-tasks. Assign a deadline and "Champion" or person in charge of each sub-task.

Sub-task	Due date	Champion
A._____	_____	_____
B._____	_____	_____
C._____	_____	_____
D._____	_____	_____

9. Estimate the percentage of completion for the sub-tasks, and assign due dates. (You may also want to establish benchmarks to know that tasks are on target.)

Sub-task #	% Completion	Due Date

10. Review sub-tasks and list the initial "to-do's." Set deadlines for each. Select Profit Champions for the to-do's. They may be different than the overall Profit Champion.

Sub-task	To-Do	Due Date	Champion
A.			
B.			
C.			
D.			

After your Profit Champions have filled out this form and planned how they will implement their particular project (one bite at a time), set a date and time for your next meeting. At the meeting you will begin to use the following form to monitor progress and establish new goals and deadlines as needed.

Implementation Coaching Meeting

Date_____ Profit Project_____

Profit Project #_____PAL_____

Team Champion_____

General status since last meeting:
What did you accomplish this week?

_____

_____

_____

_____

_____

What problems did you encounter?

_____
_____
_____
_____
_____

Benchmarks met_____
Overall % completed_____
Negotiated change in completion date: From_____To_____
Profit Project Status:
      On track _____ Behind_____ Critical___ Abandoned _____
For each existing or new sub-task that had activity this period, specify the following:

% Completed	**Status**	**Due Date**

List new "To Do's" that have been created:

To-Do	**Description**	**Due Date**	**Priority**	**Status**	**Champion**

Goals to be accomplished by our next meeting:

_____
_____
_____
_____

Date of next meeting:_____

Addtional suggestions for profit initiatives:

_____
_____
_____
_____

Profit Champions must be held accountable
and know the limits of their authority.

Profit Champions do not have the authority to change their profit projects, action dates, priority codes, or other action items agreed upon during the Profit Super Bowl. In other words, Champions must understand that failing is not an acceptable way to complete what was previously agreed upon. Whether or not the implementation process is proceeding as scheduled, Profit Champions must discuss the progress of their project at their regular meeting with the PAL. If a project is faltering, together they will alter the strategies and find solutions—before it fails.

Profit Champions must receive regular support during implementation. Profit implementation is a group effort with everyone working together to implement the company's Profit Plan.

Winning the Profit Super Bowl will bring hundreds
of thousands—even millions—of dollars
of previously unrealized profit to your bottom line.

Millions of dollars of profit potential is what it meant to one of our clients, a mega-automobile dealership. As a result of their new profit*ability*, the Profit Team found out that the company was paying the same commission for "hot" car sales as for slower-moving products. They decided it didn't make sense to pay the same commission for easy sales as for harder sells. They devised a new commission structure and brought an additional $360,000 of recurring annual profit to the company's bottom line with this one idea alone.

In addition, the Profit Team discovered that their mechanics had to wait in line at the parts counter to get the work out, sometimes for as long as 45 minutes. The company had planned to hire more mechanics! The Profit Team developed a new system for bringing parts to mechanics, keeping them doing what they should be doing—servicing cars. This new procedure brought in an extra $225,000 in profit potential.

A new utility savings procedure was put in place. Lights and power was minimized during off hours. This simple new procedure saved the company 35 percent on utility bills and brought $50,000 in profit potential to the bottom line.

Keys. There was no effective system for keeping track of car keys—on a lot with hundreds of cars! The Profit Team developed a location system for keys and added $10,000 to the bottom line.

When do you see cars advertised in the paper? Usually on Saturdays and Sundays. But this car dealership was closed on Sundays, and there was no one there to answer telephone queries from prospective customers. The Profit Team arranged for sales people who are go-getters to have Sunday calls transferred to their homes on a rotating basis. Now the sales person answers the phone with the name of the dealership in the comfort of his or her home, and gains many new leads. Their ads now read, "Call for information on Sundays." As a result, sales people generated leads even on Sundays that generated an added $50,000 in bottom line potential.

The Profit Team discovered they were losing business because customers couldn't drop their cars off the night before for servicing. They hired night service "advisors" to handle night drop-offs quickly and courteously, so that customers no longer had to wait in long lines in the morning. This initiative, costing just several people's salaries, added thousands more in profit potential.

Service writers were wasting time searching for cars on the lot. The Profit Team had each parking space numbered and added $116,000 to the unrealized bottom line potential.

A new detailing service was added to the traditional car repair and servicing items for a new $100,000 in annual recurring profit. They also added a quick while-you-wait oil change and lubrication service. Not only did this program add the potential of $75,000 in revenue, but it allowed time for the dealership employees to "get to know" their customers while they waited, to establish a "donuts and coffee" relationship that helped build customer loyalty.

These are just a few initiatives this dealership's Profit Teams carried through from idea to completion. There is absolutely no doubt that effective implementation is absolutely vital to the Profit Enhancement Process to this dealership and to your business, too.

Instant Replays

The more you get people to write down their commitments, the better chance you will have to win the Profit Game.

Project implementation is the key component of maximizing profit.

Clearly define each project and the steps needed to complete it.

Every Profit Champion needs support and the opportunity to consult with their PAL.

Each profit team is responsible for planning their own profit project.

No one, no matter how capable, will be able to implement profit strategies without the help of others in the organization.

Each team should build a consensus on how they want to work and what they plan to do, step by step, task by task.

Motivate your profit teams with a well-touted and fully understood reward program.

Bottom up—rather than top down—implementation is the key to winning the Profit Super Bowl.

Greater profitability comes when players know they are accountable, responsible, and will reap rewards for scoring profits or be penalized if they consistently fail to make it to the profit zone.

Profit Champions must be held accountable and know the limits of their authority.

Winning the Profit Super Bowl will bring hundreds of thousands—even millions—of dollars of previously unrealized profit to your bottom line.

CHAPTER 6

PROFIT IS THE SCORE

This whole experience has once again proven that you can never close the book on learning. The processes you have passed on to us for uncovering profit opportunities then setting time lines and completion dates to ensure achievement of the goals has been most rewarding to us. During my 25+ years in management, I would rank this experience among my most rewarding.

—Don Namuth, Former V.P./General Sales Manager, Forman Distributing Co.
Owned by National Distributing Company, Inc.

Great profit coaches never rest on their laurels.

Whenever you think your company is as successful as it can be, remember those old slide rules from calculus class boldly imprinted with the name of the manufacturer—Pickett Slide Rule Company. Talk about having a market cornered. But Pickett's success apparently blinded them to the microprocessor, and calculators swiftly made Pickett's little sticks obsolete. They are collectibles in antique shops now. There are those who say that the seeds of a business's destruction are sown during good times. They may also say that the seeds to business success are sown during turbulent times, but great coaches never rest on their laurels. Instead they coach and seek input and feedback during good seasons and bad seasons, utilizing their Profit Teams.

Think about the National Cash Register Company. Their NCR logo dominated mechanical cash registers from coast to coast for decades. Now most of their handsome-but-bulky old cash registers are long gone, but NCR's emblem now decorates millions of computerized retail terminals. NCR changed with the times.

Netscape Communications Corp., the Internet software

117

company that was one of Microsoft's fiercest competitors, had a rough 1997. What did their president, James L. Barksdale, do? He bucked the trend of ever-higher compensation for chief executives by forgoing his own salary and bonuses in 1997. He personally took the heat for the company's poor performance, and used this show of commitment to Netscape to spur his employees to work as hard as he does to beat Microsoft. He showed them and investors that he is willing to sacrifice because he believes in his company. That's commitment! Netscape was acquired by AOL—a true competitor.

The answer is: Find new avenues for generating new business opportunities and increasing the bottom line. Changing with the times is vital and that means being open to new ideas, being flexible, and being in tune with the marketplace. Those ideas must come from the entire company, not just from management, but from every level of employees. Each company member must understand what the company is and does, and that he or she is part of the mission and vision now and in the future. In fact, their future depends on the company's products and services evolving with the times. It is possible that 50 percent of what you'll be selling five years from now may not even exist today—or that you don't know about it yet.

We once held a Profit Super Bowl for 15 executives of a management information business, including the CFO, executive secretary, marketing director, and branch and sales managers. When asked the question, "What does your company sell?" there were fifteen different answers.

After some discussion of the problem, we broke the group into five three-member teams. Each team was asked to come up with a new description of what the company sells. There were now five explanations instead of 15, still too many. Next, these managers voted on which of the five to eliminate as not meaningful enough. Two explanations survived the cuts, and the group merged these into a clear, concise statement.

Now when asked what the company sells, every one of the 150 employees in the firm can answer, "We sell management information solutions to business problems to assist our customers in being more competitive and profitable."

This was not an easy process. The owner of the business was so elated he went to call his mother. Laughing, he said, "For years she's asked what I do for a living. Until now I couldn't tell her!"

Every company also needs a clear understanding of its customers, products, markets, opportunities and challenges. In our years of experience as Profit Advisors, we have found that many of these can only be seen clearly by an "outsider," someone not intimately involved with "the ways things are done here" at that company. Such an advisor will also help to change the company's culture—its attitude toward progress and creative solutions. When engaged as the outside experts, we facilitate the identifying of opportunities that employees may be aware of but don't know how to articulate, bring these opportunities to light, act to create a forum for communication, and then assist the CEO in his or her profit coaching throughout the implementation process.

Your profit attitude determines your profit altitude.

We've seen it time and again. Once Profit Team members are made responsible for profits and develop a sense of their profit*ability*, then an overflowing river of ideas for unrealized profit potential starts to flow. We have defined profit*ability* as the skill to analyze your business and determine what more can be done to add value to the bottom line. PEP "dams" those ideas and puts them to work. With Profit Teams working to marshal the creative forces of the entire company, your company's chances to change and grow with the demands of the times are greatly enhanced.

This chapter is all about attitudes and answers. Why attitudes? Because we can't emphasize enough how positive attitudes plus positive actions equal positive results; and the opposite is also true. For PEP to work you've got to overcome the following:

"Departmentalism" destroys teamwork
and will destroy your chances for
winning the Profit Game.

We often engage the starting team at a Profit Super Bowl for automobile dealerships by asking the question: "If you could never run another big newspaper ad, how would you bring in customers?"

We ask this question because we've found that frequently auto dealerships have absolutely no impetus for one department to work with another department. There are so many clues that a customer may need a new car. In the service department, customers decide the estimate for repairing their old car is too high. In the warranty department, a customer's extended warranty runs out, leaving them financially exposed in case of a major service problem. In the leasing department, customer leases expire regularly. These are all opportunities to sell a satisfied customer a new car. But you can't capitalize on them unless all departments are communicating with each other and working with the sales department. Why didn't the service department inform the sales department that there was a customer with a new car need? Because, "It isn't my job and there's nothing in it for me." There is no profit process.

Usually during the Profit Super Bowl, newly profit*able* managers see that tremendous additional revenue will come simply from providing a way for the departments to work together. They understand that the culture of the company has defeated this objective. Often a Profit Team is appointed to develop a commission system for all departments so that sales referrals between departments are rewarded.

In one case, during the Profit Super Bowl, the group discussed how the dealership's telephone receptionist became very grumpy in late afternoon when all the service customers call in about their cars. This dealership now pays the receptionist $2 for every car sold as a result of her successfully routing a call to a salesman. This changed her entire attitude and made her part of the company's new profit culture. Her focus became customer service and sales, not just answering the telephone.

Departmentalism, or competition among departments, will defeat a company. Can you imagine a football team where the individual players decide their own moves and compete with each other for the ball? We tried to get the CEO of a systems integration firm we worked with to recognize that competition among her departments was killing the company. We found out when we performed the Profit Audit that multiple departments were so intent on trying to get sales that in some cases they were competing for the same customer with different prices. We alerted the CEO that she had major problems with department in-fighting and that there was no system for tracking who was working with which prospective customer. She just wouldn't recognize this as a problem. She was so intent on encouraging competition, she defeated herself. Unfortunately, the company went into bankruptcy.

"Always praise a player in front of his peers.
Never criticize him in public."
— Larry Pecattiello, Former Coach, National Football League

Good people hold the answers your company needs to win the Profit Game. Managers need to encourage them, to work with them, so these opportunities will surface, not be buried under functional tasks and emergencies. What would your business be like if managers only got promoted when and if the people they supervised got promoted? You'd see a lot more managers managing the people who do the work, not just the work.

One of our most successful clients, a ready-mix, brick-and-block manufacturer and wholesale building materials company, has now held five Profit Super Bowls during the last seven years. The two years in which no Profit Super Bowl was held, their profits were static. In the five years they played in the Profit Super Bowl, profits were up. In the beginning, the CEO hired us because he knew there was much more profit potential in his company and was convinced his people had the answers, but he did not know how to tap that resource. At the end of the first Profit Super Bowl, when scores of ideas had been generated and a plan for new profit was in place, he looked us in the eye and sighed with relief. He had been right. More profit was there! It took the free forum provided by the Profit Super Bowl to flush those ideas out and renew everyone's responsibility in turning profit-generating ideas into financial results. Each year that we work with the company, we wind up with more-substantial issues than the year before because the Profit Team is now comprised of seasoned veterans who have learned to work and think profit*ably*. They are an all-star team of possibility thinkers.

Great coaches are never afraid
to admit they've made a mistake.

As an aside, this same CEO had launched the company into manufacturing concrete cemetery liners. After some years of losing money on the project, he had to admit he'd made a mistake. It was a money-losing venture. Where did he make this admission? He made it during one of the company's Profit Super Bowls. He admitted to us that this gathering of his star players gave him the courage to close the operation. That decision decreased his sales but increased his profits.

The Profit Enhancement Process is designed to provide a free forum for new profit ideas and a process for implementing them. One reason we wrote this book is because we've seen it proven so many times. When employees feel their ideas are welcome, that there is a viable way to submit them and rewards for doing so, they become profit*able*. The opposite is also true.

Unfortunately, we can't say every Profit Super Bowl has been an absolute success. An engineering firm whose business was heavily dependent on government contracts called us in because the CEO knew there was profit*ability* the company wasn't tapping. During the Profit Audit it became clear that 50 percent of the company's problems could be attributed to the vice president who was a 50 percent owner in the firm. Everyone disliked him because he was a "control freak" who bullied people. During the Profit Super Bowl he dominated every discussion and wouldn't let anyone else talk. Despite all of our efforts, he refused to let the meeting be a free forum, without fear of retribution.

Even so, discussion revealed that one of the main revenue problems for the firm was in allocating costs for government contracts. Many of those who did the work did not understand the difference between direct cost and indirect cost allocation. The Profit Team identified $500,000 in potential profits. But Harry the Bullying VP interfered again. He shouted out, "I can't believe you don't know this. It's so basic!" So, what happened? The group clammed up. Afterwards, Harry wouldn't give the Profit Team the time to discover the firm's billing opportunities. And, when we urged the CEO to step in and let his team proceed, he wouldn't do it. He chose Harry, the other shareholder, over his employees, and this firm is losing the Profit Game.

PEP focuses everyone on the profits needed
to grow the company and add value to it.

You may have founded the company and built it to what it is today. You know your business inside and out. How can someone else identify something you don't already know about your own business—whether it's a Profit Advisor like us or your very own employees? Maybe there is some hidden profit you can't find in there, but your company is doing all right, maybe even successful or super-successful.

Trust us. We've seen the Profit Enhancement Process work so many times. Most of our clients are entrepreneurial companies that have a burning desire to do it better and know it can be improved! More than half of the companies we've coached in the past have come back for additional Profit Super Bowls. PEP doesn't interfere at all with their own strategic goals for the company. It enhances them, makes them work faster, focuses everyone on the profits they need to build the company and add value to it. Our number-one successes have been with profit*able* companies with competitive coaches who know there are even more opportunities to improve the score.

Unfortunately, the opposite is also true. We were hired to facilitate a Profit Super Bowl for a news service company. Strangely enough, the COO asked that the CEO not be there, and during the meeting that COO was not very complimentary about his boss or about any part of the Profit Enhancement Process. We considered this situation so dangerous that we asked to meet privately with the CEO to inform him about this. We were convinced that the COO was truly not a leader and was, in fact, undermining the progress of the company. We warned the owner that the COO was working behind his back. He didn't want the grief of dealing with his COO, so he didn't take the time to deal with the problem. The Profit Plan developed during the Profit Super Bowl was never implemented. Unhappily, the company's sales have dropped by more than two-thirds, and it may not be around to play next season.

PEP provides the support and monitoring of
progress that effective implementation requires.

In the previous chapter we've gone through the implementation process and emphasized its importance. PEP provides the support and monitoring of progress that implementation requires. It is vital that the Profit Activities Leader meet regularly with Profit Champions to measure progress and to help them successfully complete their profit projects. The Profit Activities Leader should, of course, be a person who has the vision to see the whole picture. He or she must have profit*ability*, the ability to recognize business opportunities and the talent to turn ideas into results. They must be commited to the Profit Enhancement Process and have the project-managing and people-managing skills necessary to coach the best out of their players.

The PAL needs support, too—from the CEO and from his own profit coach. Part of our profit advising coaching role is to be "industrial psycho-profit therapists." We listen, we work with you, and we provide a fresh perspective on the profit projects because we aren't caught up with the everyday operations of the business. We do not have a vested interest in the past.

Recently we saw a big ad for a going-out-of-business sale held by a furniture store. We knew the owner. Unhappily, he had not understood the benefits of the Profit Enhancement Process when he had explained it to him some years ago. The CEO said he didn't need our services because he knew he was doing everything that could be done for the company. He didn't have profit*ability*. His team of employees probably had profit*able* solutions, but no way to present them. They were never asked. Now the business is closed.

Players play harder when they know
their work will be rewarded.

When people know what's in it for them, do you think they're eager to put in the extra effort working on new profit initiatives? You bet. And it doesn't always have to be big monetary rewards, although money is still a strong motivator. Sometimes it takes making them feel like a real part of the profit process—to make everyone an official Profit Enhancement Officer.

We worked with a family-owned catering company that had some real problems, both financial and personal family ones. They were so busy squabbling among themselves that they couldn't even agree on a common strategy for the company. Our first major task was to help the family determine which role each was to play in the company's management, then to get them motivated to win the Profit Game. Once they felt comfortable with each other, this commitment was easy to obtain.

Our client later reported that we engaged them "...in some difficult, thought-provoking and probing questions...very needed questions regarding commitment, performance, expectations and individual and collective goals for our business." He went on to say:

> My brother and I, after some coaching, and an overall meeting of minds, have taken on the leadership role of the company along with our operations manager,

now general manager, who is entering his 26th year of service with us. Our highly experienced events management staff, each with over 15 years of service, has also taken on a leadership role and now has many more avenues and opportunities for input and growth.

Then we assembled their all-star employees for the Profit Super Bowl. Many of these loyal people had never before been asked to participate in any kind of profit strategizing session for the future of the company. It was exciting to see them begin to light up with ideas and to offer them freely when given the chance.

At the end of the session, the family issues were resolved, their employees were involved in and committed to the bottom line growth of the company, and everyone's new ideas were incorporated into a true Profit Plan for action. This company went from a loss to a pre-tax profit of $200,000. Now the company has scheduled a Profit Super Bowl for each annual planning process. They use their slow time of the year to devote themselves to identifying and implementing profit-making projects. This client wrote afterwards:

> The tough issues that were affecting the company have been identified and are being dealt with. There is a renewal level and excitement and optimism now in the company. We are well on our way to realizing the profit potential of our long-held and successful family business, so that it will thrive well into future generations.
> WOW!

Often it's the shoemaker's kids who
are the ones going without shoes.

It's amazing how many service companies claim to be working to improve the profit*ability* of their clients while forgetting about their own. We were looking over the sales materials of a hospitality software firm we worked with. Their promotional brochure touted their goal as developing new products to make their customers more profitable. They even boasted, "Our employees are focused on profit."

This company has offices all around the world. When we gave our Profit Enhancement Survey to 65 of them, gathered for a meeting, their scores were in the ones and twos across the board, out of a possible 10, on the statement, "Our employees are focused on generating bottom line opportunities and have a plan to follow." What an eye-opener this aspect of the Profit Audit was to the owners!

This company provides worldwide services and advertises that they are interested in improving profit for their clients, but their employees realize that the company has no profit plan for itself or for them.

PEP supports your company's strategic goals. It doesn't change them; it enhances them with the bottom line results of additional opportunities.

The big difference between the Profit Enhancement Process and other management systems is that we're not suggesting you change your firm's strategic goals, just to define, refine, and hone them for your employees and your customers. You know who you want to be, and important members of your team need to be reading from the same playbook. PEP makes sure you achieve the results you are capable of for the benefit of the owners, employees, families, lenders, suppliers, and customers of your business.

PEP can make a difference NOW. It helps you identify unrealized profits that in many cases have immediate bottom line results, while others may take some time to achieve. We're not promising that you'll always pull in thousands of extra profit dollars immediately, although sometimes a brilliant profit strategy can do just that. Like the trash company story where all it took to realize $78,000 extra was to get the trash men to get off the truck when it was weighed at the landfill. Others do take longer. Like the automobile dealership where $225,000 was generated over a year's time when a new repair-parts ordering system was put in place so mechanics didn't waste time waiting in line at the parts counter. They're not always complex initiatives. Sometimes they are simple ones, like the restaurant chain that measured the size of its trash receptacle, found that the actual cubic yards were less than it was being charged by the hauler, and saved $60,000 by stopping this practice. The Profit Enhancement Process brings all these ideas together—the big ideas and the little ones—to provide your company with identifiable steps to obtain hidden profit opportunities. Remember TIMES x TIMES x TIMES equals Endless Profit Opportunities. Your profit journey must be on the road to continued success. If you don't know where you are going, it doesn't matter which road you take. We want you to win every season. Profit is a business's lifetime journey, not a quick destination.

As opposed to other systems, you could say ours is a "grounds up" rather than a "trickle down" approach to bringing in extra profit, because PEP makes profit everyone's responsibility. We believe that everyone can be coached and trained to be profit*able.*

Great coaches learn from other winning teams.

Here are just a few of the great ideas and opportunities for extra profit that have already come out of the Profit Enhancement Process—opportunities that might be just what you and your business have been looking for.

The Profit Advisors' Client Success Stories

1. Automobile dealership shutdown unnecessary utilities during closed hours. Estimated profit potential: $50,000.

2. Office equipment dealer created a process to eliminate billing omissions that were resulting from hand-written tickets not being entered into the computer. Estimated profit potential: $180,000.

3. Printer developed a process to verify that work orders are complete and accurate prior to being placed into production. Estimated profit potential: $40,000.

4. Professional service firm developed a procedure to catch work that was not originally authorized. This eliminated a problem with uncollectible bills. Estimated profit potential: $125,000.

5. Employment agency combined multiple invoices into one envelope rather than separately mailing them. Estimated profit potential: $4,000.

6. Automotive service agency initiated a regular customer satisfaction survey and was able to more effectively gauge customers' actual feelings. There was a noticeable improvement in additional business from existing customers. Estimated profit potential: $100,000.

7. National advocacy group reduced the paper size used for their magazine by one-eighth of an inch to a standard paper size. Estimated profit potential: $18,000.

8. Food distributor redefined the roles of their sales staff and added merchandising specialists. Estimated profit potential: $325,000.

9. Accounting firm developed a training program to educate employees in all of the products and services they offer. This cross-selling effort increased sales in all departments. Estimated profit potential: $75,000.

10. Plumbing supply distributor reduced permanent overtime through more effective scheduling and by requiring that employees get approval for extra hours before they are incurred. Estimated profit potential: $110,000.

11. Retail tire company established a "Red Carpet Service" to provide pick-up and delivery service for business people who could not get away from their office to purchase tires. Estimated profit potential: $100,000.

12. Liquor distributor segmented a third of one component of their product line that could justify higher prices than their normal markup percentage. Estimated profit potential: $350,000.

13. Law firm established a protocol to enhance the efficiency of staff meetings. The resulting guidelines better utilized the time of attending staff and eliminated necessary and/or unproductive meetings. Estimated profit potential: $ 40,000.

14. Computer training company restructured their processes for selling to customers. Estimated profit potential: $500,000.

15. Medical laboratory identified a new system to archive medical records and modified the policies relating to record retention and file maintenance. Estimated profit potential: $250,000.

16. Beverage distributor increased the on-street time of their sales force by establishing clear guidelines and limiting their role in personally handling last-minute deliveries. This resulted in additional sales without hiring additional sales people. Estimated profit potential: $250,000.

17. Trade association negotiated a credit card affinity program for their members. Estimated profit potential: $1,000,000.

18. Clothing retailer took quality employees from one branch, on a temporary basis, to help train individuals at another. Estimated profit potential: $170,000.

19. Office supply distributor identified additional items that could be sold with each telephone order and incorporated a training program for their customer service representatives to ensure successful implementation. Estimated profit potential: $200,000.

20. Computer graphics firm contacted their suppliers to help organize and fund a training program to improve their dealers' operations. Estimated profit potential: $95,000.

21. Card and gift store created sales analysis and profit*ability* reports by product line to more quickly notice pertinent trends. Estimated profit potential: $15,000.

22. Concrete block manufacturer developed a plan to eliminate paying for the weight of water in raw materials delivered in trucks during wet weather. Estimated profit potential: $50,000.

23. Landscaping contractor developed a plan to obtain more off-season work. Estimated profit potential: $72,000.

24. Cleaning service established English classes for their ethnically diverse workforce. Breakdowns in communication impacted quality control, timely deliveries and ultimately customer satisfaction. Estimated profit potential: $100,000.

25. Auto body repair shop extended hours for estimates to evenings and weekends to make the process more convenient for working customers. Estimated profit potential: $50,000.

26. Trash hauler got their drivers to get out of the trash truck while the truck and its load of trash were getting weighed at the landfill. Estimated profit potential: $78,000.

27. Lighting supply company had owners of vendor companies come to their office to pick up their accounts payable check. When on the premises, they got a tour of the facilities. Expanded business and some new customers were the results. Estimated profit potential: $27,000.

28. Medical supply company revamped their phone system to be more user-friendly for customers and allow easier access to customer service representatives. A couple of lost sales per week are now saved. Estimated profit potential: $500,000.

29. Advertising agency started using an e-mail system instead of paper memos to its staff. Estimated profit potential: $25,000.

30. Moving and storage company set up a procedure to call three days prior to appointments to confirm. This resulted in more qualified meetings and a higher close rate. Estimated profit potential: $40,000.

31. Wholesale bakery revised their shift management system to minimize inefficient interdepartmental interactions. Emphasis included: job descriptions, scheduling, accountability, measurement and training. Estimated profit potential: $700,00.

32. Specialty food manufacturer consolidated similar recipes to reduce the number of short production runs. This reduced line cleaning and raised the size of production runs. Estimated profit potential: $500,000.

33. Tool fabricator organized a maintenance and storage plan for equipment that moved between departments. Estimated profit potential: $54,000.

34. Health and beauty aids supply company increased their prices by ten cents a case. Their customers did not notice the increase because the per item cost was less than a penny. Estimated profit potential: $130,000.

35. Public relations firm started tracking when work came in versus work being delivered, so they could react more quickly to poor sales trends. Estimated profit potential: $130,000.

36. Automation control manufacturer focused on obtaining job tax credits for hiring certain types of workers. Estimated profit potential: $24,000.

37. Advertising agency developed a new system for tracking business prospects to facilitate adequate and timely follow-up. Estimated profit potential: $120,000.

38. Technical services company coordinated travel through one travel agency and established corporate guidelines. Estimated profit potential: $120,000.

39. Embroidery company created an incentive program for unused sick days. Estimated profit potential: $7,500.

40. Medical laboratory set ordering guidelines and standards for supplies. Estimated profit potential: $500,000.

41. Language school created an internal referral fee for recruiting new candidates and reduced employment agency charges. Estimated profit potential: $32,000.

42. Book distributor designed a new employee orientation and training program in order to increase retention levels. Estimated profit potential: $140,000.

43. Home accessory store converted an unused second floor into retail space and rented it to another business. Estimated profit potential: $125,000.

44. Sign maintenance company paid a referral fee to employees who informed them of the names of companies with burned-out business signs. Estimated profit potential: $15,000.

45. Temporary employment agency coordinated classified advertising with their branch offices and centrally purchased these services and consolidated ads. Estimated profit potential: $608,000.

46. Home remodeler created premium pricing for handyman jobs by scheduling jobs during evenings and weekends. Estimated profit potential: $37,000.

47. Courier service reduced vendor costs for phones, beepers and radios by consolidating contracts and establishing rules for usage. Estimated profit potential: $100,000.

48. Janitorial supply company developed a driver checklist as a means of spotting additional sales opportunities. Estimated profit potential: $75,000.

49. Hospital out-patient clinic overbooked appointments based on no-show statistics and increased the number of patients served with no staff increase. Estimated profit potential: $320,000.

50. Payroll service generated extra fees by offering customized management reports for customers. Estimated profit potential: $40,000.

51. Metal fabricating company created an "adopt-an-area" program for employees accepting responsibility for keeping their workplace clean and performing minor equipment maintenance. Estimated profit potential: $55,000.

52. Roofing contractor installed a process to retrieve unused materials from job sites. Estimated profit potential: $180,000.

How do we bring out ideas during the Profit Enhancement Process—through leadership and questions, right? Bright, creative people with positive attitudes often need just the right questions to get them digging into their own experiences and working to find the answers. One of our clients, a specialty gas supply company, hired us to help them reach their goal of growing their bottom line by 20 percent. In a wide-ranging discussion of sales opportunities, someone noted that if the company had more gas cylinders, they could sell more. The problem was having to spend $340,000 a year to replenish liquid gas cylinders. Without that expense, they could make their sales goal. Customers simply weren't returning the cylinders that were nominally rented to them. Replacements cost $160 each.

A Profit Champion was appointed to dig into this problem. The team he put together discovered that the delivery drivers were more focused on timely delivery of cylinders than worrying about making pickups of the empties at the same time. If the empties weren't conveniently there to return, they didn't worry about it. It was just a custom in their industry. The team reasoned that while drivers couldn't really help them raise sales with their customers, they could become more diligent in picking up empty cylinders and save the company $160 for each one returned. So they suggested that drivers be awarded 60 cents for each returned cylinder up to the quantity originally delivered and $1.20 for each cylinder returned in excess of those they delivered. Amazingly, the company soon had too many cylinders for their warehouse. Savings in replacement cylinders added $340,000 of profit to the company's bottom line during the first year.

PEP does not change the strategic goals of the company. It changes the culture in which people work. It encourages everyone to become aware of profit opportunities and to find ways of implementing them. It develops their profit*ability* so they will add value to the company without reinventing its mission.

Employees are your most valuable resource.
Coach them into a winning Profit Team.

A big "Eureka!" we've found from facilitating Profit Super Bowls is that in many companies no one is responsible at the end of the day for their employees' successes or failures. Many entrepreneurial companies don't even have a system for personnel evaluation. People don't know which direction to travel. They are trying to score touchdowns, but don't know toward which end zone to run.

During the Profit Super Bowl for a distribution firm, we facilitated a discussion about their problem with low employee retention. The firm employed 170 employees: two-thirds of them were telephone customer service reps, one-third filled orders, but in all only 20 percent had worked for the company longer than one year. Because of this rapid turnover, managers spent their time putting out fires, filling the gaps left by absent or resigned employees. Further discussion revealed that the phone staff had no benefits—no training, no health insurance, no job descriptions, no orientation classes. The "Improve

Employee Retention" initiative that came out of the Profit Super Bowl, was to appoint Profit Teams with Champions to address these issues. One team was established to develop orientation classes designed to help new employees understand the work of the company, the products they sold, and their place in it before they began talking to customers on the phone. Another team was charged with establishing a three-month evaluation program for new employees. Health insurance benefits were awarded to those who made the cuts and became permanent members of the team. A third team worked on a program of monthly training sessions to keep employees informed about new products and customer service techniques and to support their sense of pride in their work. The profit potential of this initiative was $190,000.

Even when they are leaving your employ, employees can tell you a lot about the state of your company. We advise our clients to hold exit interviews with employees leaving the company. Remember, perceptions are real. The way former employees view your organization may be the way things really are. Take these comments seriously! Here is a sample questionnaire we've developed for our clients.

FUTURE PROFIT OPPORTUNITIES
Employee Exit Questionnaire

Name of Company_____

Department_____

Employee_____Date_____

1. Why are you leaving the firm? (Check those items that apply.)

❑	Pay	❑	More responsibility
❑	Job Promotion	❑	Type of work
❑	More convenient hours	❑	Supervision
❑	Coworkers	❑	Office environment
❑	My physical condition	❑	Commuting distance
❑	Less responsibility	❑	Other (Specify)

_____

2. If you are going to work for another firm, what are they offering you that we haven't?

_____

_____

_____

_____

3. Please rate the following:

Quality of product or services offered for sale.

Outstanding ❑   *Above Average* ❑   *Average* ❑   *Below Average* ❑

Competence of staff and management

Outstanding ❑   *Above Average* ❑   *Average* ❑   *Below Average* ❑

Opportunities for advancement

Outstanding ❑   *Above Average* ❑   *Average* ❑   *Below Average* ❑

Training

Outstanding ❑   *Above Average* ❑   *Average* ❑   *Below Average* ❑

Compensation and fringe benefits

Outstanding ❑   *Above Average* ❑   *Average* ❑   *Below Average* ❑

4. Was your workload a problem? (Too much or too little?)

_____

_____

_____

_____

5. Did you have the support (coaching, equipment, and technology) to be as effective as you are capable of?

_____

_____

_____

_____

_____

6. What did you like most about your job?

_____
_____
_____

7. What did you find most frustrating about your position?

_____
_____
_____
_____

8. In what areas could you have benefited from additional training?

_____
_____
_____
_____

9. Will you recommend our firm to prospective employees?

_____
_____
_____
_____

10. Will you recommend our firm to prospective customers?

_____
_____
_____
_____

Please share any other comments you have to help us be a model employer in the future.

_____
_____
_____
_____

Note: *Thanks for your valued services while employed by our organization.*

Organizational Structure—
Is your staff organized to work effectively?

A moving and storage company was determined to grow their sales. They hired us to coach them through the Profit Enhancement Process. We discovered during the Profit Audit phase of our engagement that their sales representatives were spending only about 12 1/2 percent of their time actually selling. The rest of the time was spent doing administrative and other non-sales related work. The company planned to hire more sales reps. They thought more sales people would mean more sales. Their current sales staff was frustrated. When the managers gathered for the Profit Super Bowl, this was an issue they chose to address, and they appointed a Profit Champion to review all the administrative and non-sales related work their sales reps were performing and suggest which tasks could be eliminated and reassigned to the administrative staff. The sales personnel now spend 80 percent of their time selling. Estimated profit potential? $250,000 annually.

There is nothing more unprofitable than making
unnecessary work more efficient.

The Profit Audit we performed for a bank (jointly with another Institute of Profit Advisors member) revealed that they had too many employees by industry standards, but the employees' surveys revealed that they were feeling overworked. When we began to discuss this issue at the Profit Super Bowl, people were fearful that if the bank began letting the weaker people go and kept just the good people, they too would be overwhelmed and leave. So together we started focusing on what work could be eliminated, and it soon became clear that there was too much duplication and unnecessary work. There is nothing more unprofitable than making unnecessary work more efficient.

For instance, when the computer system had been installed ten years before, someone told the staff to keep duplicate records until they had confidence in the new system. They were still keeping duplicate records because no one had told them to stop!

Fortuitously, the internal auditor for the bank was one of the attendees at this Profit Super Bowl. As the discussion continued about what other work could be eliminated, people kept saying, "But the auditor requires this." More frequently than not, the auditor would speak up and say, "No, I don't!" Immediately, long-held beliefs about workload were eliminated along with work.

Every branch had their own office-supply vendors. A Profit Team was appointed to develop a central buying system to eliminate duplicate work in the branches and take advantage of bulk-purchase opportunities.

There were many, many unnecessary meetings. Few employees used their e-mail or telephones to communicate effectively, so they had meetings. A Profit Team was appointed to set up a training program for the e-mail and voice-mail systems.

There were too many duplicate reporting systems. The bank mailed out receipts for deposits made through the ATM system. Since customers can see their deposit records right on their monthly statement, this duplication was eliminated. There was a lack of efficiency in the way loan documents were prepared and too much unnecessary information was kept in the loan files. A Profit Team was established to develop a better system.

Thousands of customer telephone calls came in every month after Social Security checks were issued. Every month it was the same query: "Did my Social Security check get credited to my account?" Now the bank has an automated telephone system which answers Social Security direct-deposit questions automatically along with other common questions.

What did the elimination of duplicate work mean to this bank's bottom line? Sixty-six percent potential for improvement to their bottom line, year in and year out. They are diligently turning their unrealized bottom line potential into a financial reality.

Marketing & Sales —Are your sales people getting enough chances to run with the ball?

When we analyze the sales and marketing section during a Profit Audit, we always ask ourselves and the CEO: "Are your sales people getting enough chances to run with the ball?" We ask this because we firmly believe in the old saying, "Sales is a number's game." The more people you face, the better the chances are that you will make sales if coached properly. This is half correct. Success in sales is dependent on two things: activities and execution. If the receivers are thrown the football but aren't skilled and coached properly, it is unlikely they will execute the big plays that make all the difference in winning the Profit Game.

If you can't measure it, you can't track it and you can't manage it.

During the Profit Audit we conducted for a computer software training company, it soon became clear that there were severe weaknesses in the sales and marketing end of the business. The managers didn't know how to change the way the department was doing business in order to achieve their sales objectives. We learned from the managers that sales were posted at the end of the month, but sales people had no idea how they were performing during the rest of the month. The sales team was like a football team playing hard, not knowing what the score was until the game ended. They never knew whether they were winning or losing until it was too late to make a difference.

We coached the Profit Team on setting up a system for posting daily sales figures. Everyone on the sales staff now sees at a glance how their sales compare with delivery targets set for specific points of time during the current and future months. The numbers immediately illustrate how individuals and the group are performing. There are no surprises anymore. Everyone tracks their progress and makes adjustments to their game plan before it is too late to reach their profit goals.

A distribution company incorporated the same concept and added an additional twist—a tracking system for lost accounts that pinpoints drops in customer activity. The system alerts managers of customer accounts when there is a reduction in frequency of transactions. Now the company can more quickly discover problem accounts. They immediately determine what is causing the customer to change their buying patterns. The company now retains a significantly higher percentage of potentially lost business. This project has the profit potential of $250,000 extra for the bottom line this year, next year, and every subsequent year.

Sales feed egos, but profits feed families.

We advise Profit Teams to look at the bottom line of the income statement. A company is very fortunate to have a 10-percent bottom line net income. In other words, to earn $100,000 of additional profit, a company may have to increase sales by $1 million. So, the questions is: What if you were to cut costs by 10 percent instead? Let's check out the following hypothetical (and admittedly simplistic) example:

	Pro Forma Prior to Cost Cutting or Increasing Sales	Pro Forma After Cutting Costs 10%	Pro Forma for Increasing Sales (Equivalent to Cutting Costs 10%)
Sales	$20,000,000	$20,000,000	$38,000,000
Cost of sales	(10,000,000)	(9,000,000)	(19,000,000)
Gross Profit	10,000,000	11,000,000	19,000,000
Operating Expenses	(8,000,000)	(7,200,000)	(15,200,000)
NET PROFIT	2,000,000	3,800,000	3,800,000

As you can see, cutting costs by 10 percent almost doubled the net profit. On the other hand, to increase profits to $3,800,000 without the 10-percent cost cutting, sales would have to increase to $38 million. Imagine the effort and cost associated with a sales increase of $18 million!

Many companies cannot afford to do business at nearly twice their existing volume, simply because they don't have enough cash to finance the sales increase. A sale made at the beginning of the month, for example, might not produce cash for 60 days, perhaps longer. In fact, sales might have to be greater than $38 million in this example, because the costs to finance the increased sales activity may be substantial.

While savings can be associated with greater volume. Realistically, all costs do not go up in proportion to the increased sales. Significant sales growth, however, might strain equipment and personnel, so profits might be minimized.

Consider sales increases along with adequate expense controls. This balance will provide the greatest bottom line benefit to your business.

Cross-Sell—Sell all of your products all of the time. What are you providing free that you can charge for?

A company selling supplies and equipment to the physically challenged asked us to help them increase their sales. A department manager in attendance at the Profit Super Bowl reported the following incident. She was servicing a long-time wheelchair repair customer and noticed that it was a new chair, but not one sold by her company. She asked her customer why he hadn't bought it from them. Surprised, he said that he didn't know that wheelchairs were included in her company's product line. It seems that he had only been in the repair department. This organization's selling price per wheelchair ranges from several hundred to several thousand dollars. Imagine how many dollars of lost sales may occur in your organization because customers don't know what you sell.

The Profit Team promptly appointed a Profit Champion and committee to address this problem, soon to become an opportunity. They devised a two-step plan. First, a product folder was assembled, containing informational material on the variety of products and services offered by the company. Now whenever a customer enters the showroom, he or she is given this full-product brochure. Then the customer is offered a tour of the company's impressive facility. The Profit Team developed the major jobs and services highlights for this tour; and customer service representatives were trained in performing the walk-through so that when a customer mentions a need, they steer her to the right department. The Profit Team uncovered these missed sales opportunities, and the profit project team established simple procedures to maximize sales and services which are provided to their customers. The company wins, the customer wins, the vendor wins, the employees win!

An additional "discovery" generated substantial additional revenue for this company, with little cost. They published a free monthly newsletter on news and products of interest to the physically challenged. One employee who is physically challenged himself asked why this publication was free to subscribers when it provided such valuable information. No one had an answer. Three months later, the company began selling subscriptions. This "grounds up" initiative brought $200,000 in previously unrealized profit potential (with little additional effort or expense) which had previously been invisible to top management. They made the invisible visible.

Pricing—The customer is the driving force when it comes to selling prices.

Customers will pay you what they think your product or service is worth, not a penny more. Traditionally, many businesses have priced their goods and services based on cost. Cost is irrelevant in the buying decision of the purchaser. They never know the cost. Understanding this basic yet all-important principle is essential to determining the real profit opportunities in your business. Your organization's gross margin potential is illustrated using the following model:

Potential Sales	=	Units sold X customer's perceived value per unit
<Cost of Sales>	=	Accurately determined direct and indirect costs of product/services sold
Gross Margin Potential		The dollars left to pay all other expenses as well as generate profits

Unless your customers perceive that your product is truly unique, you've got to remain competitive in pricing goods and services. Even uniqueness, however, has limits in what customers are willing to pay. Make sure you know your competitors, what they sell, and what they charge.

Pricing decisions must work in concert with other strategic business decisions. Think about your sales goals, corporate image, marketing strategies, competitor goals, and various other related business objectives. Put those business objectives in writing and share that information with your Profit Team. Profit Team members will then be able to make informed critical pricing decisions.

Here's a last quick sales idea. In an effort to create new sales leads for their company, one of our distribution clients created a training program to help its truck drivers spot sales opportunities while making deliveries. Now the drivers track their discoveries on a form that is kept with them in their trucks. When they return to the warehouse, they give the form to their supervisor, who then forwards it to the sales staff. The drivers receive a commission on any new sales that result from their efforts, and the estimated profit potential: $100,000.

Create a whole new profit culture
where your Profit Team keeps scoring.

We've said this over and over again, the Profit Enhancement Process is a journey. It is meant to create a new profit culture, a whole new way of thinking and working that doesn't interfere with the long-term goals of the company, but produces a never-ending stream of new ideas from your people who have profit*ability*. Most often these ideas don't involve major restructuring, just profit*ability*.

For instance, the use of corporate procurement cards for purchasing is increasing because they minimize paperwork, thus eliminating unnecessary overhead. Since purchasing functions by necessity are transaction-oriented, eliminating any of these time-consuming activities while controlling costs would offer a company significant extra profits. Well-run companies have traditionally used a purchase order system to establish purchasing controls. By spending less time with unnecessary paperwork, purchasing agents can spend more time on buying strategies. Smart companies we work with have established purchasing policies that permit the use of corporate procurement credit cards for amounts below predetermined limits.

Remember the Paredo 20/80 rule? Twenty percent of the variables produce 80 percent of the results. In most cases, 20 percent of what you buy represents 80 percent of what the company spends. It represents only 20 percent of the cost associated with processing the paperwork. Using the procurement credit card for 80 percent of your purchases, which represent 20 percent of your expenditures, will save 80 percent of the company's cost of processing paperwork. Of course, the purchasing department must develop procedures for using the card, develop financial reports to assure compliance and reporting are adequate, and establish adequate internal control procedure before this program is put in place.

Our clients report that the average purchase costs from $30 to $300 in administrative expenses. Using this procedure, these costs can be reduced 80 to 90 percent, and the savings goes directly to your bottom line.

Some creative companies earn air miles by using procurement credit cards. The earned air miles reduce their travel costs. Combining travel cost savings with administrative cost savings will make the procurement credit card an excellent alternative to your other more costly methods of administratively handling the procurement functions.

Some winning plays for your playbook.

A manufacturing company changed many aspects of its operating procedures and realized millions of dollars in extra profit potential. All of these ideas came out of their first Profit Super Bowl where their starting Profit Team developed true profit*ability*.

This manufacturer sells to the giant hardware store chains. The Profit Team determined that one of their greatest profit fumbles was delivering partial loads on their trucks. They set up some real financial incentives to encourage their customers to buy full loads or share the delivery with other stores. This initiative added an extra $116,000 in previously unrealized bottom line potential by saving delivery expenses.

The Profit Team identified a weakness in their customer service department: The receptionist and other telephone-answering staff were not really trained to answer questions about the company's products, nor did they know who else might answer each question. "That's not my job," they would say as they handed the call on to the next uniformed employee. The Profit Team determined which were the most frequently-asked customer questions, and set up a program to train operators about the products and issues and who could answer each question. In addition, the company had no sales tracking database. The Profit Team established one and generated an extra $425,000 in profit potential the first year.

Consider testing your own system by calling your business phone number as a customer in disguise. You might be astonished about the sales opportunities your firm is losing because of untrained and ineffective procedures for handling customer requests and inquiries that can potentially turn into additional sales. Your phone system mannerisms and technology may need improving as well in order to ensure a predictable result.

Our client had not trained customer service representatives to cross-sell their products. The company sold certain products to some customers, and different products to others. The Profit Team developed a new sales program in which all the company's products were featured in customer promotional materials. Cross-selling has brought in an extra $300,000 in potential profit.

The company purchased its raw materials by weight. The Profit Team discovered that they were buying truckloads of raw materials with high moisture content. They set moisture content limits for raw materials. This reduced costs and saved the company $100,000.

In addition, they now have a Profit Champion in charge of repairing the wooden palettes on which their products are shipped and stored. Instead of throwing away broken palettes, this profit*able* employee repairs and recycles them. No one was in charge of managing the surface utilization of the palettes. Some were only 70-percent utilized. The Profit Team evaluated the size of palettes and compared them against the size and weight of their products. This maximized storage and minimized delivery expenses. The extra profit potential generated from these two initiatives is $80,000.

A Profit Team examined the pricing on their inventories. They looked at the pricing for their products based on availability and quality. Accordingly, they raised some prices and lowered others, and developed close-out procedures for excess inventory. These initiatives brought in $180,000 in extra cash.

The company had no procedure for validating the accuracy of orders. This created many costly errors. The Profit Team put new control procedures in place and greatly reduced those error rates.

There was no preventative maintenance plan for the company's equipment. We know that preventative maintenace prolongs the life of equipment and keeps people working instead of waiting for equipment to be repaired. The Profit Team established a plan for preventative equipment maintenance and saved the company a potential of $260,000 in excess repair costs, wasted time, and the inability to fill orders promptly.

Now add it all up. This company through its Profit Teams "found" $1,161,000 of unrealized profit for their bottom line.

Just think what you can do for your company.

---

14 Things You Can Do Today to Drive Profits to Your Bottom Line.

---

1. If your business is seasonal, ask your biggest vendors to let you stock up now, but pay when your customers buy. Also, renegotiate your leases to pay only those 8, 9, or 10 months out of the year when you experience the greatest sales. See how well your cash flow improves.

2. During the next two weeks, keep a list of products your customers would have bought had you stocked them. Then calculate how much revenue you will earn by stocking the three most-requested items.

3. Ask your employees to make a list of ten ways they would like to be rewarded for a job well done. See how much you will make by awarding these perks, instead of giving subjective cash bonuses.

4. Ask your production foreman to estimate how much you spend in lost production, manufacturing errors leading to re-work, and injuries. Then calculate how much extra profit will come by offering manufacturing crews a percentage of the savings from waste and accidents they prevent.

5. Tell your plant foreman to give you a list of equipment that is idle most of the time. Then calculate how much you will save in insurance, property taxes, maintenance, storage space and carrying charges by getting rid of it.

6. Ask your secretaries, delivery people, janitor, customer service personnel, shipping clerks, production workers, service people, paralegals, staff accountants—anyone who performs the day-to-day work in your business—to write down five ways your company can become more profit*able*. See how many bottom line ideas you receive.

7. Start sending letters to customers who discontinue doing business with you thanking them for their past patronage. See how many call you to reinstate their account.

8. Ask your accounting department to rank your customers by dollars they spend. Calculate how much more money you will make by transferring your time and dollars from servicing the lowest-producing 80 percent to "wowing" the top 20 percent of your customers beyond their wildest expectations.

9. Ask your accounting department to tell you how much you spent last year on overnight priority packages and shipping. Then calculate how much you will save if 75 percent of those are sent to arrive the following afternoon instead of morning.

10. Ask your payroll manager to give you a list of employees who were paid overtime last year. Initiate a bonus to selected employees in those departments who get their work done responsibly without incurring any overtime. See how much that will add to your bottom line.

11. If you currently bill customers a fixed amount every month, calculate how much you'll save in monthly mailing costs and how much you'll increase cash flow by billing in advance every two months instead.

12. Calculate how much you spent last year for products and services that could have been billed, but were not authorized by your customers. See how much you will make with a system to catch what is not authorized before it occurs and get your customer's approval in advance.

13. Calculate how much more you will earn if you improve your net pre-tax by just 10 percent.

14. Make a list of all the things you will do with those extra profits!

Now go on to Part II where we give you a complete playbook of our top 100 profit-generating ideas that your team can put into play right away.

Instant Replays

Great profit coaches never rest on their laurels.

Your profit attitude determines your profit altitude.

"Departmentalism" destroys teamwork and will destroy your chances for winning the Profit Game.

"Always praise a player in front of his peers. Never criticize him in public."
— Larry Pecattiello, Former Coach, National Football League

Great coaches are never afraid to admit they've made a mistake.

PEP focuses everyone on the profits needed to grow the company and add value to it.

PEP provides the support and monitoring of progress that effective implementation requires.

Players play harder when they know their work will be rewarded.

Often it's the shoemaker's kids who are the ones going without shoes.

PEP supports your company's strategic goals. It doesn't change them; it enhances them with the bottom line results of additional opportunities.

Great coaches learn from other winning teams.

Employees are your most valuable resource. Coach them into a winning Profit Team.

Organizational Structure—Is your staff organized to work effectively?

There is nothing more unprofitable than making unnecessary work more efficient.

Marketing & Sales—Are your sales people getting enough chances to run with the ball?

If you can't measure it, you can't track it and you can't manage it.

Sales feed egos, but profits feed families.

Cross-Sell—Sell all of your products all of the time. What are you providing for free that you can charge for?

Pricing—The customer is the driving force when it comes to selling prices.

Create a whole new profit culture where your Profit Team keeps scoring.

Develop your own play book with all your firm's successful strategies recorded and ready for winning the Profit Game now and in the future.

Part II: 100 Ways to Win the Profit Game

CHAPTER 7:
SALES & MARKETING

CREATE SALES AND MARKETING ACTION PLANS

A successful sales and marketing organization has a strong infra-structure in place for each of the following areas:

- Marketing and lead generation
- Compensation plans
- Hiring practices
- Sales support
- Sales processes
- Sales management
- Training practices
- Sales and other departmental interactions

The following questions will help you conduct a "self sales and marketing audit" before undertaking any business planning activity. Companies who are maximizing their sales and marketing efforts have solid answers for a majority of the following questions. The answers will come from personal interviews with marketing and communications personnel, sales people, sales managers and customers.

Answer the questions, determine where you need to begin making improvements, then implement the specific action-items following each list of questions.

MARKETING & LEAD GENERATION

1. Who are your customers?
2. What are your revenue projections for each salesperson?

153

3. Which are the key accounts you targeted to achieve revenue projections?
4. What are you selling?
5. Is mass media (TV, radio, print) appropriate for your company's advertising?
6. What form of print advertising do you use?
7. What percentage of your market do you have?
8. How effective are lead generation mechanisms?
9. What types of direct mail programs are carried out by your company?
10. How much is your marketing budget, and how is it calculated?
11. What type and how effective are your collateral materials?
12. Are trade shows appropriate to market and sell in your industry? Do you participate?
13. Which markets should you be selling to?
14. How frequently is your message presented to customers, clients and prospects?
15. Who are your main competitors and what are their strengths?
16. Are territories sensibly organized and perceived as fair by your sales staff?

MARKETING AND LEAD GENERATION:
SPECIFIC ACTION ITEMS

1. Define the role of an in-house marketing person and hire such an individual if warranted.
2. Develop a marketing strategy with goals and directions for each business component.
3. Consider an outside public relations firm when a marketing strategy is in place.
4. Develop an activity-based marketing plan for the next 12-month period.
5. Create a current, centralized list of all customers and prospects. Develop a set of criteria for including names on this list. Establish a process to identify names and roles that should be added to this list. Utilize it for direct mail programs and to record personal contacts.
6. Establish a marketing budget and empower a champion to assure its execution.
7. Create collateral materials for each business unit.
8. Evaluate a realignment of present sales territories to include a teaming concept.
9. Develop compensation plans for shared opportunities.

THE SALES PROCESS

1. Are there defined sales processes for sales staff to follow?
2. Are salespeople talking to decision-makers of your prospects?
3. Are you selling commodities, or value-added products and services?
4. Are salespeople held accountable for making a pre-determined number of sales calls and meetings?
5. Do you have a sales department? What role does it play?
6. Are salespeople able to differentiate your company's products and services from the competition?
7. How good are your salespeople at getting referrals?
8. What percentage of sales opportunities do you close?
9. What are the main reasons sales opportunities are lost?
10. How strong are your relationships with clients/customers/prospects?
11. What training takes place to enhance sales skills?

THE SALES PROCESS: SPECIFIC ACTION ITEMS

1. Develop goals and action plans for each sales representative. Determine expected levels of calling and/or meetings to attain these goals.
2. Identify key information that must be obtained from each account. Use this data to develop sales strategies for deeper account penetration.
3. Develop important sales indicators which will be monitored daily. Publicly post daily and monthly sales indicators for all sales representatives. This should be segregated by salesperson category.
4. Create a definition of the value your company provides to customers and communicate it continuously to all parts of the company.
5. Conduct a brainstorming session with representatives from various departments to identify additional value-added services which will differentiate your firm.
6. Perform an analysis of competitors' strengths and weaknesses and distribute the findings to salespeople and others that will use this information to your company's advantage.

COMPENSATION PLANS

1. What is the philosophy behind your compensation plan?
2. Are you generating the margins you need?
3. Are there adequate incentives for new business? Are there consequences for not maintaining the business of former customers?

4. Are there adequate incentives for more business from existing customers?
5. Is the plan understandable?
6. How much leeway do salespeople have in pricing orders?
7. How often do salespeople receive commissions?
8. How does your plan compare with other companies in your industry?
9. Are commissions calculated accurately and fairly?
10. Is your plan creating the desired behavior from your sales force?

COMPENSATION PLAN: SPECIFIC ACTION ITEMS

1. Create comfort in the minds of your sales staff that the factors affecting their commissions are accurately computed.
2. Pay people commissions monthly. If the calculations can't be made that quickly, pay them an estimated draw monthly with a quarterly adjustment.
3. Evaluate whether your compensation plan is motivating people to achieve desired sales.

SALES MANAGEMENT - GENERAL ISSUES

1. What are the duties of your sales manager?
2. How is the sales staff monitored?
3. How are salespeople trained?
4. Are sales projections made, and if so how effective are they?
5. How involved is your sales manager in understanding the business aspects of your company?
6. How involved is your sales manager with your most valued customers?
7. How involved is your sales manager in vendor relationships?
8. What role does your sales manager play on your profit team?

SALES MANAGEMENT - HIRING & RETENTION PRACTICES OF SALESPEOPLE

9. What is the track record of recent hires of salespeople?
10. How are their skill levels evaluated?
11. How are good candidates attracted?
12. Are specific job requirements reduced to writing?
13. Do multiple people evaluate candidates?
14. Do your new hires know specifically what is expected of them?

SALES MANAGEMENT - SALES TRAINING PRACTICES

15. What type of sales training is provided?
16. How are sales training skills reinforced on an ongoing basis?

17. How is sales training matched to staff deficiencies?
18. What considerations are made for salespeople at different skill levels?
19. Are salespeople aware of your corporate strategic direction?

SALES MANAGEMENT: SPECIFIC ACTION ITEMS

1. Develop a list of criteria for effective sales management and compare it with the attributes of those presently in these positions.
2. Identify an effective sales process for each salesperson category. Look at your "stars'" attributes in each area to develop this model. Components should include opening scripts, key probing questions, qualification variables, common objections and relationship-building techniques that will continually re-enforce selling value instead of commodities.
3. Develop an agenda format and set a frequency for sales meetings.
4. Find a qualified, passionate champion to be in charge of your sales and marketing efforts.
5. Initiate coaches notebooks to record summaries of meetings between the salespeople and sales managers. Coaching sessions should take place regularly. Progress made and action items for the next period should be recorded. Salespeople need to know what is expected of them. Sales managers should know the progress and needs of those they work with.

SALES SUPPORT

1. What does a typical day look like for your sales force?
2. How much of each salesperson's time is spent in front of customers?
3. What type of sales support and assistance is provided?
4. What administrative work could be more efficiently handled by support personnel?
5. What technology tools are available to your sales staff?
6. Is telemarketing an effective tool for your business?
7. Are you using effective contact management software?
8. Are salespeople's meetings and calls recorded in a database?

SALES SUPPORT: SPECIFIC ACTION ITEMS

1. Provide salespeople with the technology necessary to generate sales. Make sure they have access to available databases.
2. Offer pre-sales technical assistance.
3. Approve sales effectively and promptly. Record them into your sales department's system.

SALES AND OTHER DEPARTMENT INTERACTIONS

1. How well are your customers' needs communicated to those servicing them?
2. How well do salespeople understand what is needed from other departments?
3. What difficulties do salespeople create in other departments?
4. What difficulties do salespeople create for collections?
5. Is paperwork done on time?
6. Is paperwork done correctly?
7. Are complaints handled promptly and satisfactorily?
8. Do your company and customers have favorable impressions of your sales department?

SALES AND OTHER DEPARTMENTAL INTERACTIONS: SPECIFIC ACTION ITEMS

1. Develop operational models so you can gauge the effective utilization of your sales department infrastructure. Prior to a sale, use this information to ensure that work will be performed properly. When hiring additional sales staff, determine if you can operationally handle increased volume.
2. Proceed with operational improvements expeditiously. This will contribute to significant growth in sales and profits.
3. Your sales department should be given jurisdiction over customer service.

---

1. CREATE SALES AND MARKETING ACTION PLANS

HOW DOES THIS APPLY TO MY BUSINESS?

_____

_____

_____

_____

_____

Priority   1   2   3   (Circle one)

Action Date_____

Profit Champion _____

Potential Dollar Effect $_____

STRETCH ADVERTISING
DOLLARS

There's an old saying in retailing that you don't have to rent a hall to give away merchandise.

That's true in other businesses, too. **With a little ingenuity and some elbow grease, you will be able to spread the word about your business without a "mega-ton" advertising campaign.**

The key is creativity. You should start thinking beyond conventional advertising methods—newspapers, magazines, radio and television. These media are terrific vehicles for promoting a business, but they can be expensive. And nowadays there are so many new and creative ways of advertising—especially with the Internet, and by negotiating with retailers for co-op advertising dollars or with "hungry" media for a portion of the sales generated from your ad instead of your paying the full cost.

It's time to explore alternatives to stretch your advertising dollars. Our firm, for instance, signed up for a state-sponsored "Adopt-A-Road" program. The gist of the program is that to "adopt" a road—in our case the main thoroughfare in front of our office—a business is responsible for keeping the roadsides clean. Our staff went out about four times a year to pick up trash, and afterwards were rewarded with a "post-garbage" party!

What we received in return were several large road signs, courtesy of the state highway service, which read:

"THIS ROAD ADOPTED
BY THE PROFIT ADVISORS"

The signs face in both directions of the road, in plain view of the more than 140,000 vehicles that pass by every day. That's free advertising you can take to the bank! In addition to the exposure, our firm generated lots of good will in our community for keeping the highway clean.

Think of things that your organization can do right now to help your community and generate publicity at the same time.

Why not have a blood drive in your office? All you do is volunteer the space, and the Red Cross does the rest. It won't take up office time, because it can be done during evenings or on weekends. Most importantly, the media attention you get will save you advertising dollars. After all, newspapers, television and radio stations frequently announce local blood drives—including the location and business that is the sponsor. Best of all, your company blood might well end up saving a life!

Another inexpensive alternative to conventional advertising is to develop a newsletter or other communications vehicle to reach potential clients. When you consider a simple desktop newsletter costs as little as 50 cents per copy, you can see the benefits outweigh the expense.

A physical therapy clinic launched such a newsletter, which is sent to local medical practitioners. Physicians play a tremendous role in directing patients to physical therapists, and because this particular clinic made its presence known, more doctors are sending them their patients.

We could write an entire book on Internet marketing, but others already have. There is no doubt that it is the wave of the future for marketing products and services. When you are ready to launch your company on the Web—and it better be soon! —hire a competent consultant who really knows Web design and most importantly how to link your Web site to all those mysterious areas where your potential customers or clients will be looking for you. An effective Web site will not only bring in customers but give you vital information about them which can become part of your customer database and be used in other marketing campaigns by mail or phone.

Be creative. Marketing is vital, but it need not take your entire budget.

2. STRETCH ADVERTISING DOLLARS

HOW DOES THIS APPLY TO MY BUSINESS?

_____

_____

_____

_____

_____

Priority   1   2   3   (Circle one)

Action Date_____

Profit Champion _____

Potential Dollar Effect $_____

SURVEY CUSTOMERS ABOUT YOUR BUSINESS

Our clients find that a well-structured customer satisfaction survey provides a wealth of invaluable market intelligence. Properly done, it establishes performance benchmarks, builds relationships, identifies customers at risk of loss, and is a catalyst for enhancing overall satisfaction, loyalty and revenues. Done poorly, it becomes a source of misguided direction, wrong decisions and profit fumbles.

An international hotel chain wanted to attract more business travelers. They conducted a survey to identify the needs of this type of guest. A written survey was placed in each room. When the survey period was complete, the only respondents were children and their grandparents. No one recognized that business travelers usually don't have the time or the interest in participating in a survey, unless they have a major problem to report.

Survey designs and population characteristics will dramatically alter the results. Your survey process must deliver a true representation of your customers' opinions so the findings will be an accurate basis for action planning. Before embarking on a survey program, consider the following variables:

Question Types. Survey questions should be categorized into three types:

- Overall Satisfaction — "How satisfied are you overall with XYZ Company?"

- Key Attributes — satisfaction with key areas of your business, e.g. Sales, Marketing, Operations, etc.
- Drill Down — satisfaction with issues that are unique to each attribute. These are the parts of your company that touch a customer. Examples would include ordering, invoicing, problem resolution, delivery, and so on.

Question Design. The following design elements should be taken into account:

- Surveys that take more than 5-10 minutes to complete become taxing and sacrifice response rate and accuracy.
- The questions should utilize simple sentences with short words.
- Open-ended questions are generally best avoided in favor of simple, concise, one-subject questions.
- Superlatives such as "excellent" or "very" tend to lead a respondent toward an opinion. Avoid generating subjective answers. Ask questions which offer actions for operational improvement.
- Mix up the topics and force continual thinking about different subjects. Previous questions should not influence an answer.
- Questions should be presented in positive tones.

The Need for a High Response Rate. The objective of a survey is to capture a representative cross-section of opinions from a group of customers. Without majority participation, two factors will influence the results:

- A low response rate will generally produce more negative results.
- A smaller percentage of a population is less representative of the whole.

The Accuracy of Terms

Studies have shown that a "totally satisfied" customer is between three and ten times more likely to initiate a repurchase. Understanding the differences between "totally satisfied," "very satisfied" and "somewhat satisfied" provides greater insight into the causes of your company's financial results.

Customers are the lifeblood of your business. Your financial goals are linked with meeting and exceeding their expectations, but you have to know what they are! **A survey with a high response rate, accurate information, and actionable ideas is an essential part of a profit enhancement process for your company.**

Here is a brief sample Customer Satisfaction Questionnaire which we invite you to adapt to your own business. The one we use with our clients is a bit more extensive.

HOW ARE WE DOING?

Please help us serve you better by filling out this
satisfaction questionnaire.

Your Name_____ Customer Name_____

1. What does your organization do?_____
   _____
   _____

2. How long have you been doing business with us?_____

3. What types of products and services do you purchase from us?
   _____
   _____

4. How easy is it to do business with us?_____
   _____

5. What would you enhance about our business relationship?
   _____
   _____
   _____

6. What are the reasons you choose to do business with us?
   _____
   _____

7. How well do we understand your business?
   _____
   _____
   _____

8. How would you rate our salespeople who work with you?
   _____
   _____
   _____

---

9. Would you rate our salesperson as an order taker or a consultant?

_____

_____

Please explain:

_____

_____

_____

10. Should the salesperson be more involved in either direction?

_____

_____

_____

11. How would you rate our operations people that you deal with?

_____

_____

12. What percentage of our work is right the first time? Please explain:

_____

_____

_____

13. What causes the need to have work redone?_____

_____

_____

14. How responsive are we in fixing problems? Please explain:

_____

_____

_____

15. How would you rate administrative dealings with us?_____

_____

_____

16. What do you get from us that you don't get from another vendor?

_____

_____

_____

continued

17. What percentage of your business do you estimate you do with us?

_____

_____

18. What would cause you to do more business with us?

_____

_____

3. SURVEY CUSTOMERS ABOUT YOUR BUSINESS
HOW DOES THIS APPLY TO MY BUSINESS?

_____

_____

_____

_____

_____

Priority   1   2   3   (Circle one)

Action Date_____

Profit Champion _____

Potential Dollar Effect $_____

INCREASE PROFITS BY CHARGING THE RIGHT PRICE

The "right" price for your product or service isn't always "double the wholesale price" or "cost plus X percent." It is that number which effectively earns your company the profit you are entitled to—regardless of the number of customers you have or do not have, regardless of the number of salespeople you do or do not employ, regardless of what is "standard" for your industry ... even regardless of what you've always charged. **In fact, the right price might be significantly higher than you're charging now, though it may cost you sales.** Be prepared for this possibility as you read how we determine the "right" price to charge for the goods and services our clients offer their marketplace.

1. Cost. This is the most obvious component of pricing decisions. You obviously cannot begin to price effectively until you know your cost structure inside out, and that includes both direct costs and fully loaded costs, such as overhead, trade discounts and so on. And it means knowing those cost structures for each item or service you sell, not just on an average company-wide or product-line basis. Too often managers make pricing decisions based on average cost of goods when, in fact, huge margin variations exist from item to item. Your company's gross margin potential can be illustrated using the following model:

Sales = Sales = Units Sold x Customer's Perceived Value per Unit
<Cost of Sales> = Accurately determined direct and indirect costs of products/services sold
Gross Margin Potential = The dollars left to pay all other expenses as well as generate profits

---

2. Customer. Your customer is the ultimate judge of whether your price, in combination with quality of service or product, delivers a superior value. When you consider pricing strategy, ask your customers for their input. Two simple questions: What do you think this product or service is worth? Would you have bought the product or service at this price? Are your customers willing to pay more than you are presently charging? What is the customer's expected range—the highest and lowest price points—for your product or service? Within that range, what is your specific target customer's acceptable range, the highest or lowest he or she will pay? Which ways do your customers look at your selling price: The absolute price, the standard price, or the regular versus sale price? Beyond what you charge, what are the other associated expenses your customers think about as they consider your product or service?

3. Channels of Distribution. If you sell through any middlemen to get to the end-users of your product or service, then those intermediaries affect your pricing in two ways. First, you have to price so their margins will be large enough to motivate them to do what you need them to do. Second, you must consider the expenses they add that affect the price your end-users ultimately pay. Make sure your middlemen are adding value to the relationship by doing for you and your customers what can't be done without them. Should you use multiple channels of distribution?

4. Competition. This is where managers often make their fatal pricing decisions. Every company and every product has competition. Even if your product or service is unique, make sure, as you consider pricing approaches, that you think very carefully about your competitor from the buyer's point of view (the only point of view that matters). If you don't know all the alternatives against which buyers evaluate you, pick up the phone and ask a few.

5. Compatibility. Pricing is not a stand-alone decision. It must work in concert with everything else you are trying to achieve. Do you believe McDonald's can sell a lot of $10 filet mignons? Is your pricing approach compatible with your marketing objectives? With your sales goals? With the image you want to project? Those objectives have to be explicitly stated and written down. If your production goals, for instance, are to even out the process so you can better control inventory, the last thing you want is a pricing strategy that forces seasonal spikes in demand, causing stocking problems.

4. INCREASE PROFITS BY CHARGING THE RIGHT PRICE

HOW DOES THIS APPLY TO MY BUSINESS?

_____

_____

_____

_____

_____

Priority   1   2   3   (Circle one)

Action Date_____

Profit Champion _____

Potential Dollar Effect $_____

BROADEN MARKETS BY "BUNDLING" PRODUCTS AND SERVICES

Let's say a customer has indicated she's ready to buy from you. If all you do is write up the order, you've missed a golden opportunity to increase the amount of the sale.

I went to the shoe store the other day to buy a pair of oxfords. When I picked them out, the sales clerk suggested that I pick up an extra pair of laces and some polish. He even called my attention to a sale on argyle socks! Thanks to good old-fashioned "suggestive selling," I left the store loaded down with impulse purchases.

In many businesses, however, it's just not possible to have a crack salesperson on hand suggesting tie-in purchases. But that doesn't mean you can't generate extra sales volume by 'bundling' related goods or services. Instead of just one hit, you might get a double or triple sale—maybe even a home run!

There's a car wash near our office where they offer bare-bones service for $8. But for $12, they will not only wash your car, but vacuum the interior and apply spray wax. Although the big sign out front promotes the $8 wash, most customers choose the package. It's a better value for them and a more profitable sale for the car-wash owner.

Many businesses can broaden their market penetration by trying variations on this same theme. A restaurant, for example, can generate customer interest in particularly profitable menu selections by bundling an appetizer, entree and dessert at a single, attractive price.

Similarly, if you operate a service station, you can offer an oil change, lube and tire rotation at a single, reduced price. **Of course your overall profit margin percentage will be lower due to the discount. But in terms of profit dollars, you'll be financially ahead** because many customers will be purchasing additional products and services due to the financial benefit that they perceive.

One entrepreneur developed a terrific recipe for clam chowder. He had the soup canned and began marketing it locally. The response was alright, but sales didn't really take off until he hit on the idea of selling his chowder in six-pack containers like beer. Then he realized that almost everybody who bought his clam chowder was a prime customer for oyster crackers. He began packaging crackers with each six-pack, and the result was a nice, big bottom-line bonus for our client. Look what's happening with computer sales. It's not unusual to get a printer and on-line service when you buy a computer and monitor.

Car dealers use the technique of "add-on" sales all the time. As soon as you say, "Okay, I'll take it," they offer to "throw in" extended warranties, paint protection and deluxe wheels for a bundled price. You don't have to be a car dealer to do the same thing. By being alert to opportunities for add-on sales, you may be able to increase your average sale, by customer, 20 to 30 percent and perhaps even more.

5: BROADEN MARKETS BY "BUNDLING" PRODUCTS AND SERVICES

HOW DOES THIS APPLY TO MY BUSINESS?

_____

_____

_____

_____

_____

Priority   1   2   3   (Circle one)

Action Date_____

Profit Champion _____

Potential Dollar Effect $_____

IDENTIFY YOUR COMPANY'S EDGE IN THE MARKETPLACE

Every company has strengths as well as weaknesses. Recognizing these strengths and capitalizing on them is every bit as important as eliminating the weaknesses. Take the time to work with your top management to define what is unique about your business. Start out by asking, "What do we sell?" This question is not always easy to answer, especially if you sell a variety of services or products. The process of identifying and defining what it is your company does and what makes it unique or a little better than your competition will be a real morale-builder and focus everyone's attention on your strengths.

Your favorite restaurant, for example, may not have a five-star rating, but it just might serve the best pot roast in the area, and its casual atmosphere draws customers who want to relax.

Similarly, the corner pharmacist may not be able to match the discount prices of the chain store down the street, but by offering to deliver prescriptions night and day, that business will carve a niche in the market.

Your company's competitive edge might be something as complex as selling a state-of-the-art computer system or as simple as having a warm, friendly receptionist.

Identify your company's strengths and capitalize on them. **Failing to communicate the attributes that make your business special is like entering a boxing ring with one hand tied behind your back. You might come out a winner, but the odds are against it.**

Take the case of the office equipment retailer that appeared to be doing everything right. This particular firm offers 24-hour service on all business machines that it sells or leases. Customers receive a free "loaner" whenever their equipment is being repaired. In addition, the company allows businesses to renew maintenance agreements for as long as they own their equipment.

These are really valuable customer services and no other supplier in the area will match them. Yet the company was struggling because of competition from firms that offered less. The problem was that this business simply was not communicating its uniqueness to potential customers. Long-time customers took these liberal service policies for granted; new ones were never even told of the company's practices; and some of the firm's own employees were unaware that these policies were special.

Fortunately, the CEO of this business recognized the problem and took steps to communicate the company's strengths. Today, their prospective customers are supplied with a detailed brochure outlining the company's services and explaining the advantages of dealing with them.

The company is still battling for market share, but at least now it's using both fists!

Smart selling requires listening to what your customers want. Give this "Smart Sales Survey" to your salespeople to help them gather the information they need to close a sale. A savvy business owner once said, "God gave us two ears and one mouth, so that we can listen twice as much as we talk."

SMART SALES SURVEY

Company Name:_____

Phone:_____Fax:_____

Contact/Title:_____

Address:_____

Referred by:_____

Type of Business:_____

OPERATIONS
How long have you been with this organization?_____

Sales Volume:_____Number of Employees:_____

Other Locations:_____

DECISION-MAKING AUTHORITY
How is the decision process made?_____

_____

Who is involved in the decision-making process?_____

_____

USAGE
How much of our products and/or services can you use?_____

_____

Quantity: _____Stock:_____

continued

Current and previous vendors?   How long?   Why?

_____

_____

_____

SATISFACTION
What would you change about your vendor?

_____

_____

Consequences
How would the above benefit your company?

_____

_____

VALUE
What would it mean to you if our business could provide:
Better quality?_____
Easier operations?_____
Timelier deliveries?_____

Other questions to your prospective clients/customers and their industry?

_____

_____

_____

Notes regarding this interview:

_____

_____

REFERRALS
Additional people who might benefit from our services or products:
Name:_____Department:_____ Phone:_____
Name:_____Department:_____ Phone:_____
Name:_____Department:_____ Phone:_____

APPOINTMENT
Date/Time:_____

RESULTS
Date sent:_____
❏ Visit:
❏ Send literature:
❏ Not a candidate for what we sell:
Explanation:_____

_____

_____

6. IDENTIFY YOUR COMPANY'S EDGE IN THE MARKETPLACE

HOW DOES THIS APPLY TO MY BUSINESS?

_____

_____

_____

_____

_____

Priority   1   2   3   (Circle one)

Action Date_____

Profit Champion _____

Potential Dollar Effect $_____

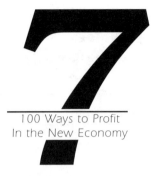

USE TRICKLE MARKETING FOR QUALIFIED LEADS

Black bamboo is a rare wood grown in Asia. In the year when its seeds are planted, the crop is weeded and fertilized and no growth is visible. During the second and third years, the process is repeated and minimal progress is observed. In the fourth year, tending the crop results in a one-foot stock emerging from the ground. Finally, in year five, continued cultivation provides a 20-foot stick. Successful marketing is very similar to growing black bamboo.

Businesses need a constant supply of new customers as well as repetitive orders from existing customers. Traditional means of uncovering viable prospects, such as telemarketing and knocking on doors, can be successful, but are time-consuming and require a significant number of contacts to realize even minimum results. When these cold-call methods result in an inquiry, the potential customer has little knowledge of the vendor's products and services, which means it will take a more complicated selling process to generate an order.

Many firms send a variety of materials to their prospects. It is customary for this information to be mailed once or twice, and it is usually product-oriented. People responding to these appeals are either curious or are actively looking for the specific product. The former are cold leads, which require a lot of education. The latter will be much more qualified and responsive leads.

"Trickle marketing," which aims to build strong and bonding relationships with prospective customers, requires a different approach. Mailing messages to a targeted audience is key to the success of the program, but there are several major differences with traditional marketing.

First, you need more than one or two mailings to give your offerings enough exposure. Second, your messages should be "educational" and make your prospects begin to *need* your products, rather than just describing the products.

On average, it takes 21 "exposures" to your company (direct mail pieces, ads, live or print media mentions) to generate a prospect—particularly if you are selling an expensive product or service. If your selling messages are strong enough, customer requests for information will take place earlier. Persistent and effective mailings combined with other forms of advertising will generate this number of contacts. We recommend that contacts be spaced no less than thirty days apart. When drafting the content of your mailings, identify the specific problem areas that your product or service can solve for the prospect. Write a one-page letter which addresses possible areas where your product will solve your potential customer or client's business problems: organizational, revenue generation, procedures and/or productivity. Reference your firm's ability to help them make improvements in these areas. All they have to do is contact you for further information. Always include another promotional piece with the letter: an article, a customer testimonial letter, or a product description, and, most importantly, a response mechanism: an order form, response card, 800 number, or e-mail address which can be mailed or phoned right back to you.

Most vital of all in your mailing campaigns are good mailing lists of prospects. Define your ideal customer in terms of geographical location, size of company, and the name of the decision-maker most pertinent to your service. These names need to be placed in a relational marketing database which is linked to one of the popular word processing programs. The letters should be personalized, and we suggest scanning your signature into the computer to avoid having to sign a large number of letters. With a good list of names, proper technology and a year's worth of effective letters, an administrative person can manage an effective direct-mail advertising campaign. The costs for such a campaign are very affordable. We recommend applying a first-class stamp, and using quality letterhead and envelopes, still keeping the total estimated cost per mailing piece under 50 cents. In many companies, the cost of mailing for a year is captured by one additional sale.

Those who respond to this type of campaign will be quality prospects. When you make contact with them, ask what motivated them to seek additional information. This opens the way for you to satisfy needs rather than just selling products.

7. Use Trickle Marketing for Qualified Leads

HOW DOES THIS APPLY TO MY BUSINESS?

_____

_____

_____

_____

_____

Priority   1   2   3 (Circle one)

Action Date_____

Profit Champion _____

Potential Dollar Effect $_____

KEEP TABS ON COMPETITORS'
PRICES

It's always important to keep close tabs on what your competitors are charging. Often this entails merely keeping your eyes peeled for newspaper ads placed by your rivals. In other cases, you may have to do a little creative snooping.

A chain of hair salons in a very competitive market regularly sends key employees out to have their hair done at competing shops. Although no company likes to send business to its rivals, in this case the practice has paid big dividends. The owner's "undercover" customers not only bring back current information on prices being charged by competitors, but also invaluable firsthand feedback on the quality of services being provided by other salons.

Some businesses run into trouble because they price their goods and services too high for the market. During a slumping economy, however, businesses are tempted to set their prices too low.

Don't think you have to be the cheapest guy in town in order to attract business. If your prices or bids are the lowest around, find out whether you're getting business because you're the cheapest, or because you're better than your competitors. If the goods or services offered by your company are high quality, you may well be able to revise your pricing strategy. While you don't want to be significantly more expensive than your competitors, you don't want to be low man on the totem pole, either.

A chain of restaurants with a reputation for offering great food and excellent service learned this lesson firsthand. They were drawing more business than ever, yet the owner was having only a mediocre year. He compared other food service establishments in the area and found that he had the lowest menu prices in town. His locations were always packed because he served good food—not because he charged low prices. As a result, he raised his menu prices by an average of 10 percent without losing business.

This chain of restaurants did about $12 million a year, so the price increases brought in an additional $1.2 million. Best of all, since the restaurant incurred no additional costs in order to realize this gain, that entire $1.2 million went straight to the bottom line! Instead of struggling through another marginal year, the restaurateur's net income more than doubled overnight!

In another case, the owner of a commercial repair business developed a sizeable customer base over the years as a result of word-of-mouth referrals. The owner assumed that his success was due to his practice of underbidding his competitors. When he surveyed his customers, however, he learned that they patronized his business because he provided reliable work, stood behind his repairs, and met deadlines.

The owner raised his prices at least 15 percent and was still competitive with other services in the area. He didn't lose a single customer because of the price hike.

Remember, prices should be established and controlled by management, not salespeople. Sales managers should be given certain guidelines for negotiating prices. Require management approval for any significant deviations.

Too many companies give their salespeople the right to give away the store. Salespeople want volume, and high prices sometimes get in their way. However, higher volume at lower prices can mean less profit.

A computer hardware company learned this lesson the hard way. The company's price guidelines had never been enforced, and its salespeople had the right to set prices at any level they chose as long as sales were profitable. In one case, a salesperson sold products with a gross margin of only 1.7 percent. When the time came for inventory to be shipped to their customers, billed, and collected, the net margin became a loss.

Luckily, management discovered that the company's margins had seriously eroded. Tighter price-setting guidelines were established. Now prices are set based on volume purchased by each customer. Sales staff are allowed no exceptions to the printed price list. This computer hardware company added $500,000 to its bottom line in the first year of its new pricing policy.

8. KEEP TABS ON COMPETITORS' PRICES

HOW DOES THIS APPLY TO MY BUSINESS?

_____

_____

_____

_____

_____

Priority   1   2   3   (Circle one)

Action Date_____

Profit Champion _____

Potential Dollar Effect $_____

MONITOR COMPETITION TO KEEP ON TOP OF THE MARKET

One of the best sources of information may be right under your nose. Maybe the other guy is doing something right! But even if your business rivals are in worse shape than you, it's important to check them out. At a minimum, you may be able to learn from their mistakes.

An automobile dealer makes it a point to keep close tabs on the activities of the other dealerships in the area. He even gets regular Dun & Bradstreet financial and business operational reports on his leading competitors. Unexpectedly, one of his key rivals slashed prices and began aggressively discounting vehicles. Ordinarily, he would have been reluctant to get into a price war, but because he had the D&B reports, the dealer knew that his rival was not capable of sustaining losses for any period of time.

Recognizing the competitor's price cuts as a desperation move, he matched them. Because he had deeper pockets, the dealership not only survived but ultimately broadened its market share.

Securing financial reports on your competitors is only one way to keep on top in the marketplace. Trade publications, industry associations, and area business groups such as the local Chamber of Commerce are all excellent sources of information on what's happening in the market.

In addition, you can often get a wealth of information about what your competitors are up to by talking with your suppliers. Hiring employees from the competition may also yield invaluable intelligence. A personnel agency client even bought stock in her publicly-traded rival. This entitled her to their annual report — and other valuable information about her rival's plans.

There's also the direct approach. Just ask other people in your industry what they're doing to be successful. You would be surprised how helpful other business people will be. Even direct competitors often swap advice—though they won't give away trade secrets.

---

9. MONITOR COMPETITION TO KEEP ON TOP OF THE MARKET

HOW DOES THIS APPLY TO MY BUSINESS?

_____

_____

_____

_____

_____

Priority   1   2   3   (Circle one)

Action Date_____

Profit Champion _____

Potential Dollar Effect $_____

INSTITUTE THE LOST SALES REPORT TO DISCOVER WHAT YOU AREN'T SELLING

Among the most important financial information your company can maintain should be the "Lost Sales Report." **Lost sales are requests from customers for products or services that your organization does not or cannot provide. There are three types of lost sales to consider: (1) customer requests for products or services that your firm does not offer; (2) customer requests for products or services that are temporarily out of stock or not available; (3) customer requests for products or services that you do have but cannot deliver on time. A regular review of this report will target opportunities for greater sales and profitability.**

Without this information, you will have no way of knowing what your customers will buy from you if you have it to sell them. With it, you have factual information, rather than guesses, on what inventory to stock or what other services you need to provide. If your customers are continually forced to do business with competitors because you don't provide what they need, the chances are that you will eventually lose all of your customers' business to them. Customers are loyal until they have a reason not to be.

Review your Lost Sales Report monthly. When there are multiple customer requests for products or services that you can't fulfill, that's when you need to act. Your customers are urging you to sell them more, so capture this valuable information.

We designed the Lost Sales Report on page 33 for an auto parts wholesaler. After careful analysis of this report, the company developed a plan to meet its customers' requests and added $250,000 to its bottom line.

LOST SALES REPORT

Employee Compiling Report_____Store/Facility/Dept_____

Date of Customer Request	Description of Unfulfilled Customer Request	Estimated Quantity Customer Would Have Purchased	Potential Sales $ Lost	Estimated Gross Profit $ Lost

10. INSTITUTE THE LOST SALES REPORT TO DISCOVER WHAT YOU AREN'T SELLING

HOW DOES THIS APPLY TO MY BUSINESS?

_____

_____

_____

_____

_____

Priority   1   2   3   (Circle one)

Action Date_____

Profit Champion _____

Potential Dollar Effect $_____

ESTABLISH A SALES PROCESS

Why does your company need a sales process? To answer this question, make a quick comparison of your sales staff. Aren't some salespeople consistently bringing in large volumes of high-margin sales? Surely you ask, "Why can't the rest of the sales staff do as good a job?" **Everyone on your sales staff will not be a superstar, but by establishing standards of performance you will increase sales as well as the profitability of your firm.**

Take the worst performer on your sales team, and compare what they do with your number-one salesperson. Success in sales requires three key ingredients; aptitude, numbers and tactics. If a salesperson struggles with establishing relationships, has inadequate customer contacts, desires routine work and does not have tolerance for failure, they probably don't belong in a sales career. There is always the possibility that people with these characteristics will slip through your screening process. No amount of training and coaching will turn them into stellar performers. If they are hard working, your best choice is to move them into other areas of your firm. During your hiring process, there are a number of sales aptitude tests which will discover if candidates possess the traits necessary to succeed in a sales career.

Once you identify the gap between your best and worst performers, use the following steps to engineer your sales process.

Determine Prospects

Your company has a responsibility to provide marketing assistance to generate leads. You should identify profiles of the ideal customers for your products or services. By creating a universe of customers who have the likelihood of benefiting from your offerings, you are adding focus to the efforts of your salespeople.

Make Appointments

If selling your product or service requires a face-to-face presence, making appointments is a crucial activity. Whether a prospect responds to some form of advertisement or is being targeted for cold calling, successful salespeople are able to get through to decision makers. The goal is to generate interest in learning more about the value of your products and services.

Maintain Sales Activity Records

Your salespeople will be interacting with many potential customers. They must keep track of what is said or promised at every part of the sales cycle. There are many good contact management systems on the market.

There is always paperwork associated with sales. Effective salespeople spend the best parts of the day calling and meeting with customers. Administrative aspects of their job are traditionally carried out either early or late in the day.

Develop Consistency

Top salespeople perform the same successful basic tasks over and over again. Experience allows them to fine tune tactics to achieve greater sales results. A process is defined as a series of related steps that lead to a desired result. When salespeople are in a slump, they can usually identify deficiencies in steps of the sales process. Many experts say that, "Sales is a numbers game." Not maintaining activities at all levels of the sales process is one of the most meaningful explanations for lagging sales.

Build Relationships

People buy from people they like and trust, and who deliver what they claim. Salespeople must develop relationships with those they serve. This applies to long-term sales as well as quick, transactional business. Doing little things is particularly effective in separating those at the top of the sales profession from everyone else.

Ask Effective Questions

When talking with prospects, your sales staff must know their motivation for needing your company. Salespeople who make great presentations but don't ask effective questions are doomed to mediocrity. Eighty percent of sales are often made by twenty percent of the sales force. The most effective salespeople spend 80 percent of their time listening and 20 percent talking. A large portion of this talking time should be used in asking intelligent, insightful questions based on research done about the customer prior to the sales call.

Qualify Prospects

The most valuable non-recurrable asset that we possess is time. Effective salespeople spend their time with prospects who are the most likely to buy from them. Five variables of qualification include: fulfilling their needs, meeting the decision maker, assuring creditworthiness, needing to buy soon, and competitive knowledge.

Overcome Objections

The worst scenario for any sales person is too spend a huge investment of time on an opportunity and at closing time an unknown issue comes out of left field and kills the deal. Closing should be the easiest part of the sale, but for many people it is the most difficult. An objection is viewed as a bad thing, but in reality it is good for the sales process. It is a customer request for more information that, if handled adequately, will educate prospects and build relationships with salespeople. It is better to proactively raise possible objections than hope that they never come up.

Present Solutions

A wonderful sales presentation is useless without satisfying a perceived need. Your product must fix a problem or help accomplish a goal. Without either, what motivation does a prospect have to spend money? Before you begin presenting, understand what your customer wants to buy.

Ask for the Order

Many salespeople feel that closing is the most difficult part of the sales process. In fact, it is the easiest. Good salespeople build rapport with their prospects, properly qualify, ask the right questions, identify and overcome objections, present solutions and treat closing as a natural transition in the process.

Put It All Together

After you have identified characteristics of strong sales performance in your company, document them. Create an ongoing training program for your sales staff and put in place mechanisms for ongoing sales coaching.

If a train rolls on a track that is missing ties, it will derail. If salespeople follow a sales process but miss a vital step, the sales opportunity will be lost. Create a sales process for your company, and your sales will consistently roll in.

11. ESTABLISH A SALES PROCESS

HOW DOES THIS APPLY TO MY BUSINESS?

_____

_____

_____

_____

_____

Priority   1   2   3   (Circle one)

Action Date_____

Profit Champion _____

Potential Dollar Effect $_____

12

JOIN THE E-COMMERCE
REVOLUTION ASAP

If you don't have a Web site and a strategy for using this revolutionary new sales and marketing tool, get with it! Thousands, if not millions, of new customers are exploring the Web, searching for products like yours. In fact, seven people all around the globe tap onto the Internet for the first time – every second. Researchers at the University of Texas determined that in 1998 about $301 billion in revenue was generated in the U.S. alone – that's close to the yearly take of the automobile industry. By 2003, business-to-business commerce could reach $1.3 trillion and 130 million Americans will be online.

Today a Web site is like a legitimate address. It has gotten so that if your business doesn't have one, prospective customers and employees will consider your company behind the times or even somewhat suspicious. They want to see your Web site before they'll do business with you.

Use your Web site to support your direct mail and advertising campaigns. Each medium should emphasize a different aspect of your products and your offers. Print ads build name recognition and inspire confidence. Who hasn't been impressed with the words, "As seen in *Time* magazine." It doesn't seem to matter that it was an ad, not an article, where they saw your product. Direct mail reaches right into targeted markets with a longer, more detailed description and a harder sell than an expensive ad. However, it doesn't offer the immediacy of the Web site, and in the near future it may be eliminated entirely as e-mail campaigns with no expensive postage and printing costs reach your customers in a matter of seconds.

Your Web site should be the easiest place to order products since mail-order catalogs. But be sure that your site is registered with every pertinent search engine and forge links with professional organizations and other noncompetitive groups in your industry. You want that customer in Omaha who is contemplating a product like yours but doesn't know where to buy it to find you right away – no matter what word he or she types into "Find." Advertise your Web site in all your promotional materials, business cards, stationary...everywhere! The Internet has intensified the need for instant gratification manyfold.

There are many experts and books on this topic, but as you decide how to present your business on the Internet, consider these few questions to get you started:

1. Why do people want to visit your Web site? Ask your current customers how they would use it.

2. What can you offer customers besides simple descriptions of your products? (Remember people expect the Internet to give them information, not advertising. Your site should not look too commercial.)

3. How will your customers order? Will you add the "shopping cart" feature so they can order online, or include an order form they can download, fill out, and fax back with their credit card information? Whatever you decide, make certain that your company's address, phone and fax are on your site somewhere. It's frustrating for many customers to feel they can only contact you electronically, and it may turn them off.

Answer these questions and you'll be ready to do business in the new millennium. There's a 24-hour Internet economy out there, use it to your company's advantage.

12. JOIN THE E-COMMERCE REVOLUTION ASAP

HOW DOES THIS APPLY TO MY BUSINESS?

_____

_____

_____

_____

_____

Priority   1   2   3   (Circle one)

Action Date_____

Profit Champion _____

Potential Dollar Effect $_____

TIE SALES COMPENSATION TO MEANINGFUL GOALS

Here is a horror story that will make any business executive shudder. A printing company was noticing an increase in the number of jobs produced, but was not benefiting from a corresponding rise in their profits.

The owner discovered that her sales force was driven more by sales goals than profit. In one instance, near the end of the month, a salesperson was still not at the required quota. He went to a customer who was considering a bid and lowered the price of the job. The only concession by the customer was an open-ended delivery date, so that the job could be produced during down time in the printing plant. One week later, the customer called and made changes to the job and demanded that delivery be made within a week. The salesperson processed the request. By the time the plant modified the order, which required extra costs, and paid overtime to get the work done on time, the printing company lost money on the job.

The control systems failed to catch a bad job from going into production. The real culprit was the salesperson who had no motivation to submit profitable jobs to the plant because he was paid on gross sales without taking costs into consideration.

Salespeople are motivated by compensation. Your business needs to generate profitable revenue by maintaining incentives for your sales force. They must push for every sale. A solid compensation plan will be the fuel for your success, but many times poorly designed plans will have the opposite effect.

Your business strategy should be the driving force behind your compensation plan. Determine your goals and devise a plan that rewards this behavior. A successful plan should incorporate the following objectives:

- **Raising margins**
- **Selling new products**
- **Generating greater sales from existing customers**
- **Acquiring new customers**
- **Moving specific items**
- **Increasing average order size**
- **Shortening the sales cycle**

It is important to think through the ramifications of your compensation plan. Evaluate which areas of your business will be affected. A wholesale liquor distributor was having difficulty in closing out slow-moving inventory. Because the warehouse was facing space problems, an extra incentive was offered for selling these items, but very few of them sold. The reason was simple, because the company had failed to look at the implications of their plan. Salespeople were paid a bonus based on their overall gross margin percentage. Close-out merchandise was included in the margin calculation. It was possible to make less bonus by selling close-out inventory. By not including obsolete inventory in the overall margin, the roadblock to this special promotion was lifted.

Effective compensation plans will be one of the variables in reducing turnover in your sales department. Obviously, there are many other factors necessary to retain your sales staff, but pocketbook issues are at the top of the list. Besides the cost of locating and training new people, the disruptions in customer relationships can harm sales. Don't become complacent with your compensation plan. Periodically review it to ensure that it is meeting your objectives and maintaining a high caliber sales force.

One final note will be helpful to you in designing your compensation plan. A computer systems integration company had the right provisions in their plan, but had very unhappy salespeople. After each sales period ended, it would take the company up to three months to calculate commissions. The salespeople were living off of minimal draws and desperately needed their extra income. The process of calculating the commissions was flawed. In addition there were compensation and underpayment errors. Avoid problems by paying your people on time and ensure the accuracy of their commissions.

13. TIE SALES COMPENSATION TO MEANINGFUL GOALS

HOW DOES THIS APPLY TO MY BUSINESS?

_____

_____

_____

_____

_____

Priority   1   2   3   (Circle one)

Action Date_____

Profit Champion _____

Potential Dollar Effect $_____

MAINTAIN QUALITY CUSTOMER RELATIONS

Success can spoil even the most well-managed organizations. When a business is flooded with orders and can pick and choose the jobs it wants, staff simply may not have much time to interact with customers. In some cases, a business "culture" develops in which some employees actually believe "the customer needs our business" instead of "our business needs the customer."

But when many competitors are vying for the same business, customers become choosy. After all, why give hard earned cash to any business where the employees are less than courteous and attentive? **Make no mistake, in any economy, good relations with customers may be the deciding factor in every sale you make.**

It's been said that you need to do something well at least ten times before a customer will recommend you to a friend. It only takes one bad experience with a rude salesperson, however, or a lackadaisical receptionist, or a delivery person with an attitude problem, and that customer will complain about you to ten others.

Eliminating such negative practices is only half the battle. To really solidify good relations with your customers, you have to deliver more than they expect to receive. Look at it in terms of the following equation:

$$\text{Customer Relations Index} = \frac{\text{Your Company's Products and Services}}{\text{Your Customers' Expectations}}$$

If your company's Customer Relations Index (CRI) is less than 1, you're in trouble. Your customers or clients believe they are being short-changed.

If your CRI is 1, customer relations at your business are neutral. Your customers or clients are getting what they bargained for—no more, no less.

If the index is more than 1, your business is a winner and so are your customers! It means you're delivering even more than your customers expect. They say WOW!

The wonderful part is that it doesn't have to cost an arm and a leg to move your Customer Relations Index into the more-than-one category.

A five-percent swing in customer retention can have a profound impact on your firm's profitability. Consider these two scenarios...

Company A has a base of 100 customers. Their average volume per customer is $5,000 per year with sales equaling $500,000. Annually, they retain 95% of their existing customers and they are able to gain 10% new ones. For planning purposes, they are assuming a three percent yearly price increase. After 14 years their total number of customers will have doubled and their sales will have grown by 291%.

Company B has a base of 100 customers. Their average volume per customer and sales are the same as Company A. Annually, they retain 90% of their existing customers and they have the same 10% growth of new accounts. They are also forecasting a three-percent annual price increase. After 14 years their total number of customers will remain at 100 and their sales will have grown by 47%. A five-percent difference in customer retention will cause a significant variance in the financial performance of both firms. As long as there is a five-percent difference in retention levels, these numbers will remain constant for any customer retention percentage.

As you analyze your business, the key question should be, "Why do customers leave?" If they still have a need and are buying from someone else a product that you provide, the value of purchasing from your firm has been lost. It is easy to place blame on your competition. We commonly hear that a customer was lost because someone else was cheaper. Sometimes this is true, but in many cases the money paid was not equal to their expectations.

Find out how well your customer service representatives are serving your customers, and get them thinking about how they can serve them better by asking them to fill out the questionnaire on page 46.

CUSTOMER SERVICE QUESTIONNAIRE

Please complete this questionnaire. Your responses are important to our organization in meeting internal and external customer needs. Answer the questions the way things are, not the way you think they should be. Also, please give us an explanation for any "no" answers. For any "yes" answers, give us an example of how you accomplished the task. We would be pleased to meet with you to find solutions to your concerns about the department.

Thank you,

The Management

Yes No

❏ ❏ Do you enjoy your work and are you dedicated to helping our customers become more productive?

❏ ❏ Do you have a proactive approach to customer service?

❏ ❏ Do you anticipate our customer demands?

❏ ❏ Do you suspend ideas until customers request assistance?

❏ ❏ Are you concerned about the interest of our customers' businesses?

❏ ❏ Do you adhere merely to assigned roles, or are you willing to go above and beyond if our customers' needs require it?

❏ ❏ Are you continually investigating ways to improve our customers' businesses?

continued

Yes No

❏   ❏   Do you absorb as much information as you can about our customers' businesses?_____
_____

❏   ❏   Are you focused on future possibilities to be of service to our customers? _____
_____

❏   ❏   Do you have open channels of communication with our customers so that you can effectively listen to their needs?_____
_____

❏   ❏   Are you receptive to suggestions from customers about how to make things better in the future?_____
_____

14. MAINTAIN QUALITY CUSTOMER RELATIONS
HOW DOES THIS APPLY TO MY BUSINESS?

_____

_____

_____

_____

_____

_____

Priority   1   2   3   (Circle one)

Action Date_____

Profit Champion _____

Potential Dollar Effect $_____

15

BUY SOMETHING FROM YOUR COMPANY

The owner of an automobile dealership had just arrived at a popular resort to begin a well-deserved vacation. Business had been great and several months of promotional work was starting to pay dividends. It was time to get away, to unwind and enjoy some of the fruits of recent successes which had been the result of a lot of hard work.

On the second day he was walking on the beach and bumped into an old acquaintance whom he hadn't seen for a couple of years. Over lunch his friend mentioned that he was in the market for a new car and was actively shopping. The auto dealer told him about a new model that was worth looking at. His friend asked if he had any in stock at his dealership and could he take a look at it. The dealer informed him that he did and invited him to visit his showroom. Since he was not going to be back from vacation for a week, he wrote the name and phone number of his sales manager on his business card along with instructions to take good care of this special customer. They finished their lunch, shook hands, and said their good-byes. The friend told the owner that he would be back in town the next day and would be calling the sales manager to make an appointment. The dealer was gratified that he had laid the proper groundwork to move another unit that month.

Several months later, the dealer bumped into his friend again, and asked how he was treated at the dealership. Appearing slightly embarrassed, the friend responded by mentioning that he had never gone there. He explained that he had called the sales manager twice over a several day period, but couldn't get through. He had been out shopping at another dealership near his home, saw a car on the showroom floor that was exactly what he wanted and bought it. Finally, a week after the original call, the dealer's sales manager called the customer, but was informed that he had already purchased a vehicle. The dealer controlled his anger and thanked his friend for letting him know of his experience.

Unfortunately, this kind of incident happens too often in the business world. Several possibilities can explain this behavior. It can be an isolated incident. Even in the best run companies, quirks in the system occasionally cause less-than-perfect service. The key concern is that mishaps are identified and systems are put in place for speedy resolutions of problems. The second scenario is that poor service is ingrained in the culture of too many companies' standard operating procedures. We know of business owners who believe that they have the market cornered and have lost the incentive to maintain high levels of service. The last scenario is that the company is oblivious to problems.

Regularly check the level of service that is provided to your customers. Areas to be monitored include telephone etiquette, customer inquiries, additional business from existing customers, and problem resolution. In the case of retail establishments, on-site shoppers are an effective monitoring strategy. It may be best to have management make fictitious inquiries and visit locations as shoppers. If this is not possible, friends or business acquaintances might be willing to assist in return for reciprocal help with their companies. Finally, profit advisors provide valuable information about customer service improvement. It is important to remember that customer service should not be sporadically checked, but be an ongoing business activity.

---

15. BUY SOMETHING FROM YOUR COMPANY
HOW DOES THIS APPLY TO MY BUSINESS?

_____

_____

_____

_____

_____

Priority   1   2   3 (Circle one)

Action Date_____

Profit Champion _____

Potential Dollar Effect $_____

PUT YOURSELF IN CHARGE OF CUSTOMER RELATIONS

When your bottom line is at stake, customer relations aren't just the job of the sales department. They're everyone's responsibility — especially the boss's. To build your business, call on customers personally.

Customers have reason to feel special when top managers take the time to visit them personally. We've seen management rekindle business relationships with customers who were thought to be lost forever. A lot of this is psychological—the charisma when the manager of one business meets with the manager of another. But there's more to it than that. In many cases, managers are the company's best salespeople. Typically, the boss started out in sales, and he or she was probably pretty good at it. If the company's founder wasn't a good salespeople to begin with, it's doubtful that the business would have gotten off the ground.

The manager of a glass installation company is just such a salesman. He built the business from scratch, and in the beginning he handled all of the sales. As the business expanded, he hired a sales staff and devoted his time to management and administration.

Sales started to decline and the owner got personally involved. He began accompanying his salespeople on calls. Within three months a number of new customers had signed, some existing customers increased their orders, and previous customers began buying from his company again. Sales increased 20 percent.

The manager of a business brings something extra into the sales process. A salesperson is restricted by company policy in quite a few areas, but the boss can bend the rules when necessary to make a sale or solidify relations with customers. The boss of a business can offer price concessions, make delivery commitments, authorize sale returns, and improve payment terms on the spot.

Keep the personal touch in everything your business does: send thank-you notes to customers who refer others and gifts to your special customers. Pretend an "invisible" customer is in attendance at every meeting where you discuss customer service with your staff, and watch how customer service improves. The "invisible" customers at your meetings will help you focus on what more you can do for them to improve customer relations.

---

16. PUT YOURSELF IN CHARGE OF CUSTOMER RELATIONS
HOW DOES THIS APPLY TO MY BUSINESS?

_____

_____

_____

_____

_____

Priority   1   2   3   (Circle one)

Action Date_____

Profit Champion _____

Potential Dollar Effect $_____

GET YOUR CUSTOMERS TO COMPLAIN

One of the biggest obstacles businesses face these days is getting their customers to complain. It's long been known that the vast majority of customer complaints are never openly expressed, yet some companies continue to hope that "keeping their ears to the rail" will tell them where they stand with customers.

Contrary to that hope, a study of customer behavior conducted by the Technical Assistance Research Programs Institute of the U.S. Office of Consumer Affairs concluded that, among other things:

- **Customers don't register dissatisfaction with products or services, because it requires too much effort for too little potential payoff.**

- **For face-to-face encounters, complaints often involve unpleasantness that most people would rather avoid.**

- **There is often very real fear that a complaint will get a service provider, perhaps an acquaintance or someone the customer has gotten to know, into trouble.**

- **Because most people have experienced the frustration of filing a complaint with someone whose principle aim seems to be to deny wrong doing, many customers believe the problem will be left unaddressed and simply keep complaints to themselves.**

Are you satisfied with a four-percent success rate? Of course you're not! If you were, your company would be out of business. So why accept only hearing four percent of your customers' complaints?

Studies consistently show that for every customer complaint you receive, on average, 27 others are not heard. Customers' hesitancy to openly speak their minds, employee filtering, and general uncertainty over how to file complaints all contribute to communication breakdowns.

How many complaints never make it to your desk, and what are they costing your business? Have you ever lost a major customer without warning or explanation? Of course you have. Every company has. If you knew before they left why they were planning on leaving, could you have done something about it? Probably!

This is why it's so important to get your customers to complain. They may be satisfied. But are they totally satisfied? What is a totally satisfied customer?

It's not enough to have satisfied customers. Totally satisfied customers are loyal customers that tell others about their good experiences, thus becoming a valuable extension of the sales force.

Somewhat satisfied customers are normally open to overtures from competitors, thus placing them at risk. They are also a nominal source of referral business, which slows your ability to grow. Dissatisfied customers are, in all probability, seeking out your competitors, looking for a way to get rid of you. Such customers tend to willingly and openly tell others about their bad experience, thus undermining the efforts of the sales force.

What is the benefit of a totally satisfied customer? To truly appreciate the impact of reduced attrition, stop to consider the "Lifetime Value" of any customer by taking their current annual volume and profit contributions, then multiplying that figure by five years, ten years or more to see what the true impact of their loss would be.

The chart on page 54, originally published in the *Harvard Business Review* in 1990 (and somewhat modified since), illustrates the point by showing what a small increase in customer loyalty will do to the bottom line. What will increased customer satisfaction and loyalty mean to your business?

In a study of some leading public companies reported in *The Service Profit Chain* (The Free Press, 1997), the authors found the stock of companies devoted to utilizing customer satisfaction as a strategic business development tool increased 147 percent between 1986 and 1995 (nearly twice as fast as the stocks of their closest competitors).

Impact of Customer Loyalty

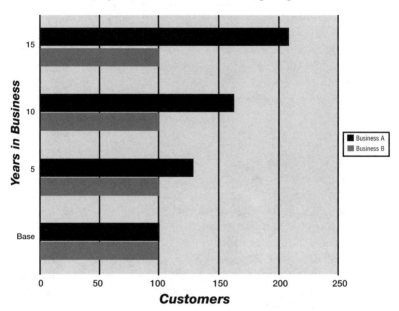

Impact of Customer Loyalty on Profits

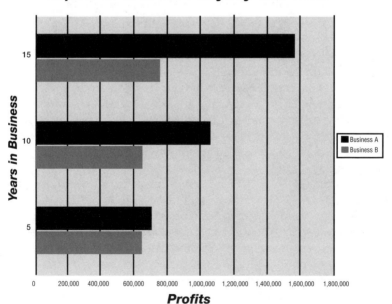

17. GET YOUR CUSTOMERS TO COMPLAIN

HOW DOES THIS APPLY TO MY BUSINESS?

_____

_____

_____

_____

_____

Priority   1   2   3   (Circle one)

Action Date_____

Profit Champion _____

Potential Dollar Effect $_____

Expand Business Hours to Rope In New Customers

Nowadays, when shoppers can go on the Internet 24 hours a day, you can't afford to continue business as usual. You can't expect your customers to take valuable time off from their jobs or businesses in order to accommodate your business schedule. Sometimes the difference between business success and Chapter 11 is a willingness to adjust your hours of operation to meet customer demand.

Look at it this way. If customers take time away from their job or business to accommodate your company's schedule, they are paying double for your services. In addition to what you charge, they may have lost income to boot.

Should you open your office at 7:00 in the morning instead of 9:00? Should you close at 7:00 in the evening instead of 5:30? Would staying open on Saturdays attract more customers? A wholesale building materials client recently surveyed its customers. To its surprise, it learned that many of them would give our client more business if they were open on Saturday afternoon. This business did what the customers wanted and became more profitable while doing so.

Customers are often willing to pay a premium for more convenient service. If you find a plumber or electrician who will commit to doing a job for you at a prearranged time, would that be worth an extra charge? If they avoid the need for you to take a day off from work to wait for them, would you pay 50 percent extra for that convenience?

The critical question is: Will expanded hours of operation make it easier for your customers to spend their money with your company? For many businesses, the answer is yes.

An automobile dealer generated significantly more service work because they extended their hours of operation. Under the new schedule, the dealer began taking cars at 7 a.m. and stayed open until 11 p.m. In fact, some customers who dropped cars off immediately after work were often delighted because their cars were ready the same evening. That's a real benefit for those who might otherwise have to miss work the next day or find someone to drive them in because their car was being serviced.

Sometimes staying open longer will open up entire new business opportunities for a company.

A dental practice began promoting cosmetic dentistry, such as teeth brightening, as a sideline. The dentist expected this to generate a lot of new and very lucrative business. But the initial reaction from patients was ho-hum. Many people regard cosmetic dentistry as a nonessential procedure — even a vanity. They would take time off from work for a root canal, but not for a cosmetic treatment. Fortunately, the dentist recognized this early in the game and hired a young dentist fresh out of school to provide cosmetic dental services in the evenings and on weekends. The cosmetic practice flourished, and because it was all done during "off-hours," it didn't interfere with the dentist's regular practice. Gravy!

When do people use their boats? On weekends, right? But how many companies that offer repair service are open on Saturdays and Sundays when weekend boaters need them? You can charge a premium of 25 percent to fix boats on weekends and no one would object. Think about these financial opportunities.

---

18. EXPAND BUSINESS HOURS TO ROPE IN NEW CUSTOMERS

HOW DOES THIS APPLY TO MY BUSINESS?

_____

_____

_____

_____

_____

Priority   1   2   3   (Circle one)

Action Date_____

Profit Champion _____

Potential Dollar Effect $_____

CHAPTER 8: OPERATIONS

MONITOR COSTS AND USES OF COMPANY VEHICLES

Many companies have vehicles; most businesses have no idea how much per mile their vehicles are costing. **Account for expense, by vehicle, and determine how cost-effective each is to operate.** You will want to determine your operating costs per mile driven. Then get rid of those that aren't making the cut!

Businesses that provide company vehicles for use by employees often incur an alarming amount of unnecessary expense. It's not unusual to find that 20 to 30 percent of the cost of providing these vehicles reflects nonbusiness use or outright waste.

Even if you lease the vehicle, when you factor in such operating expenses as gasoline, maintenance, repairs and insurance, it's going to cost your company at least $5,000 to $10,000 per year to keep each one on the road. If even ten percent of these costs are unnecessary, a significant amount of company profit is escaping down the rathole. In the best of times, a waste factor of $500 to $1,000 a year per vehicle should be considered a misdemeanor. In a bad year, to allow such losses to continue unchecked is a capital offense.

At a minimum, employees should be expected to maintain a daily travel log listing all mileage driven, destinations, and the reason for each trip.

Such procedures will not only help you reduce waste, but may also enable you to uncover more serious problems within your organization. One business that tightened vehicle-use record keeping discovered that one of its drivers was systematically siphoning gasoline from the company truck he drove home every night. We estimate that during the past two years the business lost at least $30 a week from this gas thief. Certainly, that $3,000 could have been put to better use.

A policy of limiting company vehicles to business use could do more than reduce your operating costs, however. It could also protect your business from nightmare liability. Suppose an employee driving home in a company car stopped off for a few drinks and then caused an accident. Imagine the exposure your company would face.

It may not be practical to flatly prohibit all personal use of business vehicles. But at a minimum, employees who put company vehicles to personal use should be asked to absorb a proportion of the costs.

If you permit employees to drive company vehicles home, personal use should be monitored and the driver should be charged for mileage not attributable to business. Even if you impose only a token charge for nonbusiness mileage, at least you're serving notice to your employees that you're concerned about excessive or unnecessary use of company cars.

In some ways, technological advancement is underscoring the need to keep tight control over automobile costs. A business client installed cellular telephones in each company vehicle used by his outside sales force. No doubt the car phones added to the productivity of the sales reps. But they also created new opportunities for waste and abuse of company funds.

We analyzed the client's telephone use and were able to trace at least one-third of the company's total charges to the cellular phones. We found that the car phones were being used to order pizzas, call 900 numbers, and make nonbusiness long-distance calls. The owner was astonished.

To put an end to this waste, the company adopted a new system under which the bills for all cellular phones are sent in the name of the employee using them. The employee identifies all business calls monthly and gets reimbursed from the company accordingly. The employee pays the cellular bill, thus absorbing the unreimbursed cost of their personal calls.

19: MONITOR COSTS AND USES OF COMPANY VEHICLES

HOW DOES THIS APPLY TO MY BUSINESS?

_____

_____

_____

_____

_____

Priority   1   2   3   (Circle one)

Action Date_____

Profit Champion _____

Potential Dollar Effect $_____

ELIMINATE UNNECESSARY UTILITY COSTS

Many businesses have been hurt financially because management failed to curb wasteful energy use. Nowadays, utilities include more than electricity. For instance, cell phones can now cost you less for long-distance calls than a standard business line.

Trash is a utility: Charged by bulk, size of receptacle. When we advised one of our clients to take a simple measurement of their trash containers, it turned out they were smaller than what they were being charged for. The company negotiated a new rate based on this smaller size and reduced their annual trash collection charges by $70,000. In the same way, monitor the volume that bags of garbage are taking up which you are being charged for. You can reduce the volume by resetting pressure gauges on your trash compactors.

Even if you rent your building space, chances are you have a triple net lease that will result in higher rent payments if utility costs rise. It's still worth a lot to your business to control utility usage. Consider for a starter buying your utilities in nonpeak times and using them in peak times.

For years, a furniture retailer deliberately left all the lights burning in the showroom. It cost the store at least $500 a month to do this, but the owner justified the expense as a form of "advertising." Customers who drove past the store late at night when the lights were blazing would surely remember the place, he reasoned.

Ultimately, he was convinced that there are more-cost-effective methods of building customer recognition for his business. He bought a beautiful neon sign that offered ten times the exposure of his lit-up showroom at one-tenth the cost. As it turned out, the store paid for the sign out of electricity savings during the first three years.

The management company of a medical office was wasting the owner's money because some of the tenants kept evening hours and left the air conditioning running all night. The extent of the problem didn't become clear, however, until several of the internists and gynecologists in the building began losing patients. It seemed the building was so chilly in the morning that disrobed patients were getting goose bumps!

This building operator consulted a specialist in the air conditioning and heating area, and invested more than $25,000 in a computer monitoring system to regulate temperatures in offices year-round. That was six years ago, and although it seemed like a lot of money at the time, the energy savings paid for the system in less than three years. Since then, it's been pure gravy.

You probably don't need a $25,000 computer monitoring system to shave your utility bills. There are automatic setback thermostats that will turn off your heat or air conditioning in the evening after everyone has left the building, then turn it on again in the morning before anyone arrives.

A word of caution, though: Utility experts warn that it is possible for energy-conscious building operators to outsmart themselves. The cost of reheating some facilities is so high that it more than offsets any savings from turning the utilities off at night. In these cases, the most efficient approach is to set the thermostat at one temperature and leave it there 24 hours a day.

20. ELIMINATE UNNECESSARY UTILITY COSTS

HOW DOES THIS APPLY TO MY BUSINESS?

_____

_____

_____

_____

_____

Priority   1   2   3   (Circle one)

Action Date_____

Profit Champion _____

Potential Dollar Effect $_____

21

SUBLET UNUSED SPACE

Even major "uncontrollable" expenses such as rent can be harnessed. Why not identify excess space — an empty room in an office, an unused section of a warehouse, an idle assembly line in a factory — and lease it to someone who can use it?

You'd be surprised at the kind of space that others will pay for. One business even managed to turn some unused parking spaces on a back lot into extra profits. A nearby bank with a limited parking area was more than willing to rent the vacant spaces to keep employee cars off its lot.

A moving and storage business now leases its parking lot to store boats and motor homes to area people in the winter.

Sometimes you can rent out business space or facilities for short-term idle periods. A new car dealer didn't have enough weekend business to keep his service department open on Saturdays and Sundays. He decided to rent out his service bays on those days — along with a mechanic — on a flat rate basis to businesses with their own fleets of vehicles.

For the fleet owners, it was an opportunity to have their vehicles serviced during a non-workday...and at a flat bargain rate. For the dealer, it was a chance to offset some of his occupancy costs...and to develop a business relationship with area fleet operators who, sooner or later, will be in the market for new vehicles.

Remember, too, that the market value of your idle space may increase significantly if you're able to throw in a few additional services that you're paying for anyway.

A law firm with an idle office may be able to rent it out for, say, $500 a month. But if the firm throws in access to a law library, a receptionist, a photocopy machine, a fax machine and a conference room — things that the firm is paying for anyway — the market value of that office may jump to $1,000 or $1,500 per month.

If you can't find a tenant for your unused space, perhaps you can come up with a productive use for it yourself. A retail luggage chain operates a large distribution center to service their stores. When the company began to more effectively manage its inventory, the owner found herself with excess warehouse space.

Her response was to partition off part of the distribution center and open it to the public on weekends as a clearance outlet for old inventory from the stores. The public loved the "bargain prices," and the chain was able to boost sales without incurring additional overhead costs.

One last tip, measure the actual square feet you are renting. You may be surprised to learn it falls short of the square feet mentioned in your lease.

---

21. SUBLET UNUSED SPACE

HOW DOES THIS APPLY TO MY BUSINESS?

_____

_____

_____

_____

_____

Priority   1   2   3   (Circle one)

Action Date_____

Profit Champion _____

Potential Dollar Effect $_____

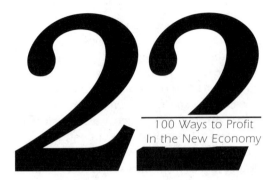

DON'T FALL IN LOVE WITH YOUR INVENTORY

Five to ten of the stock keeping units (SKUs) you have in inventory, represent 70 to 75 percent of your cost of sales. Twenty percent of your SKUs represents 20 percent of your cost of sales, 70-75 percent represents 5 to 10 percent of your cost of sales. If you want to manage inventory, manage significant dollars, not inventory items.

In every business there are hits and misses — hot-selling goods or services and real dogs that nobody seems to want. Often, the difference between a business's success or failure is the ability to distinguish between the two, and the courage to cut losses quickly by disposing of the doggies.

Because time is money, the key word is "quickly." **As a rule of thumb, we figure that the expense of maintaining goods in inventory averages about 2 percent of the cost of those goods each month not sold.** If you carry an item in stock on the shelves or in a warehouse for a year, you're down 24 percent. There aren't many businesses that can overcome this kind of a cost handicap even in the best of times. Think of inventory with recurring costs of 2 percent a month as a liability, not an asset.

For many business people, however, disposing of slow-moving inventory is difficult because it means they have to admit to making a mistake. Some have gone to the grave without making that admission. Don't fall in love with your inventory.

One businesswoman who inherited a small gift shop in a resort area was surprised when she paid a visit to the store. The shelves were crammed with a lot of dingy-looking merchandise that seemed to be priced far too low.

Upon closer inspection she discovered why. Based on the price tags, some of the goods had to have been sitting on those shelves for at least 15 years! But even at prices from that era, this shopworn merchandise was no bargain. Indeed, much of the inventory was virtually unsalable.

She junked most of merchandise, sold what she could at a distress sale, and restocked the store with fresh inventory. Today the shop is a viable business again, and the owner has an ironclad policy of getting rid of dogs. If an item doesn't sell in six months, she cuts the price 40% and moves it out. Her love affair with inventory is over.

In some industries, it's possible to work out arrangements with suppliers to limit your vulnerability to slow-selling inventories. An auto parts retailer established a relationship with a wholesaler that allowed his store to return unsold merchandise for full credit within a year.

Unfortunately, however, the company's warehouse manager failed to keep the records necessary to establish the required return date of unsold merchandise. In reviewing the business's inventory, the owner discovered thousands and thousands of dollars of old, obsolete parts sitting alongside new merchandise.

Had these old goods been identified in time, they could have been returned to the supplier in exchange for fresh merchandise. Instead, the retailer wound up disposing of them for a few cents on the dollar.

INVENTORY MANAGEMENT CHECKLIST

	Yes	No	N/A
Does your marketing department contribute to your inventory build-up by:			
Making over-optimistic sales forecasts?	❏	❏	❏
Promising unrealistic levels of shipping?	❏	❏	❏
Emphasizing sales plan targets without sufficient orders?	❏	❏	❏
Overselling product capabilities?	❏	❏	❏
Introducing new products without adequate plans to discontinue old products?	❏	❏	❏
Does quality control contribute to inventory build-up by:			
Substituting inspection for process control?	❏	❏	❏
Using inspection methods that do not detect flaws or do not inspect frequently enough?	❏	❏	❏
Establishing inspection requirements beyond the standard?	❏	❏	❏
Failing to recalibrate inspection instruments at regular intervals?	❏	❏	❏
Allowing materials or assemblies to que up at inspection stations?	❏	❏	❏

	Yes	No	N/A
Does manufacturing contribute to inventory build-up by:			
Establishing unnecessarily long cycle times to provide "padding" in materials requirement planning?	❏	❏	❏
Basing material requirements on unnecessarily long times in general, or, conversely, failing to provide adequate lead time on long-lead items?	❏	❏	❏
Providing excess buffer stocks for fear of shortages?	❏	❏	❏
Allowing excessive machine downtime?	❏	❏	❏
Tolerating poor operator productivity?	❏	❏	❏
Shipping products ahead of schedule or meeting unscheduled demands?	❏	❏	❏
Losing tight control over processes or otherwise creating scrap or rework?	❏	❏	❏
Does purchasing contribute to inventory build-up by:			
Taking advantage of volume discounts without adequate justification?	❏	❏	❏
Failing to obtain the best price and quality of material?	❏	❏	❏
Permitting delivery of material before the scheduled date or before needed?	❏	❏	❏
Establishing unrealistic procurement cycle items?	❏	❏	❏
Does corporate management contribute to inventory build-up by:			
Failing to stabilize product design?	❏	❏	❏
Not emphasizing the cost of money?	❏	❏	❏
Permitting design changes without adequate sales margins?	❏	❏	❏
Failing to control inventory other than at year end?	❏	❏	❏
Allowing slow-moving or obsolete materials to accumulate without effort to dispose of them?	❏	❏	❏
Being unwilling to take calculated risks?	❏	❏	❏
Creating an environment that doesn't allow for things to go wrong?	❏	❏	❏
Does engineering contribute to inventory build-up by:			
Creating scrap or obsolete material due to design changes, or machine or process upgrades?	❏	❏	❏
Compressing time schedules for orderly production introduction?	❏	❏	❏
Creating unnecessary start-up costs for new products?	❏	❏	❏
Requiring difficult-to-use materials to be processed?	❏	❏	❏
Setting tolerances tighter than process capabilities or than the market demands?	❏	❏	❏
Resolving manufacturing difficulties too slowly?	❏	❏	❏
Over-specifying and failing to provide materials?	❏	❏	❏

22. DON'T FALL IN LOVE WITH YOUR INVENTORY
HOW DOES THIS APPLY TO MY BUSINESS?

_____

_____

_____

_____

_____

Priority   1   2   3   (Circle one)

Action Date_____

Profit Champion _____

Potential Dollar Effect $_____

GUARD AGAINST LOSSES FROM THEFT

Make sure all employees who handle inventory or funds are bonded. No matter what systems you have in place, there is the possibility that somebody is a little more creative and devious than you might think. In addition, we urge you to review your internal controls. This is an area that managers tend to overlook. They seldom review internal controls until there are serious problems. The very simple concept of segregating duties for internal controls is as follows: Obviously, if you have an employee open the mail, make the bank deposit, and make cash entries in the journal, you have a weak system of internal control. A strong system would have one employee opening the mail, another making a list of all the money that comes in and then turning the money over to someone else who enters receipts in the cash journals, and still another employee bringing the deposit to the bank. The point is that your internal control procedures could be weak and perhaps need to be reviewed. **Make sure there is an adequate system of internal controls in place.**

Seventy-five percent of the fraud cases identified involved the theft of cash, with a sizeable fraction of those involving forged or altered checks. Fifteen percent of total cases involved stolen inventory, and approximately three percent involved the theft of property. According to findings by the U.S. Chamber of Commerce, almost $40 billion is stolen every year by employees. In rough terms, spread across a work force of 100,000,000 employees, that's an average of $363 per employee. And, employee theft is escalating at about 15 percent annually.

And don't forget stolen time! As much as $200 billion worth of employee time is also stolen annually. People steal time to do personal things like going to the bank or the cleaners, picking their children up from school, and so on. Consider implementing a new 9/80 Work Plan.

When employees work 80 hours in nine days, they are entitled to the tenth day off. This day gives them the time to do those errands — instead of taking it out of your time. It's a mutually beneficial way to avoid theft of time!

One more reminder: Customers can contribute to theft problems as well. Shore up controls to minimize this cost.

---

23. GUARD AGAINST LOSSES FROM THEFT
HOW DOES THIS APPLY TO MY BUSINESS?

_____

_____

_____

_____

_____

Priority   1   2   3   (Circle one)

Action Date_____

Profit Champion _____

Potential Dollar Effect $_____

EMAIL THAT'S EFFICIENT - ECONOMICAL - EXCITING - EXTRAORDINARY IS ESSENTIAL TO THE EXISTENCE OF EVERY ENTERPRISE

Web sites have exploded like popcorn and will continue popping up well into this millennium. No doubt your organization has already made a big investment to develop an Internet presence. But is the Internet, with its speed and easy access, generating the meaningful financial opportunities you hoped for? Is it generating the kind of revenue you were expecting from all those dollars you've paid to search engines, advertising media, and other marketing campaigns? In the New Economy, driving traffic to your site is vital—not just the first time, but for repeat business.

But have you considered "driving out" to meet your customers with your products and services, instead of waiting for them to come to you? You can do it very effectively with lists of email addresses—your own customers' and those of prospective customers. "Emailings" can be just as effective as "snail" mailings to

- Message timely and critical information to customers and prospects;
- Access pertinent information about your business, products, and services;
- Share important happenings within your company and industry;
- Enhance loyalty between customers, vendors, and your organization;
- Inform customers and prospects about value-added ideas that contribute to their success;
- Remind users of critical due dates, regulations, price changes, policy modifications, and new ways of doing business;
- Direct users back to your Web site to buy your products or services.

Even more importantly, utilizing email effectively can be economical, efficient, and effortless. For example, BizActions™, LLC, will regularly email your customers, clients, members, and prospects with timely, pertinent business tips in your organization's name. To these easy, friendly email tips, your organization can add your own messages as well as other business and industry proprietary content—all of which will be perceived as a service to your customers, not an advertisement. A multi-functioning reminder system can be added to help them turn the BizAction™ tips into financial results. It also includes a resource center where your organization can promote and sell products or services.

In effect, BizActions™, a company in which we have an association, becomes an out-sourced, proactive Web site that goes out to "meet" your customers instead of waiting for them to come to you. For businesses, not-for-profits, trade associations, and franchisers trying to compete in the volatile world of the Internet, these friendly, useful emails build member and customer loyalty, attract prospects, and generate traditional as well as non-traditional sources of revenue. Check out www.bizactions.com for more information.

Your goal in any Internet marketing campaign is to leverage your assets, people, vendors, products, services, relationships, knowledge, and technology with content, communication, and commerce unmatched by your competition. You and your marketing team need new ways of thinking and new ways of doing business in order to succeed—but that traditionally valuable customer list (with email addresses) is still a most important asset. Utilize it in a new way. Remember, it's still "all about earnings" in the New Economy.

---

24. EMAIL THAT'S EFFICIENT...

HOW DOES THIS APPLY TO MY BUSINESS?

_____

_____

_____

_____

_____

Priority   1   2   3   (Circle one)

Action Date_____

Profit Champion _____

Potential Dollar Effect $_____

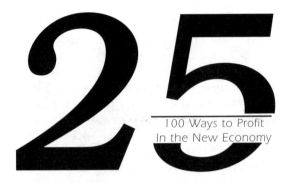

MAKE SURE YOU ARE GETTING VALUE FOR ENTERTAINMENT AND BUSINESS TRAVEL EXPENSES

Some people in business have managed to convince themselves that lavish forms of client entertainment are necessary to attract and retain customers. But even in the best of times, $100-a-plate lunches, corporate yachts, "skyboxes" at the Superbowl and similar extravagances are difficult to justify. No matter how robust the economy, prodigal client entertainment practices can backfire on a company.

This isn't to say that client entertainment serves no valid business purpose, or that all expenditures in this area should be curtailed. In many industries, customer entertainment is an essential way to establish and cement a long-term relationship with a business associate.

Indeed, a business relationship without an element of customer entertainment is like a marriage without a courtship — it is clearly possible to carry it off, but it is likely to have some awkward moments.

The objective is to use client entertainment to build a comfortable business relationship with your customers without going overboard. One approach being used by a number of companies today is to invite customers to a company picnic or outing. It's far less formal and threatening than a formal party, and much less costly.

The same goes for travel to educational seminars, conferences, and face-to-face meetings. Consider the costs of sending people to an out-of-town convention or seminar. Start with at least $200 to $300 in air fare, $100 per night for hotels, another $50 per day in meals, plus several hundred dollars in registration fees. Add in cab fares, car rentals, telephone costs and all the other incidental expenses, and you'll find that it costs at least $2,000 to send each person to such a meeting.

25. Make Sure You Are Getting Value for Entertainment and Business Travel Expenses

As a more cost-effective alternative, consider sending people to seminars held locally, or perhaps even bringing the "seminar" to them. If you have a number of people in your organization who would benefit from participating in a certain meeting, bring speakers in to meet with them rather than the other way around! Video and telephone conferencing are cost-effective alternatives to travel. The technology of computers and electronic mail has already made many face-to-face meetings possible.

When travel is necessary, renting a car may be less expensive than paying your employees a mileage reimbursement for high-mileage business trips. Use the Internet for finding discounted tickets. Some airlines are giving discounts for Web purchases. Establish written travel policies, by geographic region if necessary. Then everyone understands the limits. As part of your travel policy, negotiate preferred rates with car rental firms, preferred rates with hotels, even airlines. Travel agencies want your business. Try issuing requests for bids for planned business travel to a number of them, and see who gets you the best deals and provides the best service.

25: MAKE SURE YOU ARE GETTING VALUE FOR ENTERTAINMENT AND BUSINESS TRAVEL EXPENSES

HOW DOES THIS APPLY TO MY BUSINESS?

_____

_____

_____

_____

_____

Priority   1   2   3   (Circle one)

Action Date_____

Profit Champion _____

Potential Dollar Effect $_____

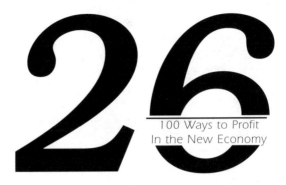

SLASH
PAPER

For years now we've been reading about how computers, laser discs and other high-tech electronic products are turning us into a "paperless society." A paperless society saves lots of paper costs, but more importantly it saves substantial labor costs. How long does it take you to walk to the file room and retrieve an important piece of information that has been misfiled?

Here are some suggestions that will help control paper costs, including labor. Whenever possible, respond to outside correspondence by jotting a reply on the face of the letter received and returning it by fax. That way, you don't even need to make a copy. Reuse large envelopes received from outside the company for interdepartmental mail within the company. Once the tab on one side of a file folder has become outdated, reverse the folder and use the other side of the tab. Once that is used, put a label over the top and write on that.

Try trimming paper costs by shifting to lower-priced recycled paper for internal use. To be sure, the quality of recycled paper is several notches below top-grade stock, so don't use it for external communications. However, since it's available at up to 40% off the cost of regular paper, by using recycled stock for internal needs, you're able to generate savings on paper costs—and help the environment at the same time!

Plan your next step, document imaging, a relatively new technology that scans documents and converts then into digital pictures that are stored on high-capacity optical disks similar to CD-ROMs. With this technology you can expect to increase your bottom line by saving precious storage space and employee time.

Document imaging allows employees to find documents quickly and efficiently. Retrieval takes minutes, no more searching for lost or mis-filed documents.

Another paper-saving exercise is to do a "Report Audit." Analyze all the reports your organization now requires for the benefit they add to the business. Are they all really necessary? Try not sending out certain reports for one, two or three weeks. See who notices and who doesn't notice. You will usually be able to trim your distribution list and eliminate some reports after measuring the reaction (or lack of reaction).

Consider giving someone the authority to approve, reject or amend all new computer reports as well. This will force everyone to justify the critical need, and cost, of each new report. Some reports are critical, of course, but many are just nice to have. Eliminate non-critical reports, and you'll find that no one misses them.

Remember, each ton of recycled paper saves 7,000 gallons of water required for new paper production. Combine that with saving trees. Look what you can do for the ecological system while boosting your bottom line.

26. SLASH PAPER

HOW DOES THIS APPLY TO MY BUSINESS?

_____

_____

_____

_____

_____

Priority   1   2   3   (Circle one)

Action Date_____

Profit Champion _____

Potential Dollar Effect $_____

100 Ways to Profit
In the New Economy

CANCEL INSURANCE ON UNUSED VEHICLES AND EQUIPMENT

Is there any reason to insure the Sherman tank sitting in your storage yard, unused for years? **If you have equipment that will not cause a hardship if it is destroyed, look closely at whether or not you need that equipment insured.** Equipment not being utilized but identified on your depreciation schedules is, in all likelihood, costing substantial insurance premiums. If you are paying expensive insurance premiums to carry equipment that has no value or serves no purpose, you are wasting your company's resources.

We represent contractors who own construction equipment that sits idle during winter months while they pay unnecessary insurance premiums. We have advised them to do as other clients have done and place minimum coverage insurance on that equipment during lean winter months, thus saving considerably on insurance premiums. Here are some profit actions we recommend:

- **Suspend insurance on idle equipment.**

- **Suspend insurance on seasonal equipment.**

- **Audit your insurance policy for nonexistent equipment.**

- **Evaluate equipment values and the cost of replacement versus the cost to insure the property.**

- **Use seasonal vehicle tags for registration.**

A word of caution: Before you drop the insurance, make sure that the equipment in question is not being used as collateral for a loan. Lenders usually require insurance coverage on items used as collateral. If you cancel the insurance, the lending institution might declare you in violation of the loan agreement and demand full payment on the note.

And, before you drop the insurance on vehicles, check to find out whether your state will require you to turn in the license plates. If you must surrender your tags, your vehicles may have to be reinspected before they can be relicensed. If your vehicles are several years old, it could cost you far more to shape them up to pass inspection than you will possibly save in insurance costs.

---

27. CANCEL INSURANCE ON UNUSED VEHICLES AND EQUIPMENT

HOW DOES THIS APPLY TO MY BUSINESS?

_____

_____

_____

_____

_____

Priority   1   2   3   (Circle one)

Action Date_____

Profit Champion _____

Potential Dollar Effect $_____

SHIFT TO SHORT-TERM LEASES TO LIMIT EXPOSURE

Prudent businesses in uncertain economic climates often choose to lease rather than buy equipment, vehicles or facilities. However, long-term leases can be the shortest route to the poor house.

The last thing you need is to be stuck with three more years of stiff lease payments on equipment or facilities that you're not even using if there is a sudden change in business. Limit your exposure with short-term leases; this way, if the worst happens, you can simply return the equipment and you're off the hook.

To be sure, you will pay a higher rate if you lease on a short-term basis. Rent a car from Hertz and it might cost you $50 or $60 a day. Lease that same car for four years and you may get it for only $300 a month. But if you only need the car for a few days, it's silly to make a long-term commitment.

You would be surprised, however, at how **many businesses become unnecessarily encumbered in long-range leasing agreements.**

A cash-strapped construction business needed a lot of earth-moving equipment. On a long-term basis, leasing a single piece of heavy equipment would have cost the company over $4,000 a month, even though it was idle for at least half that time. Worse yet the company was committed to making those payments, rain or shine, for two years.

As an alternative, the contractor sublet the equipment he needed from another construction firm on a short-term, week-to-week basis. The company wound up paying $2000 a week — but only for the two weeks each month that the equipment was needed.

The end result was that the company was paying the same $4,000 a month as before, but now had the option of walking away from that arrangement at any time, or if a better deal came along! There was no long-term financial commitment.

Of course, it's not always possible to reduce the duration of your lease commitment without increasing your net cost of leasing. But even if you end up paying a little more, it's often a prudent move to limit your exposure. Say you have an opportunity to lease a photocopy machine for five years at $300 a month, or a total of $18,000. If, instead, you are able to negotiate a month-to-month lease for that same machine at $450 a month, it could be a much better deal, considering technological obsolescence and other relevant factors.

If you take the long-term lease and business falls off, you'll be expected to continue making those payments even though there's nothing to photocopy and no revenues coming in to pay the lease. If you hedge your bets by taking the short-term option, you can walk away from that arrangement as soon as conditions change. If the danger to your company passes, you may then decide to terminate that "expensive" short-term lease and shop for a "cheaper" long-term arrangement.

Point is: When there's uncertainty in the air, keep your powder dry and your options open.

---

28. SHIFT TO SHORT-TERM LEASES TO LIMIT EXPOSURE
HOW DOES THIS APPLY TO MY BUSINESS?

_____

_____

_____

_____

_____

Priority   1   2   3   (Circle one)

Action Date_____

Profit Champion _____

Potential Dollar Effect $_____

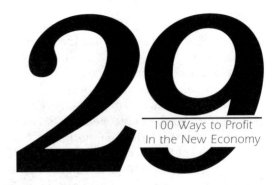

RENEGOTIATE LEASE TERMS TO MESH
WITH BUSINESS CYCLES

For many seasonal businesses it's a real struggle just to keep the doors open during the off-season. There are strategies that homebuilders, campground operators and other seasonal businesses can use to ease the pressure during slack periods. **Since companies in seasonal industries are forewarned of the worst, they can be forearmed.**

In the landscaping business, for example, you know that they will be generating virtually all of their revenues during spring, summer and fall. Little is going to be coming in during the winter. Suppose their overhead costs dried up during the winter, too? Actually, that isn't so far-fetched.

If you were a landscaper and you were leasing your equipment, it might be possible to work out a schedule to make lease payments over a nine-month period rather than 12 months. It's hard enough making it through the winter without income, why be saddled with equipment payments in those months?

A real estate development firm leased millions of dollars worth of earth movers and other heavy equipment that couldn't be used in the winter months when the ground was frozen. The company had been operating in this fashion for years. Because the company wanted to conserve cash in the lean months, they called a meeting with the lessor and negotiated a new arrangement under which monthly payments would be due only from March through October.

The leasing company agreed to this change because it didn't affect the total amount paid on the equipment each year — the company was simply making fewer, but larger, payments. Additionally, by agreeing to the new schedule, the leasing company cemented a stronger relationship with one of its largest customers.

This isn't the only way for seasonal businesses to get relief from stiff, year-round lease payments. It may be possible to restructure a lease agreement from 12 to eight monthly payments without increasing the amount of each payment. Indeed, the lessor may jump at such a proposal if you, in turn, are willing to agree to an extension of the term of the lease.

We advise our clients to develop a "tickler file" of renewal dates and terms on their leases. Sometimes the lessor imposes a penalty for not complying with lease terms. With a lease tickler file you'll be able to prevent unnecessary additional costs on your leases.

Also consider auditing the physical existence of equipment leased to the lease payments. On occasion lease payments continue in error after the leased machinery and equipment has been returned.

---

29. RENEGOTIATE LEASE TERMS TO MESH WITH BUSINESS CYCLES

HOW DOES THIS APPLY TO MY BUSINESS?

_____

_____

_____

_____

_____

Priority   1   2   3   (Circle one)

Action Date_____

Profit Champion _____

Potential Dollar Effect $_____

DISPOSE OF IDLE ASSETS

It costs substantial dollars to carry idle fixed assets. Idle assets—including unused vehicles, vacant real estate or unneeded machinery—can hurt a business's cash flow. **Even assets that you own free and clear can create a profit drain.**

For example, you may incur unnecessary but considerable insurance, as well as maintenance and storage expenses, by continuing to hold on to an asset when it is no longer needed. Adding insult to injury, in some states you may have to pay a personal property tax on that item.

By contrast, disposing of an idle asset can have an invigorating effect on your company's cash flow and your bottom line. If an unneeded asset is being financed, you may recover enough from the sale to allow repayment. Disposing of a vacant factory or an unused truck may enable you to reduce your monthly note payment.

Even if an idle asset can't be sold, it may still be advantageous for you to get it off your books. You might be able to donate it to a charitable organization and claim a tax deduction, subject, of course, to the limitations imposed by IRS rules.

If nothing else, most assets have some scrap or salvage value. Even trash may be worth something to somebody. Take the case of a medical practice which routinely purged its files of old, unneeded patient X-rays. The doctors were actually throwing away treasure with the trash. Because of the silver content in the film, this medical practice learned they could recycle the old X-rays at a tidy profit.

Perhaps the most compelling reason to reexamine the status of your business assets is the fact that you may be able to reap substantial tax benefits by unloading them. Indeed, your company may be able to claim a sizeable tax loss by disposing of idle assets — as long as they are sold for less than their "undepreciated basis" (the original acquisition cost less the depreciation claimed over the years).

For example, suppose that a dry cleaning business has taxable income of $45,000. The owner decides to dispose of some cleaning equipment no longer needed because of a store closing. Let's say the equipment was purchased some years ago for $225,000. Over the years the company was able to tax-depreciate a total of $80,000 on that equipment. The remainder—$145,000— represents the undepreciated basis of the asset.

Now let's say the operator is able to sell the surplus equipment for $100,000. The remaining $45,000 represents a tax loss—an amount that can be used to reduce the company's federal income taxes. Since the business is currently operating in the black, what good is that $45,000 tax loss? Plenty! It will eliminate the current year's tax liability completely. This business paid their tax bill in effect by getting rid of their idle equipment.

HERE ARE SOME IMMEDIATE PROFIT ACTIONS YOU CAN INITIATE:

- Look for idle assets among your inventories, real estate, equipment, intangibles (including licensing).

- Generate cash from the sale of idle assets.

- Cut your cost of ownership, including insurance, personal property taxes and real estate taxes, storage and administrative oversight.

- Move idle assets to save on personal property taxes.

- Examine the tax advantage — you can deduct the difference between cost less the depreciation if the asset is discarded.

- Consider donating equipment to a charity.

30. DISPOSE OF IDLE ASSETS

HOW DOES THIS APPLY TO MY BUSINESS?

_____

_____

_____

_____

_____

Priority   1   2   3   (Circle one)

Action Date_____

Profit Champion _____

Potential Dollar Effect $_____

ADOPT AND MONITOR CREDIT AND COLLECTION POLICIES AND PROCEDURES

Too often, businesses without proper credit procedures find themselves in deep trouble without warning, particularly during economic downturns. You can avoid such unpleasant surprises by keeping close tabs on the customers to whom you extend credit. If a customer who has always paid promptly suddenly begins paying more slowly, it can be an important danger signal. Contact that customer immediately and let them know your concerns. Go to work now shoring up your company's credit policies. Here's how:

1. Require all new customers to fill out a credit application—before any credit is extended. Such an application should request specific references sufficient to allow you to verify that the new customer is in good standing. Don't be bashful about asking your new customer to put you in touch with a specific individual at their bank who can discuss their creditworthiness. Get business references and ask them such pointed questions as: How difficult is the customer to do business with? How long has the reference had a business relationship with the credit applicant? Does the applicant dispute bills either occasionally or on a regular basis? Does the customer take advantage of purchase discounts, when available?

2. Subscribe to a credit-reporting service to provide you with such "tip-off" information about a prospective customer like collection claims, suits and judgments by other suppliers; downgrading of credit ratings; pledges of inventory or receivables to a bank or finance company; selective payment patterns.

3. Require customers to sign a statement of contract. A written agreement at the onset of a business relationship can help you avoid misunderstandings later in the game. Spell out the terms of the arrangement on your credit application form so they are clear from the start. You might want to go one step farther and have customers sign a separate credit statement or contract identifying not only when payment will be due, but also that the customer is liable for any legal or arbitration costs should the bill not be paid. Many businesses already use a standard credit contract—a form they can photocopy and use for almost any transaction. However, if you're considering an especially important deal, you might want to draw up a more explicit contract with your attorneys.

4. File a security agreement at the courthouse. If you're especially nervous about a particular customer coming through on a deal, consider a security agreement. This type of arrangement entitles you to first claim on any goods you've shipped. If the customer doesn't pay for the goods, you can recover your shipment. Even if your customer goes bankrupt, your goods will not be subject to the general claims of other creditors.

5. Secure personal guarantees from the owners of the business as well as from their spouses. If a customer goes down the tubes while owing you money, you're not going to be paid by the company. But if you have required the owners of the business to personally guarantee the debt, then the obligation is doubly secured. If the business fails, you have a legal right to recover personal as well as business assets. To be sure, business owners are often reluctant to secure business debt with personal assets — and well they should be (see #99). If you're the one extending credit to a financially troubled company, however, you should protect your business by insisting on personal guarantees.

6. Assign a due date to all bills, include them with customer shipments, and/or provide electronic transfer procedures. Remind customers of your credit terms. Check the invoices and/or statements you send out to make sure your customers are clearly informed of what is expected from them. Do they explain whether payment is due upon invoice rendered? Or within 30 days? We review the billing practices of clients and find that almost half of them fail to include specific payment terms on their statements. They might as well be asking customers to pay late! After all, if a customer receives two bills, and one says "Net 30" and the other says nothing, you can be sure which one will go on the back burner. Send your invoice with your shipment, not separately some time afterward. And try sending out semi-monthly statements, rather than monthly. Always include stamped self-addressed envelopes to speed payments. Better yet, with bank Internet technology, have your customers transfer funds electronically and cut out all the mailing delays.

7. Offer discounts to early payers. Don't overlook any opportunity to accelerate your cash flow. You should even consider offering your customers discounts of one to two percent if bills are paid within ten days of delivery. It may cost you a little, but it may also light a fire under slow payers — and that can have a major effect on your cash flow.

8. Establish an interest penalty for late payment. Once a bill becomes seriously overdue, you may have to resort to penalties. It's hard to do — especially if it's not industry policy. Start by adding a clause to your initial bill like, "A 1.5 percent a month late payment penalty will be imposed unless payment is made by (date)." Later, if your customer becomes delinquent, you'll be able to impose this penalty as an incentive to pay you.

Be just as determined about your collection procedures. While you can and should sympathize with hard-pressed customers, don't allow their problems to drag you under. Poor collection practices are a prescription for disaster in the best of times. Steps 9-14 will help put your company's collections back on track.

9. Appoint a permanent manager to handle collections. Too many businesses treat collections as a stepchild. When customers or clients fall behind in payments, the company bookkeeper or office manager or a secretary may be assigned to placing a "reminder" call. Often there's no real system, and customers or clients are sometimes allowed to fall so far behind that they may never catch up.

If you have to go outside and hire someone to handle this, so be it. The money spent on a good collections manager will come back manyfold.

10. Establish an internal review of your accounts. Structure your accounting department to prepare fast, accurate reports on overdue payments. Monitoring your own accounts can reveal erratic payments, ignored discounts, extraordinary orders, and unwillingness to provide the information you require from your accounts receivable customers. These early warning signs will allow you to identify problems. For certain long-term customers, you may decide to loosen credit to spur their sales, but for less reliable ones you'll know when you to cut credit and avoid trouble.

11. Telephone tardy customers. It's one thing to get a letter in the mail warning you that your bill is past due; it's another to hear it over the phone from a collections manager! If your customers are behind on their payments, get on the horn and let them know it. Not only are you alerting them that you are concerned, but you're verifying that the bill actually arrived.

12. Put "problem" customers on C.O.D. or stop shipments altogether. Many businesses continue to deliver service or ship goods when their customers fall far behind in their payments. It's important to let delinquent accounts know that you mean business.

13. Always obtain a payment commitment from overdue accounts. It's easy for a person to say, "I'll put a check in the mail." Set a deadline and if the customer doesn't meet it, contact the company immediately. Some businesses with effective collection procedures even send someone around to visit chronic slow-paying businesses on the day that each bill is due. When you've agreed to make a payment on a specific date, it's hard to wiggle out of your obligation if the bill collector is literally at the door.

14. Put your collections staff on commission. Collecting bills is tough work, especially in a soft economy. It's important to give your collections staff an incentive to go that extra mile on your behalf. One building contractor pays his collections personnel a base salary plus a sliding scale commission to encourage aggressive collections. Under this system the staff is paid a bonus of 1 percent on collections of 60-to-90 day old accounts, 1-1/2 percent on collections of 90-120 day old accounts, and 2 percent on receipts from accounts older than 120 days.

The contractor also sets a quota to ensure that the collections staff actively seeks payments in less than 60 days. Those who don't make quota face a possible downward revision in their base salary. As a result of these collection incentives, the average age of the company's accounts receivables has dropped by almost two weeks! The upsurge in cash flow is just what the profit advisor ordered!

31. ADOPT AND MONITOR CREDIT AND COLLECTION POLICIES AND PROCEDURES

HOW DOES THIS APPLY TO MY BUSINESS?

_____

_____

_____

_____

_____

Priority   1   2   3   (Circle one)

Action Date_____

Profit Champion _____

Potential Dollar Effect $_____

ADD VALUE TO YOUR BUSINESS: DON'T BUY A JOB

"Our goal is to be the most valuable and respected company on earth," said Steve Case, founder and CEO of America Online, Inc. years before their Time Warner merger. Most entrepreneurs love their business! They have found or created a need for their company's products and services in the marketplace. They have built their business around servicing these needs. The business is their baby. Their primary goal should be to make their business constantly more valuable.

Are you so much in love with your business that you would pay to have the same job and responsibilities you have today? Often entrepreneurs do pay to have their job because they haven't maximized the value of their business. The economic effect of not maximizing the value of your business is the cost to you of having your job.

Let's look at an example to illustrate the reality of buying a job. Assume these facts:

Entrepreneur's annual salary and fringes	$ 350,000
Value of the business — "as is"	$ 5,000,000
Potential value of the business by maximizing profits for 2-3 years prior to its sale	$10,000,000
Tax rate on the sale of the business	25%

If the value of a business is maximized by embracing profitability for 2-3 years prior to the sale, here's what can happen ...

Sales price from sale	$10,000,000
Tax (*25% of the sales price — assuming a zero tax basis*)	$ 2,500,000
Net proceeds from sale of business — after taxes	$ 7,500,000

Now let's assume that the after-tax sales proceeds will be invested in conservative, good quality mutual funds, providing a ten percent annual retur

Invested return on net proceeds from the sale of the business (10% of $7,500,000)	$ 750,000
Entrepreneurs present annual salary and fringes	$ 350,000
Economic annual cost of having a job	$ 400,000

In this example, the difference between the investment return on the net sales proceeds of the business and the amount the owner is receiving in compensation and fringes is the economic annual cost of "buying" their job.

Certainly this makes little sense. Why would anyone choose to work every day, accept the financial risks of owning a business, deal with the frustrations inherent in most businesses ... and leave $400,000 a year on the table? The answer is probably that they don't realize the economic consequences of not reaching their profit potential and thus not maximizing their company's value ... until it is too late!

Your business eventually will either close its doors or be sold, hopefully the latter. Selling your business is the preferred choice. Your job is to maximize the value of your business. Perhaps the greatest factor used in valuing your business is profits. The greater the profit, the greater the sales price. What's the down side of maximizing your bottom line but not selling the business – a profit annuity! There's not much risk on the down side, is there?

Studies indicate that more than 75% of closely held businesses are sold for less than their value. In today's affluent society created with gains from the stock market, there are many prospective purchasers of businesses. Unsolicited purchase offers occur frequently. A buyer's starting point to determine value when making an offer is most often profits. Traditionally, profits reported for tax and financial statement purposes are conservative so there are certain "add backs" that will be made to determine a more realistic bottom line. But buyers traditionally will not pay for profits that haven't been realized.

In summary, it is critical to focus on reaching your profit potential to maximize the value of your business. You never know when a purchaser will come your way. The value of most businesses is significantly influenced by the bottom line. Your job is to enhance your business's value. Stop paying for your job.

32. ADD VALUE TO YOUR BUSINESS: Don't Buy a Job
HOW DOES THIS APPLY TO MY BUSINESS?

_____

_____

_____

Priority   1   2   3   (Circle one)

Action Date_____

Profit Champion _____

Potential Dollar Effect $_____

USE A DUNNING SERVICE TO MINIMIZE COLLECTION AGENCY FEES

When in-house collection efforts fail, most business people swallow hard and turn their past-due accounts over to a collection agency. That should be a last gasp alternative, because most collection agents will keep anywhere from 25 percent to 33 percent or more of whatever they are able to recover from your customers.

Before turning unpaid bills over to a collection agent, consider using a computerized "dunning service" to recover payment. Unlike a collection agency, these services take no action to recover the debt other than to send out letters. But the letters they send are extremely official-looking documents designed to grab attention. If someone brought 100 pieces of mail to your desk, theirs would be the one you would open first.

One service offers a choice of letters ranging from a "diplomatic" message to a pretty tough one. The dunning agent sends out up to eight of these letters over a 12-week period to each account you designate, and every subsequent letter is a little stronger than the last one.

When the customer settles up or commits to a repayment schedule, you simply notify the dunning service and the letters stop. If the customer doesn't follow through on the agreement, you can contact the service and the computers start spitting out dunning notices again.

Believe it or not, this approach is extremely effective — and extremely cost-effective. There are dunning services with branches in many major markets, and they claim an average payment rate of 50 percent. For some of our clients, the collection rate has been even higher.

The cost of this service runs less than $12 per account. You couldn't send out eight letters yourself for that! And when you consider that the alternative is a collection agency that may keep a third of what they recover, a dunning service is an even bigger bargain.

Suppose you have 50 customers behind in payments to you. Despite your own letters and phone calls, these accounts are still in arrears by an average of $500 each. If you go to a dunning service and their collection letters result in payments of half of those accounts, it has cost you about $600 (50 x $12) to recover $12,500.

If you turn these accounts over to a collection agency, it will cost you over $3,000 to recover these same payments. Admittedly, a dunning service isn't going to bat 1000 for you. But the accounts that don't respond to these letters can then be turned over to the collection agency as a true last resort. At this point, negotiate your fee with the collection agency. We've been able to cut down their charges to as little as 15 percent of what they recover.

CLIENTS SENT TO COLLECTIONS

PERIOD ENDING _____

Client Name	Amount Due	Dunning Service	Collection Service	Attorney

33. USE A DUNNING SERVICE TO MINIMIZE COLLECTION AGENCY FEES

HOW DOES THIS APPLY TO MY BUSINESS?

_____

_____

_____

_____

_____

Priority   1   2   3   (Circle one)

Action Date_____

Profit Champion _____

Potential Dollar Effect $_____

34. Use Technology to Speed Sales and Collections and Trim Expenses

Take advantage of technology to speed collections and trim your expenses. Now that includes electronic mail. It goes without saying that paying bills by e-mail will catch on over the next several years. Invoices will be sent electronically, and payment made by filling out a "check" at a Web site. Many banks permit electronic banking presently. The advantage to you is faster remittances and lower costs, of course. The advantage to customers is that they can incorporate invoices into their computer system and search for details by keyword. For both, this system will eliminate some more paper and paperwork, and we're all for that.

For now, the facsimile machine and electronic faxing are some of the most cost-effective office procedures that any organization can use. Think in terms of using your fax machine or electronic fax to take orders instead of having an employee take orders over the telephone. You can save time and, thereby, money by using faxing in this way. It's a messenger service, a post office, and a newsletter distribution service all in one. One company in our building saves wasted staff time at lunch hour by faxing carry-out orders to the local Chinese restaurant!

Chow mein isn't all faxing can get you, however. Take the account-ant who has had to make changes on tax forms at zero hour—April 15th. That firm will go crazy if they have to chase people down by phone and then dictate what they needed over the line. Federal Express doesn't cut it either; it takes too long, and it costs too much. Instead, you get all the information you need zapped to you instantaneously by fax, economically.

34. Use Technology to Speed Sales and Collections and Trim Expenses

A local law firm saved a bundle when they stopped mailing their monthly client billing statements and started faxing them instead. This particular firm sends out roughly 1,200 statements a month. The cost of stamps plus stationary doesn't sound like that much, until you multiply it by the number of statements this law firm sent: 14,400 each year. That adds up to a tidy $5000-$6000 a year in mailing expenses.

The real advantage is that they get their bills to their clients the day they are prepared. The faster your bills get to the accounts payable departments of your clients/customers, the faster that money will come back.

Technology can also speed up sales. Suppose an auto dealer has a customer who really wants to buy a new car, but who needs a credit approval to do so? They don't want to give that customer a couple days to stew over his purchase — and possibly change his mind — while the credit application is mailed in, processed, and shipped back! With technology there is the opportunity for instant approval. Their customer gets his car, and they get cash in the bank immediately.

Don't forget voice mail. Do you really need an employee to sit at a desk and answer a telephone when somebody can call in an order and have it recorded on voice mail? Soon e-commerce may replace most customer service reps. We represent a business that is a large wholesaler of automobile parts. They sell to jobbers. Their customers can call in orders 24 hours a day; there's no operator. Delivery trucks are rolling early in the morning. They are able to fill their orders faster than their competitors. The point is that a customer can call orders in 24 hours a day, and not be dependent on having an employee available. Human error is minimized and orders are filled expeditiously at lower cost.

---

34. USE TECHNOLOGY TO SPEED SALES AND COLLECTIONS AND TRIM EXPENSES

HOW DOES THIS APPLY TO MY BUSINESS?

_____

_____

_____

_____

_____

Priority   1   2   3   (Circle one)

Action Date_____

Profit Champion _____

Potential Dollar Effect $_____

35

ESTABLISH CASH CONTROLS THAT
ACCELERATE DEPOSITS

Process deposits immediately! It's incredible how many businesses hold payment checks and cash receipts for days on end before getting that money to the bank. All businesses should make timely deposits. **There's absolutely no excuse for letting badly-needed cash sit idle in a drawer when it can be used to reduce the need for borrowing.** We were personally shocked to discover that the check we sent to pay our local real estate taxes in September wasn't cashed until November!

Even if you're uncertain how to record a particular payment, don't just sit on the check. As a general rule, deposit your receipts first and worry about the bookkeeping later.

Take the automobile body shop that was surprised to learn the cashier's drawer contained literally thousands of dollars in checks from insurance companies for work done. The cashier had never taken them to the bank because he was unable to match customers with the insurance payments. Some of the checks gathering dust in the drawer were more than six months old, yet the bookkeeper was still awaiting clarification from the insurer.

Obviously, those checks could have been photocopied for later investigation and then immediately deposited in the company's account. By not following this procedure, the company's cash flow problems were unnecessarily aggravated and operating costs were needlessly increased. The company might well have avoided some interest costs on business indebtedness had this money been put to use in a timely fashion.

Additionally, at many banks, interest rates on loans are linked to the balance that the business maintains at that financial institution. The more quickly your receipts are deposited at the bank, the higher your firm's average account balance will be.

Another reason for making timely deposits is to reduce the risk of loss. We've seen situations where accounting staff allowed cash receipts to pile up for several days because it was inconvenient to make daily deposits. In the event of a theft, however, the insurance company may well refuse to cover the loss on grounds that maintaining this much cash on hand exceeds the limits of the policy. Moreover, if you allow checks to gather dust for months as our auto body client did, you may discover too late that they are worthless.

When a check is months old, the bank is no longer obliged to accept it. Of course, you may be able to get the check reissued, but that's not at all certain. The customer who paid you by check six months ago might not be willing to reissue the check.

---

35. ESTABLISH CASH CONTROLS THAT ACCELERATE DEPOSITS

HOW DOES THIS APPLY TO MY BUSINESS?

_____

_____

_____

_____

_____

Priority   1   2   3   (Circle one)

Action Date_____

Profit Champion _____

Potential Dollar Effect $_____

OBTAIN BIDS
FROM VENDORS

We have a salesperson who comes to our office to sell supplies. He was giving a 40 percent discount on most supplies because we had a super-store open a block from our office. We decided to comparison shop the 40 percent discount for 12 yellow pads for which we were paying $9.80. With no discount at the superstore, the pads cost $5.90! Make sure you take advantage of opportunities to save. When you get a discount from one source, you don't necessarily know the base price the discount is applied to. A big discount may be no bargain if your supplier's prices are uncompetitive to begin with.

The mind-set of the proactive purchaser is to be a hunter, and not the hunted — view all purchases as negotiable. Price, quantity and delivery are variables, and are not set in concrete. The best purchasers/negotiators seek out situations in which they can hone their skills. Once you have developed your purchasing skills, pass them on to others in your organization. Encourage the development of your staff's negotiating skills and allow them to gain experience. When your company is consciously predisposed to proactive purchasing policies, the cost of your purchases suddenly begins to drop. Remember that effective purchasing and negotiating have less to do with price and quantity issues and more to do with human insight, personal interaction and listening skills.

Price, quantity, type, delivery, warranties, payment and other terms can be parlayed to your advantage when negotiating. The key to prudent purchasing is to become proactive in how you spend your money. How you make your purchases and control your inventory impacts your liquidity and may be your company's single largest cash trap. Here are some quick tips for finding the best deals on supplies:

- Develop multiple sources of supply.

- Continually seek favorable purchasing opportunities, then negotiate to make them even more favorable. Discipline yourself to be selective, wait, or say no, knowing that today's seemingly bargain price for goods may be exorbitant when compared with tomorrow's prices. Become known as the buyer who hunts for values.

- Effective purchasing and negotiating has less to do with price and quantity issues and more to do with human insight, personal interaction and listening skills. Your suppliers need to make sales.

- Ask your suppliers, "What is your slowest sales month, and what kind of terms will you offer if I place a large order on the first of that month?"

- Negotiate a payment arrangement with suppliers who are willing to "give" a little if it means keeping a steady, bill-paying customer on the books or making a big sale.

- Allow yourself to be courted as a customer. The person you are dealing with may not have authority to go below a certain price level, but may be able to offer other concessions. Push for them.

- Bunch your orders. Not only may you be able to secure a lower price, but you will be able to get some other cost-savings like free delivery.

- Ask suppliers for help in controlling costs. They may be able to suggest alternative materials or less expensive products or services. They have also seen what works for others, so don't hesitate to ask for better terms. If you are a good customer, your suppliers will work hard to keep you.

SUPPLY COST COMPARISON

ITEM	QUANTITY	VENDORS	COST	DELIVERY

36. OBTAIN BIDS FROM VENDORS

HOW DOES THIS APPLY TO MY BUSINESS?

_____

_____

_____

_____

_____

Priority   1   2   3   (Circle one)

Action Date_____

Profit Champion _____

Potential Dollar Effect $_____

37

MANAGE SUPPLIES AS YOU MANAGE INVENTORY

Figure out how much your business spends on supplies in a typical year, multiply that total by 40 percent, and I'll bet you would have a pretty good estimate of the amount you could save by implementing tighter supply control procedures.

Do your office supply expenses increase around Labor Day—when school starts? We are not suggesting that employees are likely to be raiding the company's supplies for their own personal use — although that certainly has happened at some firms. We are, however, suggesting that **unregulated supplies are likely to be an engine of waste within any organization.**

Look around your office or shop and notice how supplies are being used. In our office, I'm one of the worst offenders. I looked around my house one day and found 19 company pens that I had carried home over the past few weeks without even realizing it!

The first step toward correcting this problem is to control your supplies by assigning one person in the organization the responsibility for these items. To obtain supplies, employees should be asked to fill out a short requisition form. This not only gives you a way to get a handle on where these items are going, but it also serves as a reminder to employees that the availability of company supplies is not unlimited.

Be forewarned, though. If you've been allowing unrestricted access to supplies, when you finally do impose controls on these items count on some grumbling from your staff. We suggest you hold a "Supply Amnesty Day" to launch your new policy. Announce that for one full 24-hour period, employees can return all "borrowed" supplies without fear of retribution by depositing them in a box somewhere where discreet returns of supplies can be made. Just like the public library, you'll be amazed at how full that box will be at the end of the day.

A law firm was budgeting an excessive amount for office supplies. There were fewer than 50 employees at this particular office, yet the firm was spending almost $40,000 a year on stationery, pens, pencils and other routine supplies. It was easy to see why costs were so high. The supply room was unsupervised. People were allowed to walk in and grab whatever they wanted, and the place was a complete mess.

When the partners imposed controls over the office supplies, there were plenty of complaints. Some employees accused the firm of penny-pinching; others viewed the new procedures as an indication that they were not trusted.

But the partners were able to nip that resentment in the bud by pointing out that the purpose of the new system was not simply to bring expenses in line. They explained that these procedures would also streamline the ordering process and keep the supply room neat.

The staff complaints stopped, and so did much of the waste. Thanks to the new procedures, the lawyers were able to slice their supply costs in half and realize a tidy $20,000 a year savings.

Actually consider not maintaining any supplies in your firm by negotiating daily deliveries with vendors when needed. That way your suppliers carry the inventory in their warehouses, not your company.

SUPPLY REQUESTS

Date Ordered	Description	Ordered By	Date Delivered

37. MANAGE SUPPLIES AS YOU MANAGE INVENTORY
HOW DOES THIS APPLY TO MY BUSINESS?

_____

_____

_____

_____

_____

Priority   1   2   3   (Circle one)

Action Date_____

Profit Champion _____

Potential Dollar Effect $_____

SCALE BACK ORDERS, BUT POUNCE ON DEALS

How can your purchasing department find great deals? Ask your vendors! Chrysler did this in 1997, got thousands of cost-saving ideas from their vendors and boosted the company's bottom line by $325 million! Based on their poor financial performance after their merger with Daimler, perhaps it's time to repeat this exercise.

One of our clients followed their lead and wrote a letter to each vendor telling them how much the company had appreciated their service over the years and inviting the vendors to suggest ways the company might save on their products.

Dear Vendor:

Our business becomes more competitive as a result of increased competition and changing markets. We look towards your company to contribute to our needs. We don't just look to you as a resource to fill our inventory needs, but as a source of innovative ideas that will help us to meet our competition, with greater profitability in mind.

We expect you to inform us of product or service alternatives that will help us be more profitable while increasing the quality of our products. We are constantly looking at price in relation to customer needs and benefits, but price is not the only reason we do business with your company. We consider you a member of our customer service task force. We look to you for leadership in the products you distribute, timeliness of service, quality of products, and competitive pricing. We believe that you can help us in all of these ways. We are very appreciative of any assistance and advice you can offer to help us reach our objectives.

We are certain that you have the ability and experience to help us make our business more successful. With your help we will continue to remain competitive, our relationship will continue to grow and long-term benefits will be derived. Please inform us of your thoughts, concerns and suggestions, so together we can be the very best we can be.

Very truly yours,
(Company President)

The response was incredible!   Here's one example.

Dear Customer:

In response to your letter I would like to offer the following:

1. We will review all your sales literature.
2. We will assist in the cost of literature to do a customer mailing.
3. We will schedule a training seminar for your salespeople.
4. We will schedule a sales seminar for your customers.
5. We will spend time in the field with your salespeople concentrating on customers using competitors' products.

These are some of the efforts we use consistently to increase market share. Should you have a special request or an untried idea, we would be happy to work with you.

I felt your letter to be encouraging as this is the type of thought process that fosters sales and marketing ideas and strengthens relationships. It is a pleasure to do business with professional people like you and your competent staff.

Sincerely,

(Sales Manager)

Remember that there are likely to be deals available in the marketplace that you just don't know about. In particular, your suppliers might be looking for ways to improve their own cash flow, and you may have opportunities to stock up on merchandise or supplies at bargain basement prices. **The idea is to keep your inventories tight so that you can cash in on opportunities when they arise in the**

marketplace.

Ordinarily, however, you should think in terms of "just-in-time inventory." Keep minimum inventories on hand. We bet that if there are no office supplies in your facility, and you make a deal with a local office supply company, that supplier will guarantee delivery within 24 hours. They want your business. Yet you have invested dollars in inventory and supplies that are just sitting there waiting for someone to use them. Don't wind up with that inventory; scale back those orders. Then, if your purchasing department finds a deal, and only then, buy substantial quantities of products. And, when such an opportunity comes along, ask yourself the DO and WHEN questions before buying:

1. **DO I really need this quantity?**
2. **WHEN can I reasonably expect to use or sell this product?**

The U.S. Government, by the way, has a standard reference for ensuring that federal agencies are given the best prices possible. It's a contract clause that requires a supplier to certify that the prices quoted by the supplier are at least as low as those "offered to the most favored customer." This is a standard you might well emulate in your purchasing activities.

---

38. SCALE BACK ORDERS, BUT POUNCE ON DEALS

HOW DOES THIS APPLY TO MY BUSINESS?

_____

_____

_____

_____

_____

Priority   1   2   3   (Circle one)

Action Date_____

Profit Champion _____

Potential Dollar Effect $_____

Avoid Costly Equipment Buying Blunders

Have you ever purchased new "state-of-the-art" equipment only to discover that you paid dearly for those bells and whistles, yet could have managed nicely with a much more reasonably priced model?

Of course, the knife cuts both ways. It can be just as big a mistake to invest in a bargain basement piece of business equipment that can't do the job. You know the kind of gear we're talking about. The stripped-down photocopy machine that doesn't collate documents the way you need them. The bottom-of-the-line fax machine that requires an employee to constantly hand-feed it. And, of course, last season's computer system that turns out to be incompatible with every other machine in the world!

A restaurant bought a $250,000 computer system that was intended to handle a variety of different accounting, inventory control, and internal management reporting functions. Unfortunately, however, the business didn't do its homework. The selection of the system was turned over to the restaurant's procurement chief — a fellow who was a whiz at finding the best-quality prime beef and the lowest prices on Maine lobsters. Unfortunately, his expertise did not extend to computers.

The new quarter-million-dollar system arrived at the office in crates. The manufacturer offered virtually no setup or training assistance, and it was a full year before the company was able to begin using the computer for its intended purposes. It was a horrible waste of time and money.

The correct way to select equipment for your business is to undertake a "needs" analysis, examining your reasons for considering new gear and the uses to which it will be put.

Brainstorm with the people in your organization who will be using the equipment. Don't even think about shopping the market until it's clear to you what your company's needs are.

Once you've reached this point, begin comparing specifications systematically. Professional and industry associations often conduct tests of equipment, and trade publications are another potentially valuable source for product reviews.

If you are considering investing a significant sum in new equipment, ask the manufacturer or distributor for references from other companies in your line of business that have used this gear. Ask those references about the equipment's performance and reliability, and about the maintenance and repair service offered by the supplier.

If you do your homework, the right equipment choice should be obvious. If it isn't, maybe you should postpone the purchase, at least temporarily. We advise our clients to consider buying quality equipment at auctions. Of course, this means putting a trusted employee in charge. One of our clients has a full-time person responsible for buying tractor-trailers. This employee canvases the country for auctions and other ways to buy these vital tractor-trailers because the company saves so much money by making these deals. He regularly consults the services and sources that rate this equipment before he buys.

---

39. AVOID COSTLY EQUIPMENT BUYING BLUNDERS

HOW DOES THIS APPLY TO MY BUSINESS?

_____

_____

_____

_____

_____

Priority   1   2   3   (Circle one)

Action Date_____

Profit Champion _____

Potential Dollar Effect $_____

PAY BILLS WHEN THEY'RE DUE—
BUT NOT BEFORE

It's amazing how many business people pride themselves on paying their bills the moment they come in. Invariably, these people justify this practice as a means of enhancing their credit standing. Their logic is faulty. You don't wind up with any better credit by paying bills early, rather than when they're due. Creditors are very pleased to get your money when it is due. They certainly don't expect to be paid any sooner.

If your company is incurring finance costs by borrowing working capital from a bank, it makes absolutely no sense to provide your creditors with interest-free use of your funds. The people responsible for accounts payable at your company should be instructed to sort through all bills as they are received, and categorize them according to when they must be paid. Most bills are due either at the end of the month, by the 10th of the month, or by invoice. If the bill does not indicate when payment is due, it becomes your call to decide when it should be paid. It's a good idea to set up a "tickler file" to ensure that bills are paid at the appropriate time. Software is available to assist you with this opportunity.

If you're really compulsive about paying bills before they are due, then at least contact your suppliers and negotiate a special early payment discount.

Although the general rule is to pay bills when they are due, there are times when it is wise to delay payments beyond the due date. If you rent space for your business, your lease almost certainly obligates the landlord to provide certain services — heating, electricity, cleaning, maintenance, etc. If the landlord does not provide these services, you may well be justified in withholding payment until the services are restored. Check with your attorney before doing so.

For instance, a real estate brokerage company had a very difficult time getting its landlord to maintain building temperature to the specifications of the tenants. In addition, the roof leaked, and the grounds were not being maintained. After failing to convince the landlord to fulfill his obligations, the realtor began withholding rent payments. Over the course of six months, he withheld rent payments totalling some $350,000. Of course, this money was ultimately paid to the landlord when the repairs were made. But in the interim the realtor was able to deposit this money in an interest-bearing savings account for a number of months, and reap a tidy return. Best of all, the landlord learned a lesson, and building maintenance was never again a problem for our client.

Likewise, businesses should consider delaying payments for orders which have not been delivered, or in cases where the supplier ships the wrong products or materials. Your accounts payable department should always audit bills before paying them, checking all charges against the purchase order. **Be careful of price creep—being charged higher prices when lower prices were quoted.** Bills should never be paid without this audit, some may not even be real bills. Office supply scams—receiving toner for photocopy machines that was never ordered—have hit many businesses.

There is no requirement to pay a weekly payroll. Consider moving your payroll to a twice monthly schedule as opposed to weekly. Set the payment date when your business has the most amount of cash. You'll reduce administrative costs and improve your cash flow.

---

40. PAY BILLS WHEN THEY'RE DUE—BUT NOT BEFORE
HOW DOES THIS APPLY TO MY BUSINESS?

_____

_____

_____

_____

_____

Priority   1   2   3   (Circle one)

Action Date_____

Profit Champion _____

Potential Dollar Effect $_____

41

TAKE ADVANTAGE OF PURCHASE DISCOUNTS

Many businesses can easily earn a whopping 36 percent on their money — but most of them let that opportunity slip through their fingers! It's as simple as this: **schedule payments to suppliers to maximize purchase discounts.** In many industries it's customary for suppliers to discount for prompt payment. **If you pay the bill 20 days in advance and the supplier rewards you with a 2 percent discount, then you're effectively earning a better return on your money than you can get from any bank!** Figure it out for yourself.

If the terms provide for a 2 percent discount on all bills paid by the tenth of the month, that doesn't mean you have to pay the bill 30 days early to take advantage of the savings. A payment 20 days early will qualify you for the discount, assuming your payment is due at the end of the month. If you earn 2 percent for paying a bill 20 days before it is due, your early payment has earned you an effective yield of 36 percent a year! (A return of 2 percent for 20 days is equivalent to 3 percent over a 30-day period. Multiply that 3 percent by 12 months and you're earning 36 percent a year!)

If you're cash-starved, go to a bank and borrow money in order to pay a bill 20 days early and receive the two percent discount. If the annual cost of borrowing at the bank is, say, 10 percent, and you earn 36 percent on your money, then you're still 26 percent ahead!

If your suppliers don't offer early payment terms, have a talk with them. Most businesses will agree that securing timely payments and holding on to customers who do pay promptly are prime considerations, and there are plenty who can be coaxed into offering you a 2 percent discount for paying your bills by the tenth of the month. Indeed, some wholesalers or other distributors of goods or services would probably be more than willing to negotiate those kind of terms, if they don't offer them already.

A medical practice has for years paid laboratory fees religiously on the 15th of the month. The owner prides himself on how his bills are always paid in such a timely fashion. We suggested that the owner talk to the laboratory about a prompt payment discount. As it turned out, the lab was experiencing such severe collection problems that cash flow had become an overriding consideration. They readily agreed to offer him a 2 percent payment discount in return for his agreement to pay his bills on the tenth of the month rather than the 15th. Now he's enjoying a 36 percent return on his money. It created a win-win situation.

---

41. TAKE ADVANTAGE OF PURCHASE DISCOUNTS

HOW DOES THIS APPLY TO MY BUSINESS?

_____

_____

_____

_____

_____

Priority   1   2   3   (Circle one)

Action Date_____

Profit Champion _____

Potential Dollar Effect $_____

USE A BANK LOCK BOX

Have your customers send payments to the bank so the bank handles the entire transaction. The bank will post the transaction and communicate with you about what funds have been received. In some cases the bank may charge little for this service and in others a nominal amount. I have always felt that whatever they charge is a bargain. This is a way to eliminate the clerical costs of handling funds. You can talk to your banker about using the funds to pay down lines of credit immediately, thus saving interest costs as well.

Time is money. You can't afford to waste either one. When funds are in the bank, even overnight, interest is earned for the use of that money. When it's your money, that might as well be you.

Even if your company doesn't receive many checks through the mail, if those payments are large enough, a lock box account may be a great investment.

For example, a scientific equipment company didn't receive many checks in the mail, but those that did come in were usually for amounts in excess of $100,000 each. Standard operating procedure at this company was to post all of the checks received during the previous day, and then deposit them in the bank on the third business day.

Because of the large sums involved, the company decided to have these payments sent directly to a lock box at the bank. Now those funds are deposited immediately through the lock box, and the bank has standing orders to use that money to reduce the company's line of credit.

In this particular case, by using a lock box the company's interest costs were shaved by at least $20,000 a year! In addition to these direct savings, the business reduced the risk of loss through theft or embezzlement, and they eliminated some bookkeeping chores for their company as well.

Banks typically provide you with regular, computerized reports on the activity of your lock box, and some even make it possible for you to monitor your account by using your own computer and the Internet to tap into their records of your account.

A word of caution, however. If you arrange for a lock box account, be sure to instruct the bank to contact your office prior to depositing any check that's marked "Payment in Full." If you deposit such a check and it turns out to be just a partial payment or only the first of several installments, you may have difficulty collecting the balance.

---

42. USE A BANK LOCK BOX

HOW DOES THIS APPLY TO MY BUSINESS?

_____

_____

_____

_____

_____

Priority   1   2   3   (Circle one)

Action Date_____

Profit Champion _____

Potential Dollar Effect $_____

CONTROL SERVICE CONTRACT EXPENDITURES

Whenever you purchase equipment, the company tries to sell you a service contract. Most companies buy into it. But it's expensive and not always necessary. **Do another audit of your service contracts. Are you paying for any for which you no longer use the equipment?** Would a regular maintenance schedule for your equipment minimize the need for that service contract? Better yet, is there anyone on your staff who could repair it more effectively and quickly?

One printing company discovered they had a service contract on a piece of equipment their printing crew routinely fixed themselves. The print crew didn't even know there was a service contract in force, but the company was paying for one anyway.

If your delivery truck breaks down, will an outside mechanic be available immediately? Just try to find a shop to service your company vehicles on a Sunday, or after hours on a weekday. But a good mechanic on your own staff may be the answer. Perhaps having someone on staff, in this case, is more cost-effective than a service contract.

A key advantage to handling vehicle and equipment maintenance internally is that it affords you the opportunity to practice "preventive medicine" — not just "emergency room treatment." Any health insurance company will tell you it's far cheaper to keep patients healthy than to pay for their hospital bills once they get sick.

It certainly worked out that way for one building contractor who hired his own mechanics to service the 60 vehicles in the company's fleet. By handling these chores internally, the contractor was able to reduce vehicle maintenance costs by some $50,000 a year. As an added

bonus, because the vehicles were assured of receiving regularly scheduled service by the company's mechanics, the trucks experienced fewer
breakdowns and lasted longer.

A landscaping company had similar success when they brought in
their own mechanics. This business owned and maintained literally hundreds of lawn mowers — dozens more than they needed. The owner's
philosophy was "better safe than sorry," and he acquired all this extra
equipment in case the regular mowers needed repairs or servicing.

By hiring an in-house mechanic to perform needed repairs and
maintenance during the evening hours, this landscaper not only
reduced the cost of servicing these machines, but also eliminated the
need for maintaining surplus equipment. During the first year alone,
this lowered the company's operating costs by nearly $55,000.

---

43. CONTROL SERVICE CONTRACT EXPENDITURES

HOW DOES THIS APPLY TO MY BUSINESS?

_____

_____

_____

_____

_____

Priority   1   2   3 (Circle one)

Action Date_____

Profit Champion _____

Potential Dollar Effect $_____

PREVENTING PROBLEMS CREATES RECURRING PROFITS

Many organizations have systems in place to detect problems. Far fewer companies have processes in place for fixing them so that they never recur. **Recurring problems create recurring expenses and cut profits. Preventing problems creates recurring profits.** Where do you place the emphasis in your firm?

Can you identify the costly recurring problems your company has experienced over the past six to 12 months? Did they have to do with billing, delivering, pricing, production, inventory, or, of course, what is most important — customer satisfaction? Unless you know the types of problems, their frequency, and how they were ultimately corrected, your organization lacks a process for preventing recurring expenses.

Customer complaints are symptomatic of problems and are clear indications that you are spending needless dollars to put out fires that keep smoldering and eventually reignite.

Consider establishing a "PROFIT Report" or Prevention Report On Fixing It Today.

The purpose of this report is to identify problems and fix them permanently. It should not be used to assign blame to individuals. Its purpose is to identify recurring problems and make sure that they never recur. It gives all employees the opportunity to participate in solving problems instead of complaining about them. Once the cause of a problem is identified, a plan to prevent it can be established and tested; and if viable, changes put into place to prevent any recurrence. Future fire fighting expenses will be eliminated or certainly minimized. Profits rise because recurring problems are eliminated or diminished.

"PROFIT REPORT"
PREVENTION REPORT ON FIXING IT TODAY

Name of Company_____

Department Discovering the Problem _____

Customer Complaints   **Non-Customer Complaints**
(Please Describe)   (Please Describe)

_____   _____

_____   _____

_____   _____

Probable Cause
(Please furnish any information you might have that supports the above
complaint/problem.)

_____

_____

_____

_____

**In my opinion, the most qualified person to prevent this problem from
recurring is:**
Name_____

**A copy of this report was forwarded to our "Profit Coordinator",
(This person enters this form's information into a database and
determines the Profit Champion who will be responsible for fixing it.)**

Future Profits Being Initiated by _____
                                        (Your name)

Date: _____   **Time:** _____

Profit Opportunity No. _____

44. PREVENTING PROBLEMS CREATES RECURRING PROFITS

HOW DOES THIS APPLY TO MY BUSINESS?

_____

_____

_____

_____

_____

Priority   1   2   3   (Circle one)

Action Date_____

Profit Champion _____

Potential Dollar Effect $_____

BASE YOUR PRICES ON PROFIT GOALS, NOT SALES EGOS

Profits feed families, sales feed egos. Base your pricing structure on the perceived value of your product or service — not just on a desire to increase sales.

Consider this example. With sales shrinking, a business decided to discount prices and increase volume. Profit margins declined, sales increased and profits eroded. Instead of attracting new customers, their once loyal customer base began buying more deeply discounted competitors' products. The message the company inadvertently sent to their customers was that their product was just another commodity, that its value along with its price had been reduced. When your customers feel they are buying just a commodity, not a service, they begin shopping for the cheapest price. Price-cutting turns unique products and services into ordinary commodities.

Commodity businesses that discount have unwittingly encouraged cutthroat competition — and reduced their profit margin! The automotive industry has trained customers to wait for price rebates. Airlines have persuaded customers to wait for super-saver specials. The moving and storage industry offers discounted prices even though they are moving families' lifetime and lifelong possessions with high economic and sentimental values.

Loyalty is created because customers truly believe your products and services are better — not cheaper. As we've discussed, discounting can erode your customers' confidence in your products and services. Few people, if any, buy an expensive watch solely because it keeps good time. In fact, when customers buy a watch, few if any ask if it keeps good time. Accurate time-keeping is a given when a customer buys a watch. Customers buy expensive watches because of their brand and the status that goes along with wearing their purchase.

Less than a third of all consumers think of price as a major criteria when buying products, according to a study conducted by the Copernicus consulting firm. In other words, approximately 66 percent of the customers don't consider price at all when selecting a product. The study reports that approximately 80 percent don't even remember exactly how much they paid for a product acquired just one week ago.

When price is considered, several factors influence customers' buying decisions. These factors are their disposable income and how badly they want the product. Some consumers emotionally want a European car and the make they perceive will meet their objectives. These same customers might buy paper towels and napkins based on price. Thus every product has customers that buy because of its brand, perceived quality and uniqueness, and others who buy because of price exclusively. Customers who buy because of the brand quality and uniqueness outnumber customers who buy because of price two to one in every product category. Businesses that focus on uniqueness, quality and brand can charge higher prices than their discounting competitors.

Let's look at gasoline. This is certainly a commodity. Aren't you willing to pay higher prices for gas if you can get a fresh cup of coffee in the morning on the way to work, prompt service work, and clean rest rooms?

With the technological marvels of the Internet and TV shopping channels, competitively priced shopping is easier than ever before for consumers. It is essential to determine what is unique about your products and services, and communicate that to your customers in a variety of ways. When working with clients we often ask staff what is unique about what your company sells? The number one response we get is "I don't know." If employees don't know, there is no way the customer will know and there is no way to value price, goods or services.

Customers need a reason to buy. Either what they are buying is perceived to be unique or else the cheapest price will be the determining factor.

Our message is clear — know what you are selling and how it is different from what your competitors are selling. Communicate the uniqueness of your products and services to your customers. Base your price on its perceived value and uniqueness. Discounting alerts customers that your products and services are no different than others in the marketplace.

45. BASE YOUR PRICES ON PROFIT GOALS, NOT SALES EGOS

HOW DOES THIS APPLY TO MY BUSINESS?

_____

_____

_____

_____

_____

Priority   1   2   3 (Circle one)

Action Date_____

Profit Champion _____

Potential Dollar Effect $_____

MAKE EVERY EMPLOYEE A PROFIT ENHANCEMENT OFFICER (PEO)

Nearly every person who works in a business has ideas, but most businesses have no forum for communicating those ideas. How much effort is spent trying to encourage ideas? For years a major U.S. car manufacturer had problems with the quality of their paint. They hired expensive consultants. No one could help. One day a supervisor went down and asked people in the paint shop if they had ideas to improve the quality of paint on the vehicles. One bright line worker responded to this question with, "Yes, I thought you'd never ask." She had the solution and was glad to share it.

Most organizations have a CEO, a CFO, and even a COO. But how many have "PEOs"? A PEO is a Profit Enhancement Officer, charged with developing and implementing good, new profit ideas. Who should be this PEO? Everyone in your organization.

When you make everyone into a PEO, you are delegating the responsibility for improving the bottom line to all your employees. Having this title transforms them into profit leaders for the future and emphasizes the impact they as individuals have on the bottom line of your company. You'll find employees becoming excited by, and accepting the challenge of, initiating more profit-generating ideas for their own department — and for the organization as a whole.

Then you need to provide a way for all your PEOs to submit their ideas and make them part of your overall Profit Plan, as explained in Chapter 4. These sessions must be nonthreatening forums where every idea is welcomed, enhanced, and turned into a manageable profit project that fits into the goals of your company.

46. MAKE EVERY EMPLOYEE A PROFIT ENHANCEMENT OFFICER (PEO)

HOW DOES THIS APPLY TO MY BUSINESS?

_____

_____

_____

_____

_____

Priority   1   2   3   (Circle one)

Action Date_____

Profit Champion _____

Potential Dollar Effect $_____

CHAPTER 9:
ORGANIZATIONAL
STRUCTURE

IDENTIFY PROFIT CENTERS, KEEP THE WINNERS AND LOSE THE LOSERS

Every business wants to increase sales, but some organizations literally will struggle indefinitely because only more profitable sales generate profits...not more sales.

You know the old joke about the shopkeeper who sold everything in the store below his cost. "How can you stay in business?" someone asked. "Aren't you losing money on every sale?"

"Sure I am," he replied, "but I'll make it up in volume!"

Of course, you never "make it up in volume." The more goods or services you sell at a loss, the bigger your losses. A lot of businesses actually do operate this way unintentionally, because they don't bother to **identify key profit centers and eliminate marginal products or services.**

Unlike our overly generous shopkeeper, they may not sell everything at a loss. But even one or two poor pricing decisions can drain the profitability of an otherwise successful enterprise.

During good economic times when sales are booming, these problems tend to go unnoticed. But when business becomes more difficult and earnings suffer, weeding out unprofitable goods or services can be one of the keys to a resurgence of success.

When Quaker Oats divested itself of the Snapple beverage company, sales declined by about 1.5 billion dollars, but profits rose. You probably remember when Sears and Roebuck got rid of its 110 catalog stores and tripled their net income. AT&T was losing approximately $300 million a year on 10,000 of its 70,000 customers who make fewer than $3.00 in calls a month. To prevent this, AT&T implemented a minimum monthly charge. If one of these customers didn't want to pay it, fine, they could go to another provider; but AT&T wasn't losing money on them any longer.

A private label food company put this strategy to work. Their products are superior to their competition and their customer service has a high "bragability" index. But when we conducted an analysis of his operations, which included food costs in relationship to sales, we found that his prices were off the mark.

Some of the selections were priced at or below his labor and cost of ingredients. Other private label foods featured were so complicated and time-consuming to prepare that profits were wiped out by excess labor costs. Eighty percent of their sales came from 20 percent of their products. The labor costs to produce the remaining 20 percent of their sales was so high that they were losing money on those food products.

When the numbers were analyzed, the unprofitable items were exposed and either eliminated or increased in price. Our client now has profitable sales on all of his products, thus ensuring his company a fair return no matter what food products his customers choose.

In another case, when a wholesale distributor ran a detailed gross profit analysis of his operations, he discovered that some of the company's biggest ticket items yielded absolutely zero profits to the firm. After combing through stacks of customer invoices and matching them with the cost of goods sold, we determined that the goods had been priced properly and that the wholesale distributor should have been realizing a substantial gross profit on their sale. Where did those profits go? He concluded that the profit drain must be occurring as a result of pilferage. The wholesaler implemented adequate security measures and, sure enough, profits bounced back.

The point is: Unless you undertake a gross profit analysis measuring the contribution from every major component of your product line, you may not even be aware that you have a problem. Your accounting system must provide the information necessary to make prudent pricing decisions in relationship to your actual costs or else profit leaks will continue unnoticed forever.

One way to analyze your product lines is to apply the Pareto Principle, as we did with the private label food company described previously. Pareto's idea is most often referred to as the "80-20 rule," meaning that 20 percent of the known variables will produce 80 percent of the results. This simple but revealing fact is relevant to important executive decisions made daily. Analyzing a cause-effect situation makes it possible to isolate those key factors, either positive or negative, for corrective action. Pareto's principle can be used where profit managers seek to improve an operation or performance area such as costs, sales, customer satisfaction, quality control, accident reduction, employee productivity, and so on. Common examples of the Pareto Principle are the following:

- 80 percent of profits, your sales and gross margins come from 20 percent of your products or customers. To improve profitability, focus efforts on 20 percent of your products and customers.

- 80% of the absenteeism, morale problems and rework are the result of 20 percent of the employees. Focus your efforts on eliminating the 20 percent and rewarding the 80 percent for making positive improvements.

- 80 percent of your sales come from 20 percent of your salespeople. Yet you may be paying everyone the same, and the 80 percent of the low producer salespeople still incur the same overhead costs. Pay the 20 percent go-getter salespeople greater compensation to reward them and focus on reducing the costs associated with the other 80 percent.

APPLY THESE FIVE SIMPLE STEPS TO MANAGEMENT ISSUES THAT HAVE A CLEAR CAUSE AND EFFECT.

1. Develop benchmarks, a record or list of factors, units, or components involved in the matter being investigated.

2. Arrange the items in order of importance relative to the opportunity or problem. Largest first, smallest last.

3. Identify the vital few (the 20%).

4. Identify the trivial many (the 80%).

5. Act on findings. In most cases, your remedy will focus on the vital few — in others, on the many.

---

47. IDENTIFY PROFIT CENTERS, KEEP THE WINNERS AND LOSE THE LOSERS

HOW DOES THIS APPLY TO MY BUSINESS?

_____

_____

_____

_____

_____

Priority   1   2   3   (Circle one)

Action Date_____

Profit Champion_____

Potential Dollar Effect $_____

BE A HANDS-ON MANAGER

Over the years, McDonald's has been able to sell hundreds of billions of hamburgers. One of the reasons for the chain's success: McDonald's is a franchise operation and for the most part the owner of each franchised restaurant is on the premises running the business. That's not to say that every business requires the owner at the helm all the time. But when the company's success is at stake, **the owner had better be on board—not just on call.**

The litmus test is really, "Who is accountable?" Businesses should aim to eliminate work, not people. **There is nothing more unprofitable than doing unnecessary work more efficiently.** As a matter of fact, clients tell us it takes a long time in the business world to understand what they are doing and why. The job of managers is to help their employees understand their role, how it affects the bottom line, and to make them feel it is vital to the success of the company.

The difference between management and leadership is that managers focus on today and yesterday, while leaders focus on tomorrow.

Take the case of the automobile dealer with two locations. She set all the rules for that location using the first location as a standard. She seldom set foot in the second, which was not doing anywhere near as well as the first. She decided that she must spend some time at the "problem" location to learn what had to be done to improve profitability.

It didn't take long for her to identify the causes for the dealership's distress. The place was dirty. The cleaning crew claimed they didn't have money for new cleaning supplies and had been told that the owner wouldn't pay for those supplies. The showroom was cold and uninviting. There weren't even any holiday decorations during the vital Christmas shopping season; the staff had been told that the owner wouldn't pay for it. She even discovered that the showroom was routinely being closed an hour or two early every day. Obviously morale was low and the business suffered. She fired the manager and took charge of the operation personally. Within a month, sales bounded back by one-third, and within three months the dealership was operating in the black again.

Granted, this is a dramatic example. But every owner or manager can find some way to become more involved in the business. Leadership will make a real difference.

Hyatt Hotels have an "In Touch Program," where executive personnel are required to work at performing employee tasks at their various hotels, from cleaning to managing the front desk. Hyatt wants all of their managers to experience what the customer does—firsthand—so they will understand the details and complexity of the work their employees do and be able to formulate new profit strategies based on their experiences "in the trenches."

Become more of a motivational force for your organization! Start attending staff meetings that you ordinarily pass up. Write an article for your company's internal newsletter — or start an employee newsletter if you don't have one. Go on customer calls with your sales reps. Spend some time on the assembly line, or the loading dock, or the sales floor. Let your people know that you're willing to roll up your sleeves and pitch in when the pinch is on.

THE FIVE MOST IMPORTANT THINGS EVERY EFFECTIVE MANAGER SHOULD SAY, WHEN APPROPRIATE, ARE THE FOLLOWING:

"I WAS WRONG, PLEASE FORGIVE ME."
"YOU DID A GREAT JOB."
"WHAT ARE YOUR THOUGHTS?"
"MAY I HELP?" AND
"THANK YOU."

---

48. BE A HANDS-ON MANAGER

HOW DOES THIS APPLY TO MY BUSINESS?

_____

_____

_____

_____

_____

Priority   1   2   3   (Circle one)

Action Date_____

Profit Champion _____

Potential Dollar Effect $_____

DETERMINE WHETHER MANAGERS ARE MANAGING TOO LITTLE OR TOO MUCH

How many activities and/or people should managers have under their control? There is plenty of case history material around depicting managers operating in happy productivity with well-rounded staffs, others driven to exhaustion or to the limit of their competence by overloading, and still others whose command activities were insufficient to fill their time productively.

Different experts have different theories. The maximum number that should be used is never more than ten people, most experts agree. No manager should have the responsibility for more than six separate activities. The more specialized and complex the activities, the shorter the ideal span of control. The more uniform and simple the activities, the greater the span can be. Sometimes the span is defined by the number of people rather than by the activities. For example, it is not unusual for a department head to supervise 30 employees, provided they are engaged only in a few simple, related activities. A middle manager might direct six departments through supervision of their leaders.

Span of control is a factor in every manager's job. Often it is a combination of directing a personal staff and one or more subordinate managers. As a manager, having the right mix will make your "hands-on" managerial goal easier.

Sufficient responsibility can be as destructive as too much. Managers whose span of control is unnecessarily short may resort to make-work to keep busy, causing eventual damage to their motivation system, and wasting the benefits that would be possible if they were challenged and exercising their skills. Those who keep after their bosses for extended assignments may be on to a good thing, if they don't overdo it. Assess the span of each manager. List the responsibilities, people and departments reporting to each, and other assignments. For example:

Managers	Assignments	Subordinates
Office manager	Monthly sales reports	One assistant
Head of mailroom	Next quarter's outlook	One secretary
Head of printing	Promotional programs	Two general
Head of promotion	Field-staff building and monitoring	Clerical people

Review each manager's list and assess the degree of appropriateness of each of the three headings. Is there anything that should be added or subtracted under each? Span of control is usually flexible. Watch for opportunities to make worthwhile adjustments reflecting changes in the needs of the organization. Here are some suggested immediate profit action ideas:

- **Employees do properly what we inspect — not what we expect. Begin inspecting all processes, procedures, sales reports, staffing and other areas where profits can be hidden.**

- **Go into the field, shop, store, back office, front desk, kitchen, factory, warehouse and accounting department and find out how it is done if you want to get real answers.**

- **Span of control is a problem every manager encounters. Determine whether your managers are managing too much or too little.**

- **Investigate whether managers are delegating responsibilities and tasks, and then failing to hold their people responsible for timely, accurate, quality jobs.**

- **Encourage, support, assist, train and review — always trying to improve in every area.**

- **Make a list of every project you delegate but never hear another word about nor see any results from. Then follow up.**

- **Make sure your managers are trained, as well as their support groups, on how to effectively implement business ideas and strategies.**

49. DETERMINE WHETHER MANAGERS ARE MANAGING TOO LITTLE OR TOO MUCH

HOW DOES THIS APPLY TO MY BUSINESS?

_____

_____

_____

_____

_____

Priority   1   2   3   (Circle one)

Action Date_____

Profit Champion _____

Potential Dollar Effect $_____ x

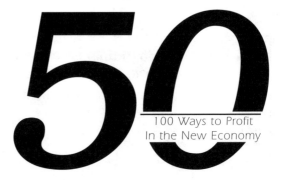

100 Ways to Profit
In the New Economy

MAKE EVERYONE IN YOUR BUSINESS RESPONSIBLE FOR PROFIT

Profit is really a state of mind. In fact, it's the fuel that powers your business.

The idea that the profitability of your organization depends solely on your organization's CEO is the traditional mindset and it, along with other ideas, has become antiquated. Profit should be the responsibility of the entire management team, properly called a "profit team." Without profits your business opportunities are restricted. Most other business activities can be designed to achieve that goal. Should a company's goal be to sell 100 widgets? No. The goal is to sell enough properly priced widgets to make a profit!

Business and financial goals are too often nondescript and arbitrary. Financial goals should be measurable, manageable, specific and understood by the management-profit team in order to relate them to the bottom line.

CEOs and managers alike share the fallacy that profitability belongs only in the hands of the CEO, and others should perform only the tasks in their job description. Wrong again. Every person on your management-profit team needs to be responsible and directly accountable for the profitability of the firm. So what if a salesperson meets his or her goal of selling $1,000 worth of appliances if their cost was $1,200? The salesperson who sold $500 worth of appliances with a $400 cost is the one who has hit the mark — increasing the organization's profits. The question to be asked in assessing the success of a sales manager is not, "How much did your salespeople sell?" but "How much profit did they make for this business?"

50. Make Everyone in Your Business Responsible for Profit.

Start working on changing your state of mind to reflect this profit philosophy. Then begin to filter that attitude down. Make sure your management-profit team accepts responsibility for contributing additional profitability to your company. Of course, attitudes and thought processes cannot be transformed overnight or by mandate. The management-profit team must be completely aware of the role they play in improving the organization's bottom line and should understand that the profit commitment must be developed. In this environment it becomes evident that "profits" are a state of mind.

Profit is not an unspeakable word — it is the reason that your organization exists. Profits pay salaries, help you expand and make going to work fun. Obvious? Not always. There is an interrelationship between your organization's profits and your managers' success. The next step is to teach your management team to redirect their thinking so that profits are a state of mind. All other tasks support the profit goal.

The CEO of a large office cleaning company we worked with expressed his enormous relief after sharing the organization's "profit picture" with his managers. No longer did he carry this responsibility alone. When his management-profit team realized their goal was profits, not cleaning offices, they contributed many valuable ideas. To date, they have added thousands of dollars to the bottom line. In fact, this company identified opportunities to boost their earnings by $1.6 million with the help of some ideas you're reading about today.

You can help your managers and your staff generate greater profitability by giving them this quiz. You will discover whether your firm has the all-important profit mentality.

PROFIT MENTALITY QUIZ

	Yes	No
1. Do we have a company-wide plan for profits?	❑	❑
2. Are our managers held accountable for various tasks that contribute to profitability?	❑	❑
3. Do we have an inventory of untapped ideas that will add to the bottom line?	❑	❑
4. Is our company sales-motivated rather than profit-driven?	❑	❑
5. Does our company have a policy regarding the types of customers it will serve?	❑	❑
6. Does our business take its long-term profit objectives into account in its hiring process?	❑	❑
7. Has our organization determined how the demand for our products or services may change based on the environment, competition, and so forth?	❑	❑
8. Does our business keep tabs on its competition?	❑	❑

	Yes	No
9. Does our organization assess customer/client product and service satisfaction levels?	❑	❑
10. Does our organization methodically and periodically reevaluate its strengths, weaknesses, opportunities, and threats?	❑	❑
11. Does our business survey our management team about their business goals and objectives?	❑	❑
12. Does our firm have formal profit goals and objectives?	❑	❑
13. Does our management discuss profit objectives regularly?	❑	❑
14. Have our profit goals and objectives been communicated to appropriate staff?	❑	❑
15. Is there a written profit plan in place to achieve our organization's profit objectives?	❑	❑
16. Does our business periodically evaluate its profit plan accomplishments and update it?	❑	❑
17. Is there a profit culture in our organization?	❑	❑
18. Is there a commitment by our management team for improved financial performance?	❑	❑
19. Does every manager know what additional profits would be used for?	❑	❑
20. Do our employees realize that profits are their responsibility?	❑	❑
21. Are employees and managers rewarded for meeting profit objectives?	❑	❑

Be proud of the "YES's." If you have any "NO's," you have room for improvement to your bottom line.

---

50. MAKE EVERYONE IN YOUR BUSINESS RESPONSIBLE FOR PROFIT.

HOW DOES THIS APPLY TO MY BUSINESS?

_____

_____

_____

_____

_____

Priority   1   2   3   (Circle one)

Action Date_____

Profit Champion _____

Potential Dollar Effect $_____

ESTABLISH EXPENSE AUTHORIZATION RESPONSIBILITIES

How many times have you paid for something that you know nothing about. Who ordered it, why was it so expensive and was it really necessary? The point is that you need a purchasing system. Only management with purchasing authority should be approving orders of supplies, products, goods, and so on. Make sure there is a purchasing system in place that fixes accountability. Tremendous savings will occur when this system is put in place.

Just what kinds of policies and procedures should you institute within your company? The following are several simple examples of the types of procedures and policies that can be implemented:

• **Have each department head identify all expenditure categories approved by his or her department. Then place a dollar limit on each type of expenditure and designate who can approve such expenditures up to that limit. Identify who is required to approve expenditures on such items over that limit. For example, supplies up to $2,000 may be able to be approved by one person. Up to $20,000 by another, and up to $100,000 by the vice president. The accounts payable department should have a company-wide list covering such limits to be used in approving invoices for payments.**

• **Establish an expense approval policy which covers the bulk of al expenditures. Then, when statements come into the accounts payable department, a clerk simply checks the supporting invoice versus the policy. Only when deviating from policy does there need be approval by the appropriate executive. This avoids the frequent costly practice of having all expenses going to a person's superior for approval, often on a subjective basis, prior to payment. This is usually a waste** of the superior's valuable time, as seldom do supervisors challenge expenses of subordinates. Instead, they usually find all reasons in the world why exceptions will be made for "their" people.

• Most importantly, consider hiring a purchasing manager. There are two ways to increase margin: increase prices and/or buy for less. Most employees are not trained to be effective purchasing agents. Certified Purchasing Managers (CPMs) are. One such CPM arranged for their employer, an automobile manufacturer, to back-charge the provider of their automotive paint a negotiated amount per minute when there were production delays caused by problems with that paint. Now this automobile manufacturer charges the paint company for these delays! It took a well-trained CPM to negotiate this.

Take a close look at your company's purchasing procedures. Are you working from a purchase order system? Can just anybody place orders? Or must they be approved in a systematic manner before supplies are requisitioned?

A commercial glass installer learned this lesson the hard way. The company had 15 different locations, and each office was individually responsible for ordering pens, pencils, paper and other office supplies. Every month they were placing orders for six to seven thousand different supply items, all various grades and prices, and the waste was enormous. The attitude at the branch office was, "If I need something, I'll just pick it out of the catalog, regardless of price or quality or quantity."

Top management finally sat down with the firm's major suppliers and together they hammered out standard supply order forms that offer one choice for each supply category. Suddenly, expenditures dropped 15 percent.

---

51. ESTABLISH EXPENSE AUTHORIZATION RESPONSIBILITIES

HOW DOES THIS APPLY TO MY BUSINESS?

_____

_____

_____

_____

_____

Priority   1   2   3   (Circle one)

Action Date_____

Profit Champion _____

Potential Dollar Effect $_____

52

DEVELOP FINANCIAL "FLASH REPORTS"

Given a little advance warning, the captain of the Titanic could have avoided the iceberg. By the same token, many businesses will thrive if management obtains early warning signals of financial opportunities. You need to develop an early warning system within your organization that will alert you of opportunities and problems in time to make adequate adjustments and capitalize on them.

Too many business owners and managers make course corrections only monthly—when the financial results are reported. But waiting until the end of the month to identify opportunities or problems within your company is like checking for icebergs once every few days.

We are firm believers in developing periodic "flash reports": up-to-the-minute snapshots of key financial information about your company to supplement the regular financial statements. The information in this report should reflect only 5-6 financial variables in your particular business— items such as payroll, billings, collections, work backlog, dollars bid on new work, and so forth.

There's no reason why a report like that can't be prepared regularly; for instance weekly or perhaps daily flash reports might prove most worthwhile.

Armed with this early warning system, financial results, either good or bad, will rarely come as a surprise to management. More importantly, if opportunities or problems arise in sales, collections, production, payroll costs and other areas, they can be attacked on a much more aggressive and timely basis.

Although most every business should develop and use flash reports, the data covered by these analyses must be tailored to your firm's specific operations. A flash report that would be valuable to a textile manufacturer would cover different items than one designed for an electrical contractor.

A law firm, for example, might develop a monthly flash report for the managing partner showing selected financial data for the period, including billings, collections, salaries, the number of new files opened, and billable hours. After a year or more of assembling these regular reports, the firm's comptroller will be able to provide the partners with historical trends by period and by year.

A word of caution: It's tempting to go overboard and compute the flash report's vital statistics periodically from various financial data. If a flash report contains too much information, the key indicators of your company's health will get lost in the clutter.

As a rule of thumb, just five or six key financial indicators will enable you to check the pulse of your business regularly and make timely adjustments accordingly.

52. DEVELOP FINANCIAL "FLASH REPORTS"

HOW DOES THIS APPLY TO MY BUSINESS?

_____

_____

_____

_____

_____

Priority   1   2   3   (Circle one)

Action Date_____

Profit Champion _____

Potential Dollar Effect $_____

SYSTEMATICALLY INCREASE PROFITS IN FIVE EASY STEPS

When analyzing your company's current financial position, ask yourself two questions: Are you comfortable with the status quo? Are you open to change? If you are not satisfied with your company's financial performance and are willing to modify existing business practices, the following steps will serve as a plan of action.

Step 1: Objectively look at your untapped profit opportunities. To improve the profit-generating capability of your company, you need to look at its fiscal parts:

Sales & Marketing
Employees
Organizational Structure
Operations, and
Financial Matters

If your firm is performing at peak efficiency, how might these components work? An aggressive marketing department stimulates product demand from new and existing customers, and your sales staff converts the leads to good margin sales. Conscientious, long-term employees perform their duties efficiently and accurately. The products and services provided by your firm reach your customers on time and exceed their expectations. Payments are promptly received, and vendors are paid within terms. Costs are held in line with your budgets, and a nice profit is left over. Doesn't this scenario look good? It should be the basis for identifying opportunities which, when implemented, help your company reach its full profit potential.

You will find it difficult to identify all of the variances from this model of perfection because you have only one set of eyes that views the same scenes day after day, in the same business and industry you have been part of for so many years. Your company's management-profit team are the additional eyes that will help you identify proactive profit initiatives.

Step 2: Expand responsibility for profit to your management-profit team. Go to the lowest level employee in your company, and present this scenario and question: Our firm is having a great year, where do you think the money is going? In too many cases, that individual will say: "It's going into the owner's pockets." Unfortunately, this misguided view of corporate profits is also sometimes shared by people at higher levels of the company as well. Making profits is too big a job to be left to the firm's top echelon. People have to know what's in it for them. This is a key ingredient in enlisting their involvement in your profit quest.

Step 3: Eliminate departmentalism. There was a car dealer who was not having a great year. Sales were strong, but overall profits were weak. Each department manager was evaluated as to their department's profitability, and on paper they were performing well and were compensated accordingly. When asked, "How are things going?" They universally replied, "We're having the best year we've had in years."

These managers were focused on buttering their department's own bread and not the overall corporation's performance. This was exemplified by the used car manager who had his inventory serviced in a garage down the street with a lower hourly rate than the dealership's own service department.

This type of behavior is called "departmentalism" and it is a cancer that can destroy your business. "My department is doing great," is meaningless if the company as a whole is not on strong financial footing. It is your obligation to continually send the correct signals to your management-profit team and employees. Individuals and departmental performance need to be rewarded, but not independent of overall corporate profits.

Step 4: Erase the fear of retribution. You want your management team to become a "profit team" and help you identify profit ideas. For this to work, there must be no sacred cows permitted to interfere with the process. Every idea has to be prefaced with "for the good of the company." If someone has an idea that would be great for the company, but might be counter to the opinion of a member of top management, the environment has to be safe enough for that individual to take the risk of raising a difficult issue. Your company will stagnate if important and unpopular statements are left unsaid. You won't be able to gain the benefit of enlisting additional sets of eyes to help you identify profit opportunities if those eyes are always protected by dark glasses.

Step 5: Implement your profit ideas. The world is full of great ideas that never went anywhere because they were difficult to expedite. The normal reasons for the failure to implement ideas are: (a) no one is responsible; (b) it's not clear when it is due; (c) no means of measuring progress exists; and (d) priority is absent.

Successful financial strategy implementation requires a process. Someone has to accept the project assignment; completion must be expected by a specific date; progress must be measured and necessary resources made available. Most important, there must be a system of accountability. If people are assigned projects which are to be completed on the 15th and 30th of the month, it is not unusual for the work to be done on the 14th and the 29th. If no one is responsible for monitoring the progress, it is likely these deadlines will be missed. Without accountability, projects will keep slipping until everyone forgets them. Someone on your management-profit team must be appointed "Profit Activities Leader" or PAL, empowered by the CEO to ensure that the ideas that have been developed by the profit team (rather than a management team) are carried out. With the unequivocal backing of the agreed upon profit initiatives by your CEO in conjunction with recognized rewards for results or consequences for lack thereof, your implementation process is destined to succeed.

Companies that follow these five systematic steps will realize a noticeable improvement in their bottom line. Empower your profit team because you don't have all the answers. Demonstrate that there is something in it for everyone when profits reach their potential. Allow issues to come out on the table and institutionalize an implementation process to turn them into financial results. These are the steps behind our Profit Enhancement Process (PEP). It has brought millions of dollars to the bottom lines of our clients. Now you try it.

53. SYSTEMATICALLY INCREASE PROFITS IN FIVE EASY STEPS

HOW DOES THIS APPLY TO MY BUSINESS?

_____

_____

_____

_____

_____

Priority   1   2   3   (Circle one)

Action Date_____

Profit Champion _____

Potential Dollar Effect $_____

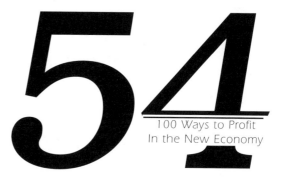

DRAW UP CONTINGENCY PLANS

Make the assumption that you are not going to receive any cash for the next 60 to 90 days. How is your company going to survive? Come up with a contingency plan. What happens if your bank is not willing to lend you money or renew your line of credit? Get your profit managers involved in this brainstorming session.

Marriott had a good contingency plan years ago. They went to Coca-Cola and asked to borrow $50 million to $100 million at below-market rates. Coca-Cola said no. Then they went to Pepsi-Cola, and they said yes. Marriott has served Pepsi ever since the loan was given.

Other companies have not been so prepared. Intel lost money as well as customer goodwill when it was revealed that their computer chips couldn't handle the most complex engineering computations. One of the most well-attended and well-bet horse races, the Triple Crown's Preakness, couldn't accept bets because the electricity went off and there was no back-up generator. FTD's computer crashed several days before Mother's Day. The United Parcel Service strike lost millions for the company and their customers, but the U.S. Post Office was quick enough to pick up some much-needed business that has remained with them long after the strike ended.

A client in the construction business had a contingency plan. When they had excess labor, they chose to create good will for the company. This business volunteered its services to remodel a camp for needy kids. The company got much publicity because it contributed its staff, who had little to do, and turned this into a community service project. The company landed some new and lucrative construction contracts from the public relations that came from this philanthropic endeavor. The kids got their remodeled camp, too!

SOME QUESTIONS TO CONSIDER WHEN DEVELOPING YOUR CONTINGENCY PLAN:

What if customers' buying habits change?

What if sales are flat? Decline by 20 percent? By 30 percent?

What if sales are accelerating? Suppose they increased by 20-30 percent?

What if accounts receivable collections slow by five days? Ten days? Twenty days?

What if lenders increase rates by one percent? Two percent? Three percent?

What if our biggest customer goes "belly up?"

What if our competitors actively go after our accounts?

Contingency planning is also an excellent way to test how financially prudent each part of your organization really is. Once a year, or every other year, ask each department head for their action plan should any of the previously discussed issues occur. Ask for their action programs that will improve the corporate results should either scenario occur.

One positive by-product of this exercise is that the managers typically realize there are areas in their departments that can be improved. Usually, they proceed to improve their departments immediately, rather than wait for "what ifs" to occur.

---

54. DRAW UP CONTINGENCY PLANS
HOW DOES THIS APPLY TO MY BUSINESS?

_____

_____

_____

_____

_____

Priority   1   2   3   (Circle one)

Action Date_____

Profit Champion _____

Potential Dollar Effect $_____

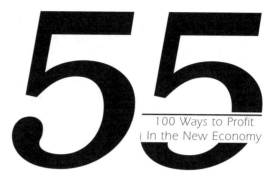

OUTSOURCING PROVIDES SIGNIFICANT BENEFITS

When in doubt — outsource wherever work can be done better, faster or cheaper. Anyone who has ever had to make a payroll knows that the wages paid to regular "W-2" employees are just part of a business's total labor costs. Payroll taxes plus the cost of health insurance, paid holidays and vacations, and other "fringe benefits" average out to an additional 20 to 40 percent at most companies.

Cost is the most obvious attraction because managers are always looking for ways to cut costs and because "support" people — those who indirectly make your product or provide your service — now account for about 40 percent of the budget, compared to 10 percent to 15 percent immediately after World War II. In contrast to regular, salaried employees, there are no fringe benefit costs or payroll taxes paid for services provided by subcontracting companies. Even if you have to lay out 10 percent or 20 percent more to secure services, you may be dollars ahead in the final analysis. Aside from the obvious payroll and payroll benefits savings, there may be other advantages to outsourcing for your business as well.

Some of those cost figures also explain why you get higher quality from an outsource vendor. Outsourced personnel often get better benefits than you can provide, indicating that they may have a level of personnel that you will not attract. Also, an outsource vendor may be able to offer employees a career track you cannot. Someone who starts in your mailroom may someday become a supervisor. Many outsourcing companies have senior management as high as the vice president who started as an entry-level employee. This opportunity attracts talented people, and you benefit, whether they're entry-level or management.

A wholesaler of lawn and garden supplies owned an extensive fleet of delivery trucks and employed a number of drivers for those vehicles. Unfortunately, the business had a terrible time attracting employees with decent driving records. The company's drivers were constantly being cited for traffic violations, and there were accidents almost every week. As a result, our client's motor vehicle insurance rates went through the roof! Literally all of the wholesaler's profit was being soaked up by sky-high insurance premiums! If this had continued, they would have been out of business in six months.

Fortunately, the CEO recognized the problem and replaced his accident-prone drivers by subcontracting with an outside delivery service company. Our client was able to get a terrific deal on this because the delivery service did not have to supply vehicles (they used our client's vehicles) just the drivers to operate them.

Best of all, the wholesaler was able to eliminate his insurance premiums altogether, because his fleet was covered under the delivery service's policy. Since the subcontractor's drivers had first-rate driving records, the wholesaler's insurance costs dropped back to earth. In the end, the shift to independent contractors saved this company over $300,000 a year.

You can also expect more management attention from an outsource company than from internal personnel. As management guru Peter Drucker stated in a *Wall Street Journal* article in 1989, "Outside contractors see your peripheral functions —whether they're mail, data entry, clerical or whatever — as their central business. They know that if they don't provide quality service at a reasonable price, you'll hire someone else."

So what can be outsourced? The obvious answer is everything that isn't central to your business.

---

55. OUTSOURCING PROVIDES SIGNIFICANT BENEFITS
HOW DOES THIS APPLY TO MY BUSINESS?

_____

_____

_____

_____

_____

Priority   1   2   3   (Circle one)

Action Date_____

Profit Champion _____

Potential Dollar Effect $_____

FORM YOUR OWN TEAM OF PROFIT ADVISORS

Nobody has all the answers. As it grows, your company's future may very well depend on the quality of advice you receive from others. Consider these people your very own team of profit advisors.

To be sure, courses in business management and books like this one can help you chart a course that can keep your company moving forward. **But they're no substitute for input from knowledgeable people familiar with your organization's strengths and weaknesses.**

Assemble a small group of trusted profit advisors, such as your attorney, CPA, consultant, banker, and insurance agent, for a meeting with your top management perhaps once every three months. Set a clear profit-generating agenda for the meeting. Talk with them about sales, profitability, operating costs, and minimizing risks that your company faces. You'll be astonished at the ideas that will come out of these kinds of meetings.

Too many people in business tend to view their outside resources as one-dimensional. The lawyer is somebody to talk to only when there is a contract to draft or litigation to discuss. The accountant is just an historical record keeper who prepares financial statements and tax returns. A banker is someone you see for financing. And so on.

If this is how you view these resources, you're missing the boat. As profit advisors ourselves, we can tell you that the professional services you pay for should not cost your business a red cent! Every penny that you pay to professionals should come back to you, by their adding value to your business...much more in value than their fees. Similarly, your

attorney, your accountant, your insurance agent, your advertising agency—these can and should be profit centers for your firm. There's no reason to look at these services as overhead.

It's up to you to make clear what you expect of them to help your company increase sales, control costs, expand markets, or improve your company's value in some other way. If they can't help you in this respect, rethink your relationship with them.

56. Form Your Own Team of Profit Advisors

HOW DOES THIS APPLY TO MY BUSINESS?

____

____

____

____

____

Priority 1 2 3 (Circle one)

Action Date______________

Profit Champion __________________________

Potential Dollar Effect $______________________

PROTECT YOUR COMPANY'S MOST VALUABLE ASSET: YOURSELF

Don't let the strain of business put you out of commission. You're the most valuable player on your team and you have a responsibility to stay healthy —both physically and emotionally.

There are a number of stress-reducing techniques that psychiatrists recommend for harried business executives. One calls for the business owner to write the names of his most frustrating customers on raw eggs. What a relief it is to smash those eggs!

In the final analysis, your health is your responsibility. Resist the urge to work yourself into a sickbed. Get enough rest and exercise, keep yourself on a decent diet, and take time off to recharge your batteries. A few days of R&R in the mountains or at the beach might end up saving your sanity, your marriage, or even your business.

Give yourself peace of mind by ensuring that all business relationships are secure. The time to prevent disputes between owners is before they occur. For instance, here are the kinds of questions you and your other owners should formally answer as part of your Buy/Sell Agreement to avoid future disputes:

Buy/Sell Agreement Checklist

	YES	NO
Applicability – Do you want your agreements to:		
Apply only to the current owners?	❏	❏
Apply to all owners throughout the life of the business?	❏	❏
Supercede all other agreements to redeem a business interest?	❏	❏
Be reviewed annually?	❏	❏
Require a unanimous vote of the owners to change prices or terms?	❏	❏

continued

Type of Agreement – Do you want your
agreement to be structured as a ...   YES   NO

Redemption agreement?   ❏   ❏

Cross-purchase agreement?   ❏   ❏

Other?   ❏   ❏

    If yes, describe_____

Provisions of the Agreement – Should your agreement ...

Require the seller to sell and the buyer to buy in?   ❏   ❏

Give the buyer an option to require the seller to sell?   ❏   ❏

Give the seller an option to require the buyer to buy?   ❏   ❏

Give a right of first refusal to the buyer?   ❏   ❏

Be a combination of any of the above?   ❏   ❏

Upon the Death of an Owner – will your agreement ...

Require an automatic buyout of the owner's interest?   ❏   ❏

Allow his or her family to remain as an owner?   ❏   ❏

Buyout Price and Time for Payout – Will your agreement address ...

Buyout price from the estate or heirs of a deceased owner?   ❏   ❏

    If yes, when will it be paid?_____

    What will be the interest rate of the obligation?_____

Buyout price to a disabled owner?   ❏   ❏

    If yes, when will it be paid?_____

Buyout price in an amicable parting of the ways?   ❏   ❏

    If yes, when will it be paid?_____

Buyout price to an owner who goes bankrupt?   ❏   ❏

    If yes, when will it be paid?_____

Whether the buyout price will reflect that the company is being sold

to a long-time business associate rather than an outsider?   ❏   ❏

Funding – Will the buyout be funded by ...

Life insurance?   ❏   ❏

    If yes, will the type of life insurance used be
    addressed (i.e., term life, ordinary life, last to die, paid-up life,
    universal life or an endowment policy?_____

57. Protect Your Company's Most Valuable Asset: Yourself

	YES	NO
Will a life insurance trust be used?	❏	❏
Will all of the policy proceeds be required to redeem the interest?	❏	❏
Can part of the proceeds be used to help the entity recover from the loss of the owner?	❏	❏
Will whole life insurance policies with cash values be transferred to the owner at termination or retirement?	❏	❏
Some other investment vehicle?	❏	❏

If yes, what?_____

Security – Will the agreement be guaranteed or secured in the form of ...

	YES	NO
A pledge of business assets?	❏	❏
A personal guarantee by the other owners?	❏	❏
A provision obligating the entity to refrain from increasing salaries, paying dividends, if applicable, or making loans until all outstanding liabilities to the beneficiaries are repaid?	❏	❏

Loans (Receivables or Payables) – Will the agreement address ...

	YES	NO
The disposition of an owner's loans in the event of death or disability?	❏	❏
The disposition of an owner's loans in the event of termination other than death or disability?	❏	❏

Other – Will the agreement ...

	YES	NO
Contain a covenant not to compete?	❏	❏

If yes, what are the geographic and time limitations?_____

| Specify a period of disability before the other owners of the business have the right to buy out a disabled owner? | ❏ | ❏ |

If yes, what is the specified period?_____

Allow an owner to transfer or assign to a trust his or her rights and interests in the business for estate-tax planning purposes?	❏	❏
Require spouses of the owners to sign?	❏	❏
Include other family members who may own stock?	❏	❏

Speaking of insurance, establish a regular insurance audit for yourself and your business. Protect yourself and your estate with long term care insurance. Protect your business with "offensive" insurance, the kind that helps your business pay those huge attorney bills should you be forced to sue another person or business for such things as copyright infringement.

Take care of yourself!

57. PROTECT YOUR COMPANY'S MOST VALUABLE ASSET: YOURSELF

HOW DOES THIS APPLY TO MY BUSINESS?

_____

_____

_____

_____

_____

Priority   1   2   3   (Circle one)

Action Date_____

Profit Champion _____

Potential Dollar Effect $_____

100 Ways to Profit
In the New Economy

RESHUFFLE STAFF DUTIES AND CROSS-TRAIN EMPLOYEES TO CONTROL COSTS

Written job descriptions are valuable tools for any organization. But they aren't carved in marble. Is it time to reevaluate your personnel costs and broaden the work responsibilities of your employees? Technology companies caught in the down draft of a slowing economy should consider reshuffling duties so that employees become more multi-skilled and thus more valuable to their employer. This helps minimize lay-offs should these become necessary since valued employees can be moved to other positions, not let go.

The management of an employment agency saved nearly $12,000 by rethinking the duties of just one employee. The office manager was told to trim some fat from the firm's budget. That same day she discovered an employee camped out in the office conference room poring over the latest novel. Business had become so slow, he explained, that he always had lots of spare time in the afternoons.

Some managers would have reacted by simply reprimanding the employee. To her credit, though, the office manager gave the situation a good bit of thought and decided to put this worker's "spare time" to work for the agency.

His new job duties, she decided, would include delivering payroll packages to each of the agency's five branch offices. Previously, the firm had used an outside messenger service to make those deliveries. By assigning these responsibilities to an otherwise idle employee, the office manager saved our client $12,000 a year in delivery charges.

Practically every business can come up with ideas to make better use of idle employees. Couldn't some of your company's maintenance work be done by your own employees? Why not assign existing staff people to paint offices, landscape grounds, maintain company equipment, shop for office supplies or make minor building repairs?

Another client, a wholesale bakery, was paying overtime to bagel makers on weekends. By cross-training the pastry staff to make bagels, thousands of dollars of overtime were eliminated.

Some employees may balk at such suggestions, but others will welcome new assignments as a break from the ordinary work routine. In any event, there's no reason why employees can't pitch in and assume additional duties to make their business more successful.

Make a list of services that you're currently paying outsiders to provide, then list the names of your employees who have the skills or experience to handle those chores in house. You may be in for a surprise! It's never wise to have only one person in the office who knows the computer system, deals with customer quality issues, or negotiates with vendors. Keep your options open by cross-training employees to perform multiple duties.

Cross-training doesn't have to be a big production. Ask your experienced employees, for instance, to train new personnel in several job skills. Your employees can create procedure manuals outlining the nuts and bolts of their jobs.

Most importantly though, cross-training employees in various job skills is a way to make sure that your organization will never be held hostage by employees who regard themselves as "indispensable." Everyone has heard horror stories about employees who feel they are too good to be let go.

For years, one business suffered with a controller who knew her job but simply drove everyone in the company crazy. Although she was clearly a disruptive influence on the entire organization, the owner was afraid to let her go because she was the only person in the company who knew the accounting system.

Finally, the CEO began cross-training. He urged one of his assistants to learn more about the company's finances, and after a few months the assistant knew enough to permit the company to "encourage" the controller to consider "early retirement."

The result was a healthier office atmosphere, increased employee morale and significant payroll savings. The previous controller had been making $70,000 a year. Although the owner offered his assistant a $15,000 raise to replace the controller, the business was still over $20,000 ahead in payroll savings.

58. RESHUFFLE STAFF DUTIES AND CROSS-TRAIN EMPLOYEES TO CONTROL COSTS

HOW DOES THIS APPLY TO MY BUSINESS?

_____

_____

_____

_____

_____

Priority   1   2   3   (Circle one)

Action Date_____

Profit Champion _____

Potential Dollar Effect $_____

59

100 Ways to Profit
In the New Economy

ELIMINATE WORK, NOT PEOPLE

Job-centered — rather than profit-centered — organizations record job-related expenses, rather than those that are activity-related. Only after determining the real cost of employee business activities is it possible to make valuable business decisions and develop meaningful strategies based on facts.

Financial accounting recognizes job-related costs, not actual work activities performed. Companies are bullied into reducing work forces, rather than work. The dilemma is that work performed to accommodate customers' needs has value, but work performed to take care of business is overhead that is a non-recoverable expense.

When employees are laid off but the amount of work remains the same, greater demands are thrust upon fewer employees who become overworked, grumpy and discouraged. Not only does their work quality suffer, but so do those customers you've worked so hard to get. Ultimately, this reduces profitability, because dissatisfied customers leave, while sales diminish and profits erode.

In the short-term, working "lean and mean" does reduce costs by reducing employees. But consider this scenario. You reduce the number of employees, but the same amount of work must be done. Now you have laid off some good employees, and others might quit because of overwork and low morale. And still the work must get done. So you hire new employees who are untrained in your work methods and may even have fewer skills. At least until they can be trained, the quality of your services is reduced. So layoffs are often followed by increased costs.

316

Typically, management then decides to scale down operations, rather than incur increased salaries. But which expenses should be reduced? You and your managers are stumped because your traditional job-centered financial reporting system has not defined what "value added" versus "non-value added" work is. So your organization becomes like the dog chasing its tail. Managers are at a distinct disadvantage without activity-based information systems. Poor decisions have long-term financially disastrous effects.

A far better alternative to eliminating people is eliminating work. Successful businesses emphasize value creation, world-class customer service, and continuous profit improvement. This can only be accomplished by maintaining or expanding the work force and eliminating "non-value added" work.

Cutting unnecessary work produces greater productivity, significantly greater profits, additional research and development for new projects, expansion of employment, satisfied staff, delighted customers that brag about your company, and never-ending improvement.

---

59. ELIMINATE WORK, NOT PEOPLE

HOW DOES THIS APPLY TO MY BUSINESS?

_____

_____

_____

_____

_____

Priority   1   2   3   (Circle one)

Action Date_____

Profit Champion _____

Potential Dollar Effect $_____

60

TURN YOUR MANAGEMENT TEAM INTO A PROFIT TEAM

Your staff probably knows more about the day-to-day problems that chip away at the business's profitability than you do. They are also likely to be a wealth of information and advice on correcting those problems and offering other great new ideas for making your business more profitable. But unless you provide a forum for generating these new opportunities, ideas and problem-solving solutions, they will be lost. Far better to build a management team into a "profit team" that is able to complete these statements: I believe that profit is ... I believe our people can ... I believe our business is ... Few managers make things happen. Many watch things happen. Far too many say, "What happened?" Profit teams make things happen that enhances the bottom line.

Start out by asking each of your profit team members for a written plan to improve your business. In order to effectively elicit this useful information from your people, you need to go about it in a systematic way. Here is a questionnaire to help you and your profit team get started.

ATTENTION ALL PROFIT TEAM MEMBERS:
HELP US IMPROVE OUR COMPANY!
PLEASE LIST FIVE IDEAS FOR EACH OF THE FOLLOWING:

SUGGESTIONS FOR IMPROVING THE COMPANY
1._____
2._____
3._____
4._____
5._____

SUGGESTIONS FOR IMPROVING YOUR DEPARTMENT
1._____
2._____
3._____
4._____
5._____

SUGGESTIONS FOR IMPROVING YOUR ROLE WITHIN THE COMPANY
1._____
2._____
3._____
4._____
5._____

SUGGESTIONS FOR IMPROVING CUSTOMER SERVICE
1._____
2._____
3._____
4._____
5._____

The first ideas they write down may be the obvious ones. Invariably, the suggestions you can take to the bank are the fourth or fifth ones. And they'll get even better if you have your profit team bring their ideas into a brainstorming session. There's no telling what ideas will ultimately emerge from this process, but we guarantee you will learn a lot about your own organization. You'll also start your profit team thinking in the right direction, and that will pay dividends at your company. Indeed, the basic ideas for every one of the chapters in this book came as a result of exactly this kind of employee brain-picking and led to the development of our Profit Enhancement Process (PEP), a five-step process for making your entire organization more profitable.

In the meantime, try some of these brainstorming techniques and be sure that you let your people know which of their suggestions were adopted, how they were put to use, and why others were rejected. The key is to help them understand that all of their ideas were appreciated and received serious consideration.

Brainstorming is essentially a procedure to mobilize groups' creative resources to solve problems and develop opportunities. When properly thought out, quantified, and assigned responsibility and deadlines, these ideas will provide the basis for a Profit Plan that will invigorate your entire organization. Here are the basic steps for brainstorming.

1. **Focus on problems or opportunities that need a remedy. Break them down into four areas such as: (a) ideas for making my job more profitable; (b) ideas for making my department more profitable; (c) ideas for making the entire company more profitable; and (d) ideas for making our customers more profitable.**

2. Get yourself a conference room, a profit coach facilitator familiar with brainstorming techniques, and a qualified group of conferees. It is all right to include peripheral or offbeat people, but exclude those who have no competence that relates to the problem or opportunity. Their silence will make them uncomfortable and may dampen momentum. Still worse, they may try to participate and throw the meeting off track.

3. Appoint someone to record the suggestions. You have several options, but don't use a tape recorder alone. You may want to refer back to something that has been said, and that would cause an undesirable delay. Have someone write the basic idea on an easel chart which can be displayed throughout the meeting. A tape recorder may be used in conjunction with the written notes as a backup. Our Profit Plan software works well for this purpose.

4. Set rules against negativism: no criticism or negative comments. People should feel free to be as spontaneous as possible and offer ideas as fast as they come, the more the merrier.

5. Evaluate. This is best done by a small group capable of separating the useful ideas from all those gathered.

6. Refine, combine, improve. The "evaluation committee" should regard the retained ideas as raw material for further improvement and weaving them into your Profit Plan for action.

7. Report back. The group should get feedback on the results of their efforts. This is desirable in any event, but essential if you plan to ask the members to participate in the future.

---

60. TURN YOUR MANAGEMENT TEAM INTO A PROFIT TEAM

HOW DOES THIS APPLY TO MY BUSINESS?

_____

_____

_____

_____

Priority   1   2   3   (Circle one)

Action Date_____

Profit Champion _____

Potential Dollar Effect $_____

61

SHOW YOUR EMPLOYEES HOW A BIGGER BOTTOMLINE BENEFITS THEM AS WELL AS THE COMPANY

Profit is not a dirty word. It is the main reason you and your employees are working. It is imperative that you make this the goal of every employee and that they understand why.

What does profit mean to your organization? **There are common threads that unite all employees in a company: the desire for success as well as security.** Profit is the mortar and bricks that build longevity into a business to ensure job security. Owners of businesses have deep seated fears about the very existence of their company. Even the healthiest firms have difficult financial periods, which can have an unnerving effect on daily operations. In fact, 46% of the companies that made the Fortune 500 in 1981 had been removed by 1991. Employees of companies share this fear that tough economic times will mean the loss of their jobs and income. All people in a company want to plan for the future. They have dreams for themselves and their families. A company on shaky financial footing does not provide the peace of mind to allow for any focus other than short-term survival.

All employees in a company share the effects of poor profitability. Instead of dealing with issues on a proactive basis, everyone must concentrate on fighting fires. The main symptom is poor cash flow and a lack of working capital. When companies don't have sufficient cash, a myriad of problems are the result: product delays, cutbacks which affect customer service, reactive rather than proactive management, human needs not fulfilled, paying more for goods and services, lack of overall focus and not having fun when you go to work. These issues cause extreme pressure all through the ranks. Even the lowest person on the totem pole can feel the effects when they bear the brunt of getting orders out late because of insufficient inventory or the lack of resources to deliver or install.

We spend at least one-third of our adult life working, whether as an owner or employee. This time can be enjoyable. If employees look forward to their work, rather than being tired and constantly beat up, how much more productive can they be? Your greatest resource is yourself and your employees. What is the cost of this resource when it is not effective because of the debilitating effect of unprofitable operations? Moving to an environment of greater profits in a company creates feelings of success, accomplishment, enhanced egos, heightened self-esteem, and provides a real mechanism for personal gain.

Owners benefit as well, because profits create return on investment and the opportunity to reap the cash benefits from your financial risk-taking and hard work. In fact, owners earn their salary because of the grief they are willing to take. Better-performing businesses have the means of taking care of their most valuable resource, their employees. Everyone can share in the luxury of spending work hours in an atmosphere that is energizing, exciting and fun.

We worked with a business experiencing financial difficulty. We were invited to meet with the owner and six members from the key executive team. As we reviewed the company's business goals, we discovered that they excluded being more profitable. It was like pulling teeth to get the owner to state his number one goal is to make his business more profitable. His initial focus was on growth in new business, net of lost sales. His management team was frustrated because they had concentrated their efforts on sales, but the company's bottom line had not dramatically improved.

As the meeting continued, an evolution in the participant's perspective of the company began to occur. We repeatedly asked the owner, "What is your most significant agenda item and goal for this company?" Finally, after much encouragement, he answered, "To make money." Everyone was relieved, because the words were never mentioned before. When the words, "I'm in business to make a profit," came out of his mouth, it was like, "Eureka, we've got it!" Everyone on the management team became very excited. Their enthusiasm had long been dulled due to the business's lack of profitability, but was reawakened as the possibilities of business and personal gain became obvious.

A new vision appeared which would bring focus to the direction of the company's financial affairs. When the CEO came to the realization and communicated his thoughts on how the business could be making more profits, it was the beginning of the solution that improved his company's financial performance. This company's management team – and every employee in the company – are now focused on what must be done to improve profitability. They realize that they are the benefactors of positive bottom line results as well as the company.

322

61. SHOW YOUR EMPLOYEES HOW A BIGGER BOTTOMLINE BENEFITS THEM AS WELL AS THE COMPANY

HOW DOES THIS APPLY TO MY BUSINESS?

_____

_____

_____

_____

_____

Priority   1   2   3   (Circle one)

Action Date_____

Profit Champion _____

Potential Dollar Effect $_____

62

FORM AN INTERNAL COST-CONTROL COMMITTEE TO TRIM WASTE

If you don't already have one, we strongly advise you to establish a cost-control committee. Appoint people from your organization, no two people from the same department. Give them a permanent assignment to meet monthly and present a written report suggesting ways to control costs. You will get some very interesting and financially beneficial ideas. **Staff people have ideas to save money and control costs in your own organization, from perspectives different from you.** Cost-control committees come up with many cost-saving ideas during the first several months. You can bring in a dozen time-and-motion experts with stopwatches and clipboards, but it will take those outsiders weeks to discover what your own people already know!

The make up of your new cost-control committee is critical. Too often, people assigned to solving company problems are so wrapped up in their own job duties and responsibilities that they fail to recognize the more global concerns and opportunities of the organization. That is why we suggest you counteract this sort of tunnel vision by staffing your committee with representatives from various departments and divisions. By securing broad, multi-disciplined representation on this internal task force, you will encourage fresh viewpoints and creative solutions.

A large construction company can testify to the benefits of getting fresh perspectives from employees. This particular company engages in different types of specialized construction work — everything from road work to commercial construction to residential building. Different cost estimators are assigned to each specialized department. In addition to preparing bids on jobs, these estimators are responsible for determining the cost of all materials and subcontract work for each project.

Individually, each of the estimators was doing a good job of getting the best value on materials and labor for his particular division. But nobody was looking at the situation from the standpoint of the company as a whole.

A decision was made to hire a procurement manager, who promptly set up a committee composed of the estimators from each of the divisions. At the first meeting, it quickly became apparent that the lack of central coordination had cost the company dearly.

One division was buying materials from several local distributors. Another was dealing directly with key manufacturers. Still another was buying much of its materials from local building supply outlets. By coordinating purchases and buying from a single designated supplier, the company could achieve significant economies of scale.

In addition to obtaining volume discounts, the company was able to negotiate more favorable payment terms and delivery schedules. The firm also reduced construction site waste significantly as a result of the committee's coordination. Instead of disposing of leftover building materials at the end of a job, this surplus is now shuttled to other divisions where building projects are still underway.

These changes alone save the company more than $200,000 a year. And the suggestions for cost savings are still coming in.

---

62. FORM AN INTERNAL COST-CONTROL COMMITTEE TO TRIM WASTE

HOW DOES THIS APPLY TO MY BUSINESS?

_____

_____

_____

_____

_____

Priority   1   2   3   (Circle one)

Action Date_____

Profit Champion _____

Potential Dollar Effect $_____

63

USE TECHNOLOGY TO MONITOR YOUR COMPANY'S PERFORMANCE

Thanks to today's technology, it is possible for even small businesses to prepare a variety of performance measures and management analyses internally.

Use your computer to get a firm grip on the operation of your business. There are programs available that will allow you to track employee performance, measure sales per customer as well as salespersons, monitor delivery times, use geography to determine buying habits of customers, determining true costs of manufacturing products or product services, graphs to illustrate financial results, general sales plans and business plans...the list is endless. Through sophisticated, but easy-to-use, software packages, your business can monitor performance and much more.

Even the smallest businesses with a very basic office PC can easily generate their own sophisticated management reports and financial statements with little effort.

Look at spreadsheet software. With it you can sort through various options by identifying the consequences of a variety of alternative actions. In effect, you can play a "what-if" game that will help you chart the best course for your business under selected conditions.

Try reviewing your bottom line projections for the quarter or the year and use this program to determine how profits will be affected by different factors. What if sales increase or fall by 20 percent? What if interest rates rise? What if raw materials become scarce? What if employee productivity increases or decreases?

Spreadsheets are only one of the computer tools available to you.

There are time-management programs that can boost your organization's productivity, project-management software to allow you to track the progress of various activities, and other programs that will help you do everything from control inventory to print employee newsletters. We caution our clients, however, to make sure that all their databases interface and are useful to all who need them. Technology that is difficult to access and use is just as frustrating as none at all.

And now there is the Internet. Do you have a Web site so that customers and prospects get a good feel for your business? Take a look at ours: www.weprofit.com. It was cost-effective to develop and it is professional in its message—our first two objectives in its development.

If your business is not prepared to do business on the Internet, you'd better hang up your hat. One-quarter of all Chrysler's sales will originate as a result of the Internet over the next several years. The information now available on the Web for managers is increasing exponentially every day. It's a technology marvel and revolution that your business must tap.

63. USE TECHNOLOGY TO MONITOR YOUR COMPANY'S PERFORMANCE

HOW DOES THIS APPLY TO MY BUSINESS?

_____

_____

_____

_____

_____

Priority   1   2   3   (Circle one)

Action Date_____

Profit Champion _____

Potential Dollar Effect $_____

64

100 Ways to Profit
In the New Economy

TRIM TRAINING COSTS WITH
PROCEDURES MANUALS

In good times as well as bad, one of the biggest hidden expenses for many businesses is the cost of bringing new workers up to speed or training existing employees for new job duties.

If your company is anything larger than a mom and pop operation, we can almost guarantee that it's costing a lot more than you think to train employees. This won't show up as a line item on any ledger, but that doesn't mean these expenses don't exist. And it certainly doesn't mean that you shouldn't be taking action to control these costs.

A detailed jobs procedures manual is one of the most direct routes to lowering employee training costs. Don't confuse an occupational procedures manual with a job description—another valuable tool for any organization. Job descriptions outline the duties to be performed by employees. A procedures manual explains how to do those jobs and why they are being performed.

Such a manual can be extremely useful in recruiting and interviewing job applicants. But more importantly, it can streamline employee training and allow new people to become productive more quickly. The out-of-pocket payroll savings alone is substantial.

Suppose it takes eight weeks to bring a new employee up to speed in a particular job, and the person's supervisor must devote 25 percent of his or her time to training during that break-in period. A good procedures manual should reduce the necessary training time by at least 20 percent. At, say $10 per hour for the new employee, and $20 an hour for the supervisor, in the example above the training time costs would come to $4,800 ($10 X 40 hours X 8 weeks = $3,200 + $20 X 40 hours X 8

328

weeks X 25 percent = $1,600). A 20 percent reduction in training costs would save you nearly $1,000 for each new staff member—enough in itself to justify the effort involved in developing a procedures manual.

Aside from these training cost-savings, there are other reasons to develop a procedures manual for your organization. Indeed, the very process of preparing such a manual can provide invaluable insight into the operations of your business. You'll be surprised and maybe even shocked at what you will learn!

Inevitably, you will discover that your people are doing things a particular way for no reason other than that's the way their predecessor did them and taught them to do as well.

A large, nonprofit organization developed a procedures manual for its staff. The process was a real eye-opener. In preparing the manual, the managers discovered that the group's accounting department routinely logged each incoming check in a cash-receipt journal, then photocopied it as a safeguard. This organization depends on outside donations for funds, and it receives an enormous number of checks in the mail. It took one clerk four hours every day just to photocopy the daily influx of checks.

But it was all wasted time! All the information about the contributors had already been recorded in the journal, so copying the checks served no purpose! Nobody was sure how or when this senseless procedure began, but it had been going on for at least ten years. In effect, the organization wasted the equivalent of one employee's salary for five years—$125,000!

If it were not for the procedures manual, this waste would still be taking place. We believe that there is nothing more unprofitable that doing unnecessary work more efficiently! **Eliminate unnecessary work and save your good people!**

64. TRIM TRAINING COSTS WITH PROCEDURES MANUALS

HOW DOES THIS APPLY TO MY BUSINESS?

_____

_____

_____

_____

Priority   1   2   3   (Circle one)

Action Date_____

Profit Champion _____

Potential Dollar Effect $_____

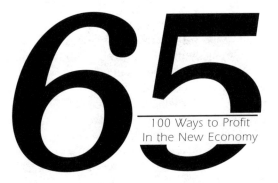

100 Ways to Profit
In the New Economy

ELIMINATE UNPRODUCTIVE MEETINGS

Make meetings productive. Prepare agendas and time allotments for each agenda item. Ask attendees to prepare for certain aspects of the meeting ahead of time. Otherwise, **meetings will eat up your staff's valuable time instead of launching them ahead on new profit projects or monitoring their progress on continuing ones.**

Suppose your department managers work like beavers, ten hours a day, six days a week. But at the same time, let's assume that 20 minutes of their day is spent on pointless or nonproductive activities. In effect, 1/33rd of their work time is wasted.

But it isn't just time that's wasted. They could have spent those 20 minutes generating new business for your company, or controlling costs, or otherwise improving your organization. So in a very real sense, 1/33rd of the salaries that you pay to these people is wasted plus the opportunities not being captured.

If you pay these department heads an average of $60,000 annually, those nonproductive 20 minutes a day are costing your business almost $2,000 a year per manager.

To be sure, you can't eliminate all wasted time on the job. But you certainly can make sure that the policies and procedures you require your people to follow aren't wasting time!

At many organizations, a significant cause of wasted staff time is poorly planned and administered meetings. Some businesses seem to have meetings all the time — whether they're needed or not. Every employee is assigned to six different internal committees, and they all meet three times a week for long, rambling sessions at which nothing seems to get resolved.

If a supervisor who wastes 20 minutes a day can cost you almost $2,000 a year, imagine the cost of a pointless, two-hour daily meeting involving a dozen staff! More to the point, imagine how much more productive and efficient your organization would be if you stopped squandering the equivalent of 24 hours of executive brainpower every day!

Make no mistake. We're not saying that meetings don't serve a purpose. Internal communication and planning is critical to every business. But make sure your staff meetings are effective. Here's how:

1. Set an agenda. Scheduling a meeting without an agenda is like trying to drive cross-country without a road map. You'll get where you're going eventually — but not without a lot of wrong turns, blind alleys and detours. An agenda, on the other hand, keeps you on track.

2. Table off-track issues. If an extraneous issue pops up in a meeting, resist the urge to pursue it. If it's important enough, schedule it for discussion at a future meeting.

3. Designate a chairperson. Without someone to take charge of the session and keep the discussion on track, the meeting is almost certain to ramble. You don't need a parliamentarian with a powdered wig every time three or four employees sit down for a discussion. Typically, the meeting participants will defer to the highest ranking "general" in the room. But at a meeting where all the participants are "lieutenant colonels," one should be designated to chair the session.

4. Set the meeting length in advance. It's important to let participants know how long a meeting is likely to last so they can schedule their day. If people are given unlimited time to speak on a subject, they just may take it.

5. Keep notes of the discussion. It's a good practice to have a secretary sit in on meetings to keep notes on what was discussed and what was decided. Six months or a year after the meeting, it might be important to know how a particular decision was reached, or why one course of action was approved instead of another.

6. Let participants plan the next meeting. At many companies, the agenda for the next meeting is set at the conclusion of the current session. This will save time by enabling the participants to provide input while issues are fresh in everyone's mind.

SAMPLE MEETING AGENDA
NAME OF GROUP
MEETING DATE AND TIME
AGENDA

1. Past Topics Revisited
    a. Topic/Speaker/Time allotted
    b. Topic/Speaker/Time allotted
    c. Topic/Speaker/Time allotted

2. Current Topics
    a. Topic/Speaker/Time allotted
    b. Topic/Speaker/Time allotted
    c. Topic/Speaker/Time allotted

3. Open Discussion/Time allotted

4. Good & Welfare (recognition of others in the group for extraordinary contributions to a particular project or to the firm in general)

5. Suggestions for the Next Meeting

65. ELIMINATE UNPRODUCTIVE MEETINGS
HOW DOES THIS APPLY TO MY BUSINESS?

Priority   1   2   3   (Circle one)

Action Date_____

Profit Champion _____

Potential Dollar Effect $_____

TAP INTO INDUSTRY TRADE AND PROFESSIONAL ASSOCIATIONS AS WELL AS FRANCHISORS

No organization needs to be alone. Others in your industry share most of the same opportunities and challenges. The experiences of these companies represent invaluable intelligence on operating a successful business.

Today there is a trade association, professional society, or franchisor that represents virtually every type of business. In fact, there is even an umbrella organization – the American Society of Association Executives (ASAE). With 75,000 executive members, this organization offers a wide selection of programs, training courses, products and services to help associations "win the Profit Game" for all their members. All associations offer a wealth of opportunities to their members.

The next time you're in the Washington, D.C. area, open the phone book and look under "National Association of..." or "American Association of ..." You will be astonished at the diversity of the industries represented by these groups.

In addition to these national organizations, there are corresponding state and local groups representing a wide range of businesses. These run the gamut from broadly-based chambers of commerce to tightly-focused, industry-specific groups. Their goal is to increase the business capabilities of their members.

Chances are your firm already belongs to one or more of these organizations. But if that's not the case, start checking out the benefits of membership immediately. **Almost invariably, our clients have found that trade and professional associations and franchisors are a business lifeline, always looking for meaningful opportu-**

nities to improve the business capabilities of their members or franchisees.

Many of these organizations develop operating statistics for businesses in their industry, and these serve as invaluable benchmarks for companies. Comparing your sales per employee, or sales per advertising dollar, with the average of other firms in your industry will help you identify financial opportunities for your business. That alone will justify the cost of membership.

Additionally, however, associations and franchisors provide a variety of other benefits to members and franchisees. Typically, they offer:

- **Surveying members' needs to determine how to better serve them;**
- **Educational meetings or seminars that will sharpen the skills of your employees;**
- **Industry newsletters and publications containing valuable business information;**
- **A structure for influencing regulatory or legislative activity affecting your company; and**
- **Prepackaged employee insurance programs and other group "fringe benefits".**

Most importantly, though, industry trade and professional associations and franchisors offer the opportunity to share experiences, problems and solutions with other businesses in your field.

You have plenty to do growing your business. Don't waste time trying to reinvent the wheel.

---

66. TAP INTO INDUSTRY TRADE AND PROFESSIONAL ASSOCIATIONS AS WELL AS FRANCHISORS

HOW DOES THIS APPLY TO MY BUSINESS?

_____

_____

_____

_____

_____

Priority   1   2   3   (Circle one)

Action Date_____

Profit Champion _____

Potential Dollar Effect $_____

CHAPTER 10: EMPLOYEES

LINK BONUSES TO PERFORMANCE

Complacency begins when incentives end. But the same is true when there are no consequences for doing it wrong.

Make no mistake, an employee bonus — whether it's cash or a gift or time off or something else of value — can be a powerful tool to motivate your work force. But an employee bonus can also be a colossal waste of money. Worse yet, the wrong kind of bonus can backfire on a business and become a minefield of employee resentment and hostility toward management.

Take GTE, for instance, where one-third of each executive's compensation has been tied to customer satisfaction. Between 200,000 and 300,000 customer service calls are made every year, so these executives are really put to the test!

Campbell Soups has also tied bonuses to performance, and the company itself has gone from a poor to a top performer in their industry. David Johnson, CEO, says: "What drives our results is a deep-seated belief that your top talent does better when they think their accountability is high. We have very tough thresholds before execs get a bonus." Their system rewards people for beating targets and penalizes them for not achieving their goals.

When we discussed the pros and cons of bonuses with the executive director of an association, he stated that Christmas bonuses create goodwill within the organization. He was determined not to change the bonus system.

The assistant CFO was bold enough to state that Christmas bonuses were creating bad will in the organization. The executive director asked the assistant CFO for an explanation and heard the following: "People are upset ... If you've been here for ten years, you get basically the same bonus as if you were here for five years. If you've taken on a lot of responsibility during the year, you get the same bonus as employees who have assumed little responsibility. People are really upset." He told us that people were in the coffee room after bonuses were paid, complaining. The hallways were full of complainers as well.

In summary, try to create an incentive bonus system in which there are two winners — the employer and the employee. If that can't be achieved, don't compound the problem with future employees by continuing to give bonuses.

There are two types of employee bonuses: those that encourage your people to become more productive or maintain high standards of performance, and those that do not. The rule of thumb is simple in this case: either link employee bonuses to performance or eliminate them altogether.

Fortunately, it's easy to distinguish between the two types of employee bonuses. Remember, you're trying to encourage certain types of behavior by rewarding it. For example, consider offering a bonus to:

- **Salespeople who exceed their quotas for the year;**
- **Service department personnel who complete a higher-than-average number of procedures;**
- **Accounts receivable staffers who achieve high levels of collections;**
- **Production line workers who suggest product design improvements; or**
- **Employees who consistently report to work on time, or use less than their allotment of sick leave, or suggest ways to reduce expenses.**

In each of these examples, extending bonuses creates two winners: the employee who receives the compensation and the employer who benefits from the worker's positive performance.

On the other hand, what does an employer accomplish by offering Christmas bonuses or year-end bonuses or other forms of extra compensation not dependent on the employee's performance? Free-floating bonuses that aren't attached to positive performance can create problems for unwary businesses.

What happens, for example, when the business takes a nosedive and management can no longer afford to offer holiday bonuses? Employees who received those goodies in the past continue to expect them. And the bigger these bonuses are, the more potentially dangerous they become. I've seen corporations face outright mutiny because they attempted to discontinue their practice of offering hefty end-of-the-year bonuses.

While the best policy is not to offer nonperformance-linked bonuses in the first place, how do you dismount from the tiger once the ride has begun? Our advice is to do it very gingerly.

You can't take a benefit away from a veteran employee. If you gave them each a turkey last year, you'd better give them a turkey this year, or else you'll be the turkey. But if you've been routinely passing out substantial cash bonuses unrelated to performance, put an end to the practice. Explain to your employees that from now on, the amount that they had been receiving at year end will go into their paychecks in the form of a salary increase spread over 52 weeks. That way existing employees don't feel they're losing anything, and you're not obligated to offer future bonuses to new employees.

The objective is to pay bonuses for results, not to eliminate them. **When done properly, the greater the bonuses you pay when tied to performance, the greater your company's financial results.**

---

67. LINK BONUSES TO PERFORMANCE

HOW DOES THIS APPLY TO MY BUSINESS?

_____

_____

_____

_____

_____

Priority   1   2   3   (Circle one)

Action Date_____

Profit Champion _____

Potential Dollar Effect $_____

GIVE EMPLOYEES A RAISE WITH THE GOVERNMENT'S MONEY

The concept of giving your employees a raise with the government's dollars rather than yours can be illustrated by this simple analogy. The suit that you are wearing is attractive. If it costs $200, you would have to earn approximately $300 in salary, pay $100 in taxes and have $200 remaining to buy the suit. The tax is 50 percent more than the object costs. A similar observation can be made with medical expenses, child care, elderly care, group life and group disability insurance. Imagine the benefit if the government gave you a tax deduction to buy a suit. They don't do that, but if they did you could pay for a suit with $200 instead of $300 of earnings and would have saved $100.

The government gives you a similar opportunity with a Section 125 cafeteria plan. **A cafeteria plan reduces compensation by the cost of medical expenses not covered by insurance including health insurance premiums, child care and elder care expenses, group disability insurance, life insurance and various other specified expenses.** Here is how it works: If you have an employee who is making $50,000 a year and has $5,000 of qualified Section 125 cafeteria plan expenditures, the taxable compensation can be reduced to $45,000 — $5,000 of this income would go untaxed. The tax savings would be approximately $2,500 per year or $50 per week. In other words, the employee's net compensation would be increased by $50 per week at no cost to the employer.

Did it cost your business any more in this scenario than by paying the employee $45,000 in salary and paying $5,000 for the above mentioned items? You pay him or her the same amount of money. How does this help your employees? They save federal and state income taxes as well as Social Security taxes. What does it do for you, the employer? You are paying Social Security, Unemployment and Workers' Compensation on the employee's gross wages. If a Section 125 cafeteria plan had been adopted, you would have saved payroll taxes and, in some states, workers' compensation on the employee's benefit deductions. An existing client of our firm is saving $240,000 a year in Social Security, and Unemployment taxes because they adopted this plan. Can you imagine giving a benefit to your employees that gives them $50 more a week in their paycheck and saves the company $240,000—all at the government's expense? Check this out for your business ... it's a win-win situation for you and your employees.

---

68. GIVE YOUR EMPLOYEES A RAISE WITH THE GOVERNMENT'S MONEY.
HOW DOES THIS APPLY TO MY BUSINESS?

_____

_____

_____

_____

_____

Priority   1   2   3   (Circle one)

Action Date_____

Profit Champion _____

Potential Dollar Effect $_____

69

REWARD EMPLOYEES WITH NONCASH COMPENSATION

What three things do your employees need and want the most from your business? You might be surprised. Studies show they want (1) recognition for work performed; (2) a feeling of being "in" on things, and (3) interesting work.

Employees always need to have their achievements recognized, but cash is not their only reward. In fact, it isn't always the most effective motivator. Numerous studies have found that non-cash compensation is an even more important factor for many people. These studies have almost summarily determined that the satisfaction that comes from being recognized as an important and valued associate is an extremely powerful motivator for employees. A new job title that reflects an individual's increased contributions to the organization, a private office, business cards, a person's name on the door, the opportunity to attend professional meetings in resort locations — these are all motivators that cost a company little, if anything, out-of-pocket. Yet they will help maintain or even enhance staff morale.

There are also more tangible forms of compensation you can offer employees. One way is to award employees "phantom stock" in lieu of cash bonuses. Unlike regular common stock, phantom stock does not convey any equity in the business, but still allows the employee to share in the future appreciation of the business.

For example, let's take the case of a business worth $500,000. The owner issues one share of "phantom stock" equal to 1% of the future appreciation of the business to each of 10 employees. If the value of the business eventually increases to $800,000, each share of "phantom stock" will then be worth $3,000 (1 percent of the $300,000 appreciation).

It's a wonderful opportunity for employees because they will be able to participate in the increased value of the company, and motivated to enhance the profitability of the business. A phantom stock program is a good deal for the owner, as well, because the business will conserve cash by deferring cash compensation to a future date without giving away any ownership in the company.

Another technique we recommend is to form an Employee Stock Ownership Plan (ESOP) enabling your workers to earn a retirement nest egg which will grow as the business prospers. This is another approach that offers employees a real incentive to help the company succeed. But an ESOP can also be a great deal for the owner of a business. The owner can sell his or her stock in the company to the ESOP, reinvest the proceeds in publicly-held securities, and not pay any tax on the gain until the stock is sold.

It's a win-win situation!

---

69. REWARD EMPLOYEES WITH NONCASH COMPENSATION

HOW DOES THIS APPLY TO MY BUSINESS?

_____

_____

_____

_____

_____

Priority   1   2   3 (Circle one)

Action Date_____

Profit Champion _____

Potential Dollar Effect $_____

PAY PEOPLE WHAT THEY ARE WORTH

Years of experience should not be based on years alone. Ask your employees to justify their wages. In fact, ask them to justify the need for their position as well as department. In other words, how does what they do affect the profitability of the company. Invite them to discuss with you what is working well in their department and what isn't. Invite them to give you their ideas for improving the profitability of their department and the company as a whole. **We reckon an employee's years of experience, not in years, but as a multiple of their competency times the complexity of their job. This is the figure upon which salary should be based.**

Overstaffing is a lot more common than you may think. Many businesses get used to keeping surplus employees on the payroll in good times, almost as a kind of security blanket for management. You really don't need all those people, but it feels good to know that they're around just in case.

An apparel retailer had 47 people on the payroll. If you had asked the personnel director, he would have argued you into the ground justifying the need for every one of them. The store's profitability began to be affected. The owner didn't lay off anyone, but he did put a freeze on all new hiring. As people quit their jobs, they were not replaced and normal employee turnover did the job for him.

Since then, seven people have left the company, the staff is down to 40, and all the work is still getting done. The employees who are still with him understand that they must put forth greater effort. As a result, they are willing to pitch in, work a little harder and pick up the slack.

For his part, this businessman avoided painful layoffs yet still managed to reduce his payroll costs by almost $100,000.

---

70. PAY PEOPLE WHAT THEY ARE WORTH

HOW DOES THIS APPLY TO MY BUSINESS?

_____

_____

_____

_____

_____

Priority   1   2   3   (Circle one)

Action Date_____

Profit Champion _____

Potential Dollar Effect $_____

FARM OUT PAYROLL CHORES

Some organizations have payroll personnel in their firms that are busy three or four days a week. They don't have much to do the rest of the time. **Automated payroll services are very cost-effective and should be investigated.** As a rule of thumb, if you have more than 10 employees, you're probably money-ahead to use an outside payroll service. You can then put your payroll people to work on more profitable projects.

These services are highly automated and make it easy to prepare payroll checks and quarterly tax reports. From this information the service can generate year-end payroll reports, produce W-2s for your employees, and provide you with other valuable management information such as payroll cost by project or department.

These automated services will be able to handle your payrolls regardless of whether your employees are paid a salary, on an hourly basis, by commission, or whatever. Many are set up so that you can phone or fax payroll information to them, and they will then calculate each worker's salary and deliver their checks to you on payday.

These automated services will even increase staff productivity by providing electronic payroll check deposits directly into each employee's checking account. If you figure that the typical employee spends an average of 15 minutes out of the workday to deposit each paycheck, and there are 26 paydays a year, a direct deposit payroll system can boost your organization's productivity by almost one full workday per employee per year!

There are lots of payroll services available to you, including some local as well as national organizations. Finding the right one for your company requires some research on your part, however. Trade publications and professional association journals often carry ads for payroll services that specialize in your type of business. Or ask your profit advisor to recommend one that has been used successfully by some of his other clients.

Even if your organization is smaller, it's frequently worthwhile to consider using a commercial payroll service. Indeed, even if an outside service doesn't save you a dime, it may offer other valuable benefits, including:

- **Enhanced payroll confidentiality (fewer people in your organization will have access to this information);**
- **Insulation against late payroll tax filings and the IRS penalties they can produce;**
- **Relief from constantly having to track and adjust to changes in local, state and national payroll tax ground rules; and**
- **Availability of customized, comprehensive and easy-to-read management reports.**

71. FARM OUT PAYROLL CHORES
HOW DOES THIS APPLY TO MY BUSINESS?

Priority   1   2   3   (Circle one)

Action Date_____

Profit Champion _____

Potential Dollar Effect $_____

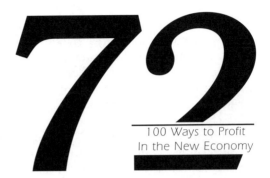

STAFF WITH LEASED EMPLOYEES

Can you imagine your workers employed by an employee leasing company? They are known as professional employer organizations. **For small business owners bogged down with government paperwork, payroll hassles and expensive fringe benefits, employee leasing provides an attractive way to eliminate red tape and paperwork expense.** The leasing firm not only takes care of all payroll and tax filings, but will frequently offer employees better benefits than you could. Sign only two checks a month—one to cover the payroll costs and one to pay for the leasing company's services—it couldn't be much easier. Leased employees are long-term workers for you who receive a full range of benefits, including, in many cases, a pension plan.

When you look for an employee leasing firm, be sure to get answers to the following questions:

- **How long has the company been in business? Will the leasing company provide bank references to verify financial stability?**

- **Are the benefits offered by major insurance companies?**

- **How long does it take for the employee leasing company's insurance companies to pay off claims?**

- **Will fringe benefits be tailored to meet your company's needs?**

- **Do you have to sign a long-term contract? Can you cancel with only 30 days' notice if you are not satisfied with the service?**

- **Will they furnish monthly statements showing that payroll taxes, pension fund contributions, and insurance premiums have been paid?**

72. STAFF WITH LEASED EMPLOYEES

HOW DOES THIS APPLY TO MY BUSINESS?

_____

_____

_____

_____

_____

Priority   1   2   3   (Circle one)

Action Date_____

Profit Champion _____

Potential Dollar Effect $_____

MAKE EVERYONE RESPONSIBLE FOR CUSTOMER SERVICE

You'll recognize this scenario. You visit a store or contact a company with a specific question that needs answered or a problem that requires solving. You explain the situation to the first person you speak with and hope to get a quick resolution. Then your troubles begin!

During your first exchange, you remain calm and clearly describe your issue. The person listens intently, and you are hopeful that he or she will help you. In well-run businesses, you will be satisfied at this level. In many companies, you will get one of the following responses:

"That's not my department."

"I've never heard of that before."

"I don't have the authority to deal with this."

"Let me transfer you to …."

"I'll take your name, and someone will get back to you."

"There is nothing I can do."

How do you feel when you get this kind of treatment? If you were expecting a problem, you were right. If you were optimistic that your issue would be efficiently resolved, your impression of the company has been tainted. Your level of aggravation and frustration will grow depending upon how many levels of the company you must navigate in order to obtain satisfaction.

Customer loyalty is built not just by supplying a good product or service, but by ensuring that all people who affect a customer are sensitive to the impact that they have on a relationship. Take a test in your company. Ask people what their main responsibilities are. In too many cases you will get task-oriented answers, which are technically correct, but miss the point of why your organization is in business. You are there to serve customers. An often used phrase, "The customer pays your salary," is absolutely correct.

There are three steps that can be taken to raise your customer satisfaction capability. First, there has to be a culture that promotes the customer as king, and representative deeds reinforce the point. Many companies will state that they value customer service, but will break all of the rules when confronted with a difficult situation. A fine line has to be drawn between being reasonable and too accommodating. There will be times when you lose battles but win wars. There will be cases when you lose money on a transaction in order to salvage a relationship. You must walk the talk.

Next, determine all possible places in your firm where your employees come in contact with a customer. This could be anywhere from accounting, credit, production, dispatch, scheduling to delivery. Anticipate possible customer service issues that could arise in each of these areas and provide policies for dealing with them.

Finally, make sure that all of your employees are fully trained in dealing with issues. Cross-train departments in solving problems from other areas. A good policy is to use good judgment in all situations. If a higher authority is needed, ensure that access is timely. Avoid bouncing customers to multiple people.

When in doubt about a component of your customer service method, put yourself in the shoes of a customer and determine how you would feel.

In today's competitive environment, every business has to provide value above and beyond just their basic product or service. If the interaction with a customer does not meet or exceed their expectations, they can choose not to buy at all, demand a cheaper price or choose a myriad of competitors who are waiting for them with open arms.

---

73. MAKE EVERYONE RESPONSIBLE FOR CUSTOMER SERVICE

HOW DOES THIS APPLY TO MY BUSINESS?

_____

_____

_____

_____

_____

Priority   1   2   3   (Circle one)

Action Date_____

Profit Champion _____

Potential Dollar Effect $_____

SHAVE LABOR COSTS WITH PART-TIMERS

In today's competitive climate, your business needs the best people it can get. But many of these excellent workers simply aren't available for full-time employment.

A mother with small children may be unwilling to return to the work force full-time, but she may be very interested in a job for few hours each day or a job at her home, telecommuting.

A retiree may not be interested in rejoining the rat race five days a week, but may well accept employment for a couple of days a week. A college or professional school student may be unable to work regular hours, but might be a perfect candidate for evening or weekend employment.

Nowadays, employers are able to choose from an army of part-time job candidates who make motivated and dedicated workers. Many have strong job experience, top skills and a great work ethic. It would be a shame to close off consideration of such people just because they're unable to work 40 hours a week, Monday-through-Friday.

But there's another good reason to consider employing part-time employees: They will help you hold down labor costs! Indeed, you may well discover that some of the positions you were filling with full-time workers don't really require 40 hours a week!

If a job can be done in 30 hours a week instead of 40, the employer may be able to reduce the cost of labor for that function by 25 percent a year. Save 10 hours each week at $10 an hour, and by the end of the year you're ahead $5,200!

Moreover, in many states if an employee works part-time (as determined by employment law), it's not necessary to provide that person with fringe benefits, even if you offer them to full-timers. Remember, these benefits are costly—20 percent to 40 percent of compensation.

A manufacturer was really feeling the squeeze as a result of the rising cost of employee benefits. The company was spending an average of $6,000 a year per worker just for "fringes." The manufacturer responded by converting 20 full-time positions into 40 part-time jobs. All the stations are being manned, just as before, and the company is paying just as much in wages as it was previously. But because the company doesn't provide fringe benefits to part-timers, the manufacturer is money ahead. Indeed, eliminating $6,000 in fringe benefits to 20 employees is the same as adding $120,000 annually to the bottom line.

74. SHAVE LABOR COSTS WITH PART-TIMERS

HOW DOES THIS APPLY TO MY BUSINESS?

_____

_____

_____

_____

_____

Priority   1   2   3   (Circle one)

Action Date_____

Profit Champion _____

Potential Dollar Effect $_____

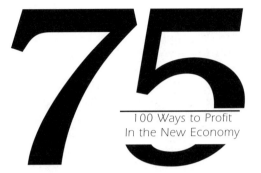

CONTROL EMPLOYEE OVERTIME

In too many businesses, overtime work has become the rule rather than the exception. In effect, these companies are operating on "permanent overtime!" After a while, **some employees tend to regard overtime pay as a "fringe benefit" to which they are entitled,** whether the company needs extra work or not. Indeed, some workers come to depend on that extra income, and they become very creative at finding ways to make sure it continues.

Although state overtime ground rules vary, the national standard is clear: Unless your employees are exempt from the Federal Fair Labor Standards Act because they hold managerial, professional or administrative status, you must pay them time-and-a-half for any hours worked in excess of 40 per week. The exception to this rule is fixed-salary compensation for fluctuating hours.

At 150 percent of an employee's normal hourly wage, overtime pay scales can put you in the poorhouse. Before that happens, impose a company-wide moratorium on overtime pay. At a minimum, require written authorization from a key management official before any nonexempt employee works more than 40 hours per week. Such a policy will eliminate a lot of misunderstandings as well as a lot of unnecessary payroll costs. If work can't be done during normal hours, analyze why. Do you need to reshuffle job responsibilities, cross-train your employees, hire a part-timer to catch up? Consider paying an employee or the department a bonus for coming up with ideas to eliminate overtime — or better yet, finish the work on time.

A medical clinic learned this the hard way. For years the doctors employed an office assistant who routinely worked 50 hours a week.

Her regular salary came to around $20 per hour, but at time-and-a-half for those additional ten hours, this practice was paying her $300 dollars extra every week. When you add it all up, that comes to a $15,000 annual bonus on top of her regular salary!

When the doctors finally put an end to all employee overtime, there was no noticeable decline in productivity. But there was a whopping $15,000 bottom line savings to the clinic.

The point to remember is that the opportunity to work overtime should not be something your staff takes for granted. Don't give them the unfettered right to a weekly bonus at their discretion. If employees don't get the job done in 40 hours, then they should be prepared to explain why.

OVERTIME APPROVAL

Employee Name:_____

Department:_____

Project:_____

Estimated Overtime Hours: _____

Reason Overtime is Required: _____

_____

_____
Signature/Department Supervisor

_____
Date

---

75. CONTROL EMPLOYEE OVERTIME

HOW DOES THIS APPLY TO MY BUSINESS?

_____
_____
_____
_____
_____

Priority   1   2   3   (Circle one)

Action Date_____

Profit Champion _____

Potential Dollar Effect $_____

BE CREATIVE WITH EMPLOYEES' WORK SCHEDULES

It can take an organization years to recruit and develop a first-rate staff. But how much time do you lose when they have to take a long lunch hour or even a "personal day" to get all their personal business done, things like going to the bank and the cleaner, doctors' appointments, and so on?

Some enlightened organizations, including the federal government, have come up with a very civilized solution to this dilemma. "The 9-80 Rule," allows employees to work nine hours a day for nine days, and take the tenth day off. In effect, you're getting an extra hour a day from your employees and "giving" them their time back every two weeks to perform their personal chores and avoid their commutes.

During slow periods, switch from five days a week to four. **Asking people to swallow a temporary 20 percent pay cut may sound like a hard sell, but you just might be surprised.** They're likely to be very supportive, particularly if they get long weekends for themselves.

Still another approach is to offer your staff the option of switching to part-time status. Many employees prefer working fewer hours, but simply have never had the nerve to ask.

A computer software design firm, for instance, made such a proposal to its staff in response to declining sales, and it worked like a charm. As an alternative to reducing the staff by 20 percent, the COO offered each worker the option of working fewer hours. As it turned out, almost a third of the staff wanted to be part-timers, and they jumped at the offer.

As a result, the part-time "wanna-bees" were happy, the "busy bees" who wanted to continue working full-time were able to do so, and nobody lost their job. Everybody won, including our client.

---

76. BE CREATIVE WITH EMPLOYEES' WORK SCHEDULES

HOW DOES THIS APPLY TO MY BUSINESS?

_____

_____

_____

_____

_____

Priority   1   2   3   (Circle one)

Action Date_____

Profit Champion _____

Potential Dollar Effect $_____

EVALUATE STAFF PRODUCTIVITY OBJECTIVELY

No business can afford to carry people who can't or won't pull their own weight. In addition to the obvious drain on your company's scarce resources, unproductive employees tend to have a demoralizing effect on the rest of your staff. Keeping a slacker on the payroll is a slap in the face of all your hard-working employees.

Remember: Your organization is only as strong as its weakest link. Your job is to find the "weak links" by measuring the productivity of your employees. Too many managers evaluate staff performance subjectively. **Develop an objective yardstick to measure the productivity of your employees and you may be surprised at what you discover.** Some people you regarded as only marginal employees may be among your "Most Valuable Players." Conversely, the ones you thought were the company "stars" may not be "MVPs" after all.

There are dozens of different ways to measure employee performance objectively. You can develop statistics showing how much each worker produces, sells, delivers or collects for your firm. You can analyze staffers based on their attendance record, customer complaint history, overtime wages, travel and entertainment spending, or many other variables.

A retailer conducted an effective analysis of staff productivity. This particular business employed about 60 salespeople, who earned salaries and commissions averaging $30,000 each. It became increasingly difficult for the retailer to justify this $1.8 million payroll.

Belatedly, the CEO undertook an analysis of sales and profitability by employee, and discovered a wide range of performance among his sales staff. Indeed, about one third of his people were carrying two thirds of the weight!

The owner eliminated the dead wood, brought in some talented newcomers, and upgraded his veteran "MVPs." He wound up with a much smaller staff of 30, but they were all highly motivated professionals who were earning an average of $40,000 each — about 30 percent above the "going rate" for the industry.

Even at the higher salaries, however, the total payroll costs dropped by a third, thanks to the staff reductions. Best of all, the new "tighter ship" was also a more productive one. Within a year the new, more highly motivated sales staff increased revenues 25 percent, and generated $750,000 in additional gross profit for the business.

Coupled with the $600,000 the company saved in labor costs, plus even more savings from reduced payroll taxes, fringe benefit costs, and additional sales, the company managed to improve its bottom line by more than $1,350,000!

In any employee evaluation, ask him or her what they like best about their job, what they find most frustrating, what their business goals are, in what areas would they benefit from training, what profit ideas they have to contribute. Use an evaluation to gain knowledge about your company!

SAMPLE WORK TEAM
PERFORMANCE EVALUATION

1. Individual demonstrates a positive and professional approach toward work.

Initials of work team members|____|____|____|____|____|____|
- Always
- Usually
- Sometimes
- Never

2. The individual responds to your questions in a way that produces positive results.

Initials of work team members|____|____|____|____|____|____|
- Always
- Usually
- Sometimes
- Never

3. The individual schedules time to direct the work and keeps you aware of changes in the assignment.

Initials of work team members|____|____|____|____|____|____|
- Always
- Usually
- Sometimes
- Never

continued

4. The individual acts as a team player in working on the completion of projects.

Initials of work team members|____|____|____|____|____|____|____|

- Always
- Usually
- Sometimes
- Never

5. The individual displays positive attitudes towards the firm.

Initials of work team members|____|____|____|____|____|____|____|

- Always
- Usually
- Sometimes
- Never

6. The individual has adequate knowledge of internal and external resources to accomplish the work.

Initials of work team members|____|____|____|____|____|____|____|

- Always
- Usually
- Sometimes
- Never

7. The individual responds to your questions by assisting you in developing strategies to solve problems and create opportunities.

Initials of work team members|____|____|____|____|____|____|____|

- Always
- Usually
- Sometimes
- Never

8. The individual encourages additional responsibility and works to his or her potential.

Initials of work team members|____|____|____|____|____|____|____|

- Always
- Usually
- Sometimes
- Never

9. Whenever possible the individual includes you in planning the work.

Initials of work team members|____|____|____|____|____|____|____|

- Always
- Usually
- Sometimes
- Never

10. The individual is open-minded and makes suggestions.

Initials of work team members|____|____|____|____|____|____|____|

- Always
- Usually
- Sometimes
- Never

11. The individual works with you so jobs are carefully and thoroughly planned.

Initials of work team members |____|____|____|____|____|____|____|
- Always |____|____|____|____|____|____|____|
- Usually |____|____|____|____|____|____|____|
- Sometimes |____|____|____|____|____|____|____|
- Never |____|____|____|____|____|____|____|

12. The individual works with you to develop reliable and analytical approaches to problem solving.

Initials of work team members |____|____|____|____|____|____|____|
- Always |____|____|____|____|____|____|____|
- Usually |____|____|____|____|____|____|____|
- Sometimes |____|____|____|____|____|____|____|
- Never |____|____|____|____|____|____|____|

13. The individual communicates in an understandable manner.

Initials of work team members |____|____|____|____|____|____|____|
- Always |____|____|____|____|____|____|____|
- Usually |____|____|____|____|____|____|____|
- Sometimes |____|____|____|____|____|____|____|
- Never |____|____|____|____|____|____|____|

14. The individual understands the ground rules being used in the decision-making process.

Initials of work team members |____|____|____|____|____|____|____|
- Always |____|____|____|____|____|____|____|
- Usually |____|____|____|____|____|____|____|
- Sometimes |____|____|____|____|____|____|____|
- Never |____|____|____|____|____|____|____|

15. In a group environment (i.e. team meeting, quality control meeting, etc.) the individual contributes, directs, and helps to sustain the objectives of the group?

Initials of work team members |____|____|____|____|____|____|____|
- Always |____|____|____|____|____|____|____|
- Usually |____|____|____|____|____|____|____|
- Sometimes |____|____|____|____|____|____|____|
- Never |____|____|____|____|____|____|____|

16. When the individual is required to display job expertise, he/she is up-to-date, thorough, interested, resourceful and creative.

Initials of work team members |____|____|____|____|____|____|____|
- Always |____|____|____|____|____|____|____|
- Usually |____|____|____|____|____|____|____|
- Sometimes |____|____|____|____|____|____|____|
- Never |____|____|____|____|____|____|____|

17. From a technical point of view, the individual is independent and uses creative thinking.

Initials of work team members |____|____|____|____|____|____|____|
- Always |____|____|____|____|____|____|____|
- Usually |____|____|____|____|____|____|____|
- Sometimes |____|____|____|____|____|____|____|
- Never |____|____|____|____|____|____|____|

continued

18. From an economic point of view, the individual takes steps to control expenses of the firm and the customers while maintaining quality and service (i.e. exhibit entrepreneurial skills).

Initials of work team members |____|____|____|____|____|____|____|

• Always							
• Usually							
• Sometimes							
• Never							

19. The individual writes and speaks in a clear and concise manner.

Initials of work team members |____|____|____|____|____|____|____|

• Always							
• Usually							
• Sometimes							
• Never							

20. The individual delegates work effectively.

Initials of work team members |____|____|____|____|____|____|____|

• Always							
• Usually							
• Sometimes							
• Never							

21. The individual wants to excel and succeed with our firm.

Initials of work team members |____|____|____|____|____|____|____|

• Always							
• Usually							
• Sometimes							
• Never							

22. The individual accepts challenges and sets high goals.

Initials of work team members |____|____|____|____|____|____|____|

• Always							
• Usually							
• Sometimes							
• Never							

23. The individual provides you with adequate feedback on the job.

Initials of work team members |____|____|____|____|____|____|____|

• Always							
• Usually							
• Sometimes							
• Never							

24. The individual takes actions to improve his/her performance.

Initials of work team members |____|____|____|____|____|____|____|

• Always							
• Usually							
• Sometimes							
• Never							

25. The individual complies with our firm's standards.

Initials of work team members |___|___|___|___|___|___|___|

- Always |___|___|___|___|___|___|___|
- Usually |___|___|___|___|___|___|___|
- Sometimes |___|___|___|___|___|___|___|
- Never |___|___|___|___|___|___|___|

26. The individual demonstrates enthusiasm and actions in support of our firm's motto and mission statement.

Initials of work team members |___|___|___|___|___|___|___|

- Always |___|___|___|___|___|___|___|
- Usually |___|___|___|___|___|___|___|
- Sometimes |___|___|___|___|___|___|___|
- Never |___|___|___|___|___|___|___|

27. The individual sets the proper example by assisting our customers with world class service.

Initials of work team members |___|___|___|___|___|___|___|

- Always |___|___|___|___|___|___|___|
- Usually |___|___|___|___|___|___|___|
- Sometimes |___|___|___|___|___|___|___|
- Never |___|___|___|___|___|___|___|

28. The individual supports our firm's decisions.

Initials of work team members |___|___|___|___|___|___|___|

- Always |___|___|___|___|___|___|___|
- Usually |___|___|___|___|___|___|___|
- Sometimes |___|___|___|___|___|___|___|
- Never |___|___|___|___|___|___|___|

29. The individual provides constructive suggestions which help develop our firm's strengths.

Initials of work team members |___|___|___|___|___|___|___|

- Always |___|___|___|___|___|___|___|
- Usually |___|___|___|___|___|___|___|
- Sometimes |___|___|___|___|___|___|___|
- Never |___|___|___|___|___|___|___|

30. When new duties are assigned (i.e. promotion, new job assignments), the accompanying responsibilities are adequately executed.

Initials of work team members |___|___|___|___|___|___|___|

- Always |___|___|___|___|___|___|___|
- Usually |___|___|___|___|___|___|___|
- Sometimes |___|___|___|___|___|___|___|
- Never |___|___|___|___|___|___|___|

31. The individual's year-round work is consistent with his/her annual evaluation.

Initials of work team members |___|___|___|___|___|___|___|

- Always |___|___|___|___|___|___|___|
- Usually |___|___|___|___|___|___|___|
- Sometimes |___|___|___|___|___|___|___|
- Never |___|___|___|___|___|___|___|

continued

32. There is a feeling that the individual is responsible for advancement.
Initials of work team members |____|____|____|____|____|____|____|
- Always
- Usually
- Sometimes
- Never

33. The individual assists in developing closer relationships with customers.
Initials of work team members |____|____|____|____|____|____|____|
- Always
- Usually
- Sometimes
- Never

34. The individual is able to identify trends and opportunities in practices, marketing efforts, potential areas for new business, etc.
Initials of work team members |____|____|____|____|____|____|____|
- Always
- Usually
- Sometimes
- Never

35. The individual understands marketing and his/her role in the process?
Initials of work team members |____|____|____|____|____|____|____|
- Always
- Usually
- Sometimes
- Never

36. The individual understands our firm's philosophy and its resources to attain its goals.
Initials of work team members |____|____|____|____|____|____|____|
- Always
- Usually
- Sometimes
- Never

37. The individual improves personal communication skills, both written and oral?
Initials of work team members |____|____|____|____|____|____|____|
- Always
- Usually
- Sometimes
- Never

38. Overall, the individual displays effective management leadership and entrepreneurial skills?
Initials of work team members |____|____|____|____|____|____|____|
- Always
- Usually
- Sometimes
- Never

Additional Comments:

_____

_____

_____

_____

_____

_____

_____

_____

_____

---

77. EVALUATE STAFF PRODUCTIVITY OBJECTIVELY

HOW DOES THIS APPLY TO MY BUSINESS?

_____

_____

_____

_____

_____

Priority   1   2   3 (Circle one)

Action Date_____

Profit Champion _____

Potential Dollar Effect $_____

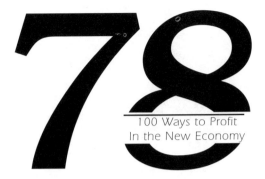

SEIZE OPPORTUNITIES TO UPGRADE YOUR STAFF

The team that wins the Superbowl is regarded as the best in their sport. But even Superbowl winners draft new players and make off-season trades to strengthen their organizations. Why? Because you don't get ahead by standing still. It's the same in business. **You need the best people you can get just to keep pace with the competition.** Take the time now to add some real "All-Stars" to your profit team.

In a booming economy when the job market is tight, recruiting good employees can be a major challenge, and finding great ones might be all but impossible. While in a depressed economy there may be a surplus of excellent prospects available, how do you find them?

No matter what the state of the economy, upgrade your staff and get rid of the slackers, troublemakers, dishonest employees, people who can't or won't learn to do their job properly.

We were making this point recently in a seminar for business owners when one person in the audience abruptly stood up and walked out of the room. After the meeting I asked her whether I had said something that disturbed her. "On the contrary," she replied. "Your talk inspired me to make some long overdue staff improvements at my company."

It seems several employees in her organization had not been doing their jobs for almost a year. Despite repeated warnings, these people were just not making a contribution to the firm. The owner had intended to discharge these individuals months ago, but kept putting off the unpleasant task. Our point about the availability of first-string job prospects struck a nerve with her, and galvanized her into action. She left the room in the middle of the talk, marched straight to a telephone and called in orders to terminate the unwanted employees.

"What a relief," she told me later. "I feel like I just put down an 80-pound suitcase!" She felt even better a few weeks later when she saw all the topnotch applicants eager to work at her firm. She even found new recruits from the Internet.

Employee Categories

Now, what would you do? "Feed the Work Horses, shine the Super Stars, fix or fire the Problems, and SHOOT THE DOGS!"

---

78. SEIZE OPPORTUNITIES TO UPGRADE YOUR STAFF

HOW DOES THIS APPLY TO MY BUSINESS?

_____

_____

_____

_____

_____

Priority   1   2   3   (Circle one)

Action Date_____

Profit Champion _____

Potential Dollar Effect $_____

REWARD EMPLOYEES FOR BRIGHT IDEAS

One of the best shoeshine men at the recently-renovated Reagan National Airport told us that completely new shoeshine stands had been installed there as part of the renovation. The poor design now makes it difficult to shine shoes, and they are uncomfortable for the customer. They are being redesigned. Of course no one asked the chief shoe-shiner for his opinion before they were designed the first time.

You can read this book cover-to-cover, but the best source of advice on how to be successful is right under your nose. It's your own work force.

Your employees know where the bottlenecks are in your organization, and they have some very interesting ideas for trimming costs, building sales and improving products or services.

But employees aren't always willing or able to articulate those ideas. Face facts: If the atmosphere in your organization discourages people from reporting or acknowledging problems, it's also going to discourage them from suggesting solutions. **Your job is to halt the profit torpedoes, to create a climate where your employees are motivated to make suggestions that will help the business. Do these profit torpedoes get fired off by your managers?**

CHECKLIST FOR PROFIT TORPEDOES

Does your management team use the following phrases?

	Yes	No
• Don't be ridiculous.	❏	❏
• Let's shelve it for now.	❏	❏
• We're not ready for that.	❏	❏
• It won't work here.	❏	❏

Does your management team use the following phrases?

		Yes	No
•	Our business is different	❏	❏
•	Let's think about it some more.	❏	❏
•	We did all right without it.	❏	❏
•	It's too radical a change.	❏	❏
•	Management won't like it.	❏	❏
•	Where did you dig up that idea?	❏	❏
•	It's not practical.	❏	❏
•	We've never done it before.	❏	❏
•	I have something better.	❏	❏
•	It's too risky.	❏	❏
•	Let's be sensible.	❏	❏
•	We can't afford that.	❏	❏
•	We'll never get it approved.	❏	❏
•	It's good, but...	❏	❏
•	Let's check on it later.	❏	❏
•	Too much work.	❏	❏
•	Let's get back to reality.	❏	❏
•	That's been tried before.	❏	❏
•	You can't be serious.	❏	❏

If the "Yes" answers are greater than the "No" answers, your organization is firing profit torpedoes.

Feeling part of the business is satisfying and eliminates some of the "stinkin' thinkin'" that permeates too many organizations.

---

79. REWARD YOUR EMPLOYEES FOR BRIGHT IDEAS

HOW DOES THIS APPLY TO MY BUSINESS?

_____

_____

_____

_____

_____

Priority   1   2   3   (Circle one)

Action Date_____

Profit Champion _____

Potential Dollar Effect $_____

CHAPTER 11:
FINANCIAL MATTERS

100 Ways to Profit
In the New Economy

TAKE ADVANTAGE OF TAX OPPORTUNITIES

Consult your tax or profit advisor. There may be a number of tax opportunities you have overlooked:

•   For instance, if your business was incorporated before August 1993 and you are ready to expand, instead of establishing new divisions to handle that business, consider setting up new C Corporations with "qualified small business stock." This could allow you to take advantage of a 50% tax reduction under the Revenue Reconciliation Act of 1993, in the event you sell the stock in your company, providing you qualify for this exceptional tax opportunity. While the Act excludes certain kinds of business, yours may qualify. In fact, under the 1998 tax bill, it may be possible for you to defer the tax completely by reinvesting in another business.Consult your tax or profit advisor.

•   If you have excess inventory, it may be possible to donate that inventory to certain types of charitable organizations and receive a tax deduction greater than its cost. If the fair market value of the donated property is greater than the cost, the tax deduction can be computed by deducting the cost plus 50 percent of the difference between fair market value and cost. Why not consider donating inventory rather than cash to your favorite charity? (Certain limits apply.)

Here's another idea. You probably have a retirement plan for your employees and yourself. It takes a lot of effort to earn the dollars to fund that plan. Much of that will be dissipated at your death, just because you've named the wrong beneficiary. If you name your estate as your beneficiary instead of a person, income taxes are incurred by December 31st of the year following the date of death. By naming an individual as beneficiary, it is possible to extend the payment over their life expectancy. In effect, you'll be receiving an "interest-free loan from the government."

A New Hampshire factory caught on fire in December some years ago and was badly damaged. The owner knew it would take him months to rebuild it. He was able to take advantage of a special provision of the tax law that allowed him to use the expected loss for the following tax year to offset the income from the current tax year. He did not pay the current year's taxes. In effect you extend the time of payment of the current year's tax liability because the expected net operating loss for the subsequent tax year, when carried back, will either reduce or eliminate the current year's tax liability.

Believe me the paperwork, though complex, is worth the trouble. When you're struggling to keep your business alive, there's no excuse for offering the government an interest-free loan!

A lot of businesses that have experienced nothing but success and growth over the years simply don't know how to sustain it. For many companies accustomed to nothing but black ink, a loss at the end of the year can come as a real shock.

With a little creative planning, a loss at the end of the year can actually generate a healthy transfusion of cash for your business!

An important (though often overlooked) section of the tax code allows corporations to "carry back" losses and effectively recalculate their tax liability for the previous two years. If your company paid taxes in any or all of the last two years, the government allows you to carry that loss back and retroactively reduce your tax liability for those profitable years.

You can actually recoup every penny of the taxes you paid over the past two years. This opportunity can be money from heaven!

Suppose your company is having an uninspiring year, but not actually running in the red. Since there is not a loss to carry back, you're out of luck. Or are you? Let's say your profitability has plunged to the break-even point after experiencing two successful years during which you paid an average of $37,500 in federal income taxes on income averaging $100,000 annually. With creative tax planning in the current year, you might be able to postpone some sales until the following tax year, while at the same time accelerating expenses.

As an example assume you're on the accrual basis of accounting for tax purposes, and that you are able to delay a sale that will generate $150,000 in gross profit until the subsequent tax year. Additionally, suppose that you can accelerate $50,000 of next year's operating expenses into the current tax year. With this tax planning you will go from a break-even situation this year to one in which you're able to report a tax loss of $200,000. That loss can then be carried back to each of the two prior years, and your business will be able to recover the entire $75,000 in taxes that you paid to IRS during those years!

There is a catch, of sorts. Carrying back a tax loss can make a business appear financially weaker on paper. Be sure to explain what you're doing to your banker (see #87) to protect your credit standing.

These ideas are just a few of many things that are less known that can have a dramatic effect on your tax liability. **Don't just sign your tax returns, rather make sure you are taking advantage of the tax opportunities afforded you. Your profit advisors can be a big help to you in this area. Tap their knowledge.**

---

80. TAKE ADVANTAGE OF TAX OPPORTUNITIES

HOW DOES THIS APPLY TO MY BUSINESS?

_____

_____

_____

_____

_____

Priority   1   2   3   (Circle one)

Action Date_____

Profit Champion _____

Potential Dollar Effect $_____

81

COMPARE INCREASED SALES WITH DECREASED COSTS

Every new sale is accompanied by additional costs. The costs are numerous. There are personnel to make the sale, trucks or freight charges to deliver the merchandise, billing clerks to send invoices and statements, and collection people to coerce late-paying accounts.

Look at the bottom line of your income statement. Your company is fortunate if it has a 10% bottom line net income. In other words, to earn $100,000 of additional profit, you might have to increase your sales by $1 million. So, the question is: Do you have the financial resources to be able to carry the costs associated with the additional sales volume? What if you were to cut costs by 10% instead? Let's check it out in the following table:

	Pro Forma Prior to Cost Cutting or Increasing Sales	Pro Forma after Cutting Costs by 10%	Pro-Forma for Increasing Sales (Equivalent to Cutting Costs by 10%)
Sales	$20,000,000	$20,000,000	$38,000,000
Cost of Sales	(10,000,000)	(9,000,000)	(19,000,000)
Gross Profit	10,000,000	11,000,000	19,000,000
Operating Expenses	(8,000,000)	(7,200,000)	(15,200,000)
NET PROFIT	$ 2,000,000	$ 3,800,000	$ 3,800,000

As you can see in this overly simplistic example, cutting costs by 10% almost doubles the net profit in this example. On the other hand, to increase profits to $3,800,000 without the 10% cost cutting, sales might have to be increased to $38 million. Imagine the effort and cost associated with a sales increase of $18 million!

Many companies cannot afford to finance nearly twice their existing volume, simply because they don't have enough cash to carry the receivables. A sale made at the beginning of the month, for example, might not produce cash for 60 days, perhaps longer. In fact, sales might have to be greater than $38 million in this example, because the costs to finance the increased sales activity would be substantial.

While savings can typically be associated with greater volume, all costs do not have to go up in proportion to the increased sales. Significant sales growth puts substantial strains on equipment and personnel, so profits are minimized.

It doesn't cost anything to control expenses. In fact, cost controls can provide immediate bottom line results and put little strain on personnel and equipment when done properly.

---

81. COMPARE INCREASED SALES WITH DECREASED COSTS

HOW DOES THIS APPLY TO MY BUSINESS?

_____

_____

_____

_____

_____

Priority   1   2   3   (Circle one)

Action Date_____

Profit Champion _____

Potential Dollar Effect $_____

BUDGETS MAY LIMIT FINANCIAL PERFORMANCE

We agree with the assessment of Jack Welch, legendary CEO of American giant General Electric, on the budgeting process:

> "The budget is the bane of corporate America. It never should have existed. A budget is this: If you make it, you generally get a pat on the back and a few bucks. If you miss it, you get a stick in the eye — or worse ... **Making a budget is an exercise in minimalization**. You're always trying to get the lowest out of people, because everyone is negotiating to get the lowest number."

When you and your staff put together a Profit Plan, complete with prioritized projects, accountability and projected bottom line results, you are looking toward the future. Standard budgeting produces only probable results based on the past, it limits your profitability.

In addition, many businesses make the mistake of establishing an overall company budget, but then fail to break that budget down by department. As a result, some divisions of the organization are chronically running over budget, while others are constantly being squeezed. Once you've worked out an operating budget for your organization as a whole, set individual budgets for each department or branch, and hold managers and department heads accountable for those budgets.

Let your divisional managers know that the rewards they can expect will depend on how successfully they use the resources budgeted to them. If the manager marshals those resources effectively and the department is successful, that individual deserves to share in the fruits of success through bonuses or other forms of compensation.

That's only good business sense, but you would be surprised at how many organizations don't operate this way. Failing to establish budgeted goals on a department-by-department basis will create lack of accountability in your business. We know of businesses that have been literally crippled because they neglected to do this.

Expectations create results. For instance, the shipping department of a business that had budgeted profit accountability by department discovered a way to recycle incoming shipping materials from materials received and using them as packing materials on outgoing shipments—instead of paying for trash hauling.

Or, take the case of the publishing company that budgeted $100,000 for legal expenses during the year. The company's magazine division encountered some legal claims which could have been resolved quickly for well under $5,000. Instead of settling, however, the department decided to fight the claim and retain a law firm. Unfortunately for the publisher, the legal expenses exceeded estimates and by the time the dispute was finally resolved, the company's entire legal budget had been exhausted.

Later that same year the publisher's textbook division encountered a legal pothole of its own. At that point, however, the cupboard was bare, the publisher's legal budget was gone. Through no fault of their own, the people in the textbook division were left to choose between several equally unappealing options.

The root cause of these problems was the fact that the publisher did not set departmental budgets and did not hold its divisional managers accountable for those budgets. The people in the magazine division regarded the corporate legal services budget as OPM (other people's money!) Rather than spending $5,000 of the division's "own money" to settle a claim, they chose to spend $100,000 in "OPM" to fight it!

The failure to hold business managers responsible for their own budgets can create other problems within an organization.

Suppose, for example, we take an automobile dealership and organize it into a new car department, a used car department, and a service department. Let's say the dealer's overall advertising budget for the year is $500,000. If at the start of the year the new car department contracts for ad placements costing $500,000, there's nothing left in the kitty for the used car manager or the service manager to promote their departments. The company would then have to decide whether to come up with additional money for advertising, or to allow the used car sales and service departments to suffer for lack of promotional funds.

In this case, besides creating serious problems for the company, the absence of departmental budgets led to a grossly unfair situation for middle managers whose income is linked to the performance of their departments.

The correct way to handle this situation would be for the dealership to earmark, say, $300,000 for new car advertising, and $100,000 each for used cars and service. But then what's to stop the new car manager from spending most or all of department's ad budget during the first quarter, leaving little left for the rest of the year? Nothing! But perhaps that would be a wise decision given the market conditions at the time, even though you've hired that manager to make those decisions. If you lack confidence in a particular manager's judgment, coach that person so that they learn how to make proper financial decisions for your company. Most of all, make your department chiefs aware that they will be held accountable for using the resources budgeted to them to perform successfully.

---

82. BUDGETS MAY LIMIT FINANCIAL PERFORMANCE

HOW DOES THIS APPLY TO MY BUSINESS?

_____

_____

_____

_____

_____

Priority   1   2   3   (Circle one)

Action Date_____

Profit Champion _____

Potential Dollar Effect $_____

NEGOTIATE SPECIAL TERMS TO STRETCH CASH FLOW

Someone once said that everything is negotiable. We don't know about that, but we do know that if your business regularly purchases substantial quantities of goods from another company, you're in a good position to negotiate favorable payment terms.

Indeed, your goal should always be to negotiate with suppliers for special terms that accommodate your cash flow requirements. Whenever possible, arrange to make payments after your busy season.

For example, if you're a retailer and you generate a significant proportion of your sales during the holiday season, try to arrange for special dating that will allow you to pay for your merchandise after the end of the year. This is particularly true if you are in an inventory-intensive business.

Why would suppliers offer such terms? In many cases, they are more than willing, in order to cement a long-term relationship with a good customer. It's certainly worth raising the issue with your sources of supply, particularly if you are in a position to increase your business with a company in return for better payment terms.

We have clients who have been buying merchandise since August that they don't have to pay for until after the Christmas season. For example, we have a client who sells rock salt for melting snow. In the spring they sell mulch, and in summertime they're into something else altogether. Because of cash flow considerations, the company makes it a point to negotiate payment terms that coincide with the nature of these seasonal operations. As a result, the distributor may receive a shipment of fertilizer in February, but won't be required to pay for it until

May—after he has received payment from his customers.

The prize for negotiating favorable payment terms goes to a high-volume auto parts distributor. This company worked out an arrangement with its principal supplier under which it agreed to substantially increase orders. In return, the manufacturer agreed to extend what amounts to a permanent $500,000 dating. Under their agreement, as long as the distributor's auto parts purchases remain above an agreed upon level, the $500,000 does not have to be repaid.

For example, if the distributor ordered parts totalling $1.2 million from the supplier, the amount payable to the supplier would only be $700,000. The other $500,000 will never have to be paid unless, of course, the distributor switches suppliers or goes out of business. In this case, the distributor is enjoying free use of $500,000 worth of inventory. The parts manufacturer is effectively financing the wholesaler's operations in return for a commitment for continued business from that company.

83. NEGOTIATE SPECIAL TERMS TO STRETCH CASH FLOW

HOW DOES THIS APPLY TO MY BUSINESS?

_____

_____

_____

_____

_____

Priority   1   2   3   (Circle one)

Action Date_____

Profit Champion _____

Potential Dollar Effect $_____

100 Ways to Profit
In the New Economy

REVIEW SPENDING FOR PUBLICATIONS AND MEMBERSHIP DUES

At our house, we subscribe to a magazine we've been receiving for 27 years. We have probably looked at very few issues in the past ten years because our interests have changed. But that subscription form keeps coming in, and the magazine keeps getting renewed.

The same thing happens in business. There are magazines, journals, newsletters and other publications that companies receive, but nobody reads. Similarly, you may be paying dues to a business group or other organization out of habit rather than because of the benefits of membership. Certainly, you must have had a good reason for joining the group or subscribing to the publication originally. But if they no longer serve a purpose, cut your losses.

I know of a real estate firm that subscribes to the *Federal Register* —a thick book of new rules and regulations published every business day by the government. The *Register* comes in every morning with the mail, and goes out unread every evening with the trash.

And we're not talking nickels and dimes here. *The Federal Register* costs over $300 per year. An annual subscription to investment publications will run you almost $150, and it's not unusual for industry newsletters to charge $500 or more per subscription. Unless you are trying to win the sweepstakes, though, there may be better things to do than that with your money.

The real problem is inertia. Subscriptions tend to continue to be renewed unless someone makes a conscious decision to cancel them. Review your publication subscriptions and keep only those that continue to serve a purpose.

Even if you decide to maintain a subscription, you may find that you can cut down on the number of copies you're paying for. At our firm we reduced the number of copies of some publications by 50 percent and now route them from desk to desk.

One business that we are familiar with has come up with an especially creative way to reduce or eliminate publication costs. For years, this major chain of beauty shops spent upwards of thousands annually on magazines for customers to read under the hair dryers. Providing these publications was good business for the chain because it fostered good will among its clients. But it was also good business for the publishers of these magazines, because the publications received considerable exposure among the beauty shop patrons.

Recognizing this, the chain was able to approach the several leading publishers and negotiate free subscriptions for their shops—a maneuver that saved the chain hundreds of dollars every month.

Of course, your business may not be the type that would enable you to negotiate free subscriptions from publishers. But there are other ways that you may be able to trim your company's publication costs.

Start by giving one person in your organization responsibility for determining which publications as well as how many are being ordered on a monthly basis, and who is receiving them. Determine whether they are beneficial to your firm, and whether several employees can share a subscription.

Give similar close scrutiny to membership dues that your company pays to various organizations. Our office, for example, was paying $500 each year in dues to provide membership for one of our employees in a local business organization. Our hope, of course, was that the individual would make contacts with area business people and ultimately attract new clients for the firm. When we discovered that our employee had stopped attending the group's meetings, we wasted no time in putting that $500 to better use.

Make sure that the benefits you reap from organization memberships and publication subscriptions exceed their cost. If employees want to order or continue receiving a particular publication, require that they explain in writing why this publication is important and how it will help them and your business. Ditto for organization memberships. If they're unable or unwilling to justify these expenditures, put your capital to better use.

EMPLOYEE REQUEST FOR MEMBERSHIP

Employee Name_____

Organization Name_____

Organization Address_____

ANNUAL DUES _____

NUMBER OF MEETINGS/YEAR_____

NUMBER OF MEETINGS ATTENDED LAST YEAR_____

NAME(S), ADDRESSES, AND PHONE NUMBERS OF CONTACTS MADE THROUGH THE ORGANIZATION

1_____

_____

_____

2 _____

_____

_____

(Use additional paper if required)

PLEASE STATE YOUR GOALS VIS-A-VIS THIS ORGANIZATION FOR THE NEXT YEAR. (For example, the number of meetings you anticipate attending, the number of contacts you anticipate making, speeches or presentations that you plan to make, etc.)

_____

_____

_____

_____

Please sign here as an indication of your commitment to the above stated goals.

_____

Watch how many of these come back to your company with the dues invoices for payment. We bet far less than you are presently paying.

84. REVIEW SPENDING FOR PUBLICATIONS AND ORGANIZATION DUES

HOW DOES THIS APPLY TO MY BUSINESS?

_____

_____

_____

_____

_____

Priority   1   2   3   (Circle one)

Action Date_____

Profit Champion _____

Potential Dollar Effect $_____ _____

DEVELOP, UNDERSTAND AND MONITOR
KEY OPERATING STATISTICS

Many companies are literally drowning in financial information but are thirsty for knowledge. There are so many computer-generated reports, but do your associates know how to use the valuable information reported in them? Don't just look at numbers—find out what they truly mean. Your task is to sort through the financial information available to you and decide which factors are really important to the success of your operation.

In some respects, the most valuable way to express business information is in the form of operating statistics—a shorthand expression of the relationship between numbers. It enables you to convey a tremendous amount of information with abbreviated numbers. They can be a very powerful tool in measuring your business.

Developing and maintaining certain operating statistics allows you to monitor the pulse of your business.

In order to develop meaningful business operating statistics for your operations, you must figure out what the pulse of your business is about. Then compute the necessary data to give you the vital signs necessary to assure you that things are financially well or if your business is off course.

Financial statements report the present value of the past. The point is that interpreting and understanding the relationship of financial information may mean more to you than financial statements. Begin by developing business operating statistics that you need to know regularly to sleep well at night. Those that provide meaningful clues about what is happening in your business and in your department. Ratios which are widely used by businesses today include:

- **Current Ratio** - The current assets of a business divided by current liabilities. This ratio is particularly meaningful to a short-term creditor, because it is a yardstick of the ability of the borrower to meet his current debts.

- **Acid Test Ratio** - The sum of a company's cash, marketable securities and net receivables divided by current liabilities. This figure, sometimes called the "quick ratio," measures the overall debt-paying ability of a business.

- **Advertising-to-Sales Ratio** - The company's total advertising expenditures divided by total sales. This figure will provide you with a warning signal if promotional costs are becoming excessive, or if advertising strategy is off target.

- **Equity Ratio** - Stockholders' equity divided by the sum of total liabilities plus stockholders' equity. This ratio is a measurement of the long-term solvency of a corporation. It is considered by many credit professionals as a key indication of credit strength of a business.

- **Daily Sales to Receivables Ratio** - Total trade accounts receivable divided by net sales on accounts, multiplied by 365. This figure provides an indication of how many days it takes your company to collect its receivables.

- **Inventory Turnover Ratio** - Total cost of sales divided by the average inventory on hand over the course of a year. This ratio is an important gauge of profitability because it shows the number of times inventory turns during a business year.

Although ratios are useful in themselves—particularly if you compare them with the results from previous periods—they may be especially valuable as a device for evaluating your company's performance with those of others in your industry. Many professional and trade associations produce key operating statistics for their industry. You may also purchase surveys published by such firms as Dun and Bradstreet, and Robert Morris.

Some other important statistics might include number of sales opportunities related to number of sales closes for the company as well by salesperson. Others might be average sale per order, per customer, per salesperson. What about a schedule of business lost and why? Imagine timely statistics showing when customers begin to buy less from your company.

You get a good or bad feel for your favorite sports team when you read the game statistics in the sports section of your favorite newspaper. The same opportunity is available when you share business operating statistics with those that you work with.

---

85. DEVELOP, UNDERSTAND AND MONITOR KEY OPERATING STATISTICS

HOW DOES THIS APPLY TO MY BUSINESS?

_____

_____

_____

_____

_____

Priority   1   2   3   (Circle one)

Action Date_____

Profit Champion _____

Potential Dollar Effect $_____

---

100 Ways to Profit
In the New Economy

MEASURE THE EFFECTIVENESS OF YOUR BUSINESS IN KEY AREAS

What you can measure, you can manage. Are you measuring your business's effectiveness in critical areas? Do you have a Profit Plan to increase your organization's performance effectiveness in these areas?

Let's look at what can be measured in your organization to determine your performance effectiveness. Complete the following checklist to learn what more you can do to achieve greater profitability by improving measurable performance results.

CHECKLIST FOR MEASURING PERFORMANCE EFFECTIVENESS

Yes	No	N/A	Sales
❏	❏	❏	Discount from standard pricing
❏	❏	❏	Sales per customer
❏	❏	❏	Gross profit dollars per customer
❏	❏	❏	Sales closes per number of sales calls
❏	❏	❏	Average size of order per sale
❏	❏	❏	Time elapsed from date of customer order to delivery
❏	❏	❏	On-time deliveries and not-on-time deliveries as a percentage of total deliveries
❏	❏	❏	Average number of sales calls necessary to obtain a sales appointment, by salesperson
❏	❏	❏	Identification of steps in the sales process necessary to close a sale

Yes	No	N/A	**Customer & Relationship Satisfaction**
❏	❏	❏	Survey of customers to determine the percentages that are totally satisfied, partially satisfied and dissatisfied
❏	❏	❏	Number of new customers
❏	❏	❏	Reasons new customers decide to do business with us
❏	❏	❏	Number of former customers lost
❏	❏	❏	Reasons former customers ceased to do business with us
❏	❏	❏	On-time deliveries
❏	❏	❏	On-time handling of customer complaints
❏	❏	❏	Special requests from customers handled without problems
❏	❏	❏	Percentage of sales returns and the reasons why
❏	❏	❏	Referrals by referral source
❏	❏	❏	Thank you letters and/or gifts sent to referral sources
❏	❏	❏	Unkept customer promises

Yes	No	N/A	**Operations**
❏	❏	❏	Timely shipments
❏	❏	❏	Time it takes to receive inventory
❏	❏	❏	Time it takes from the order date to receive materials used for manufacturing
❏	❏	❏	Percentage of on-time deliveries of materials and goods coming to us as well as going from us to our customers
❏	❏	❏	Percentage of time we perform various activities right the first time
❏	❏	❏	Cost of materials per unit manufactured
❏	❏	❏	Cost of labor per unit manufactured
❏	❏	❏	Utilization percentages of our equipment and people
❏	❏	❏	Dollars invested in inventory as a percentage of sales
❏	❏	❏	Time per task related to total time
❏	❏	❏	Supplier relations
❏	❏	❏	Paperwork handled free of errors
❏	❏	❏	Time spent on filling orders
❏	❏	❏	Accuracy of estimates

Yes	No	N/A	**Employees**
❏	❏	❏	Measuring customer service by employee
❏	❏	❏	Staff performance evaluations
❏	❏	❏	Quantity and quality of suggestions per employee
❏	❏	❏	Value created for our business by each employee
❏	❏	❏	Rework required per each employee that caused the problem

We hope you have checked mostly "yes" on this checklist, but experience indicates that perhaps you didn't. You can help your business by measuring and monitoring key factors effectively which in turn will contribute to your financial success.

---

86. MEASURE YOUR BUSINESS'S EFFECTIVENESS IN KEY AREAS

HOW DOES THIS APPLY TO MY BUSINESS?

_____

_____

_____

_____

_____

Priority   1   2   3   (Circle one)

Action Date_____

Profit Champion _____

Potential Dollar Effect $_____

KEEP YOUR BANKER
INFORMED

When a major corporation is having a great year, the company is likely to churn out press releases announcing the results, and play up sales and earnings growth on the front page of the annual report. It obviously needs the banks' help to finance its growth. But when the results are less than predicted, you don't hear a peep from management. It's human nature to share good news and keep bad news to yourself, but ignoring poor financial performance won't make the situation go away. **Whether your business is having a good or bad year, it's better to share the facts either way with your banker.**

Remember, bankers don't like surprises or last-minute requests. If your company has an outstanding loan or line of credit at a bank, your banker went to bat for you with the institution's loan committee. Give early warning signals so that he or she can prepare the bank for your cash needs long before the time you need the funds.

No matter what your company's financial picture, you just can't risk losing your bank's support. It should be standard operating procedure to keep your banker posted on your company finances—good or bad. Indeed, it's good practice to send the bank interim financial statements and follow up with phone calls and meetings to avoid misunderstandings down the road.

Too many businesses with poor financial performance often suffer from serious "bank-o-phobia." They're concerned that the banker will see only the bad news and none of the good. Often, however, these concerns are misplaced.

For example, we were able to work with a client that had large tax loss carryback. The owner of this construction company did a thumbs down on our plan for fear of his banker's reaction. The principal was concerned that the loss would weaken the firm's financial relationship with its bank and limit his borrowing capacity.

With our client's permission, we called his banker and explained the situation. In essence, we left the decision up to the bank. On the one hand, the company could minimize the loss, which minimized the tax, and present the lender with a more attractive financial statement. On the other hand, they could maximize the tax loss and claim a significant refund.

The bank pondered the situation for almost a week, and finally called back with instructions to go for the tax loss carryback and forget about how the company looks on paper.

When the year-end financial statements were prepared, they came as no surprise to the banker. He was expecting the large loss. Our client's credit standing with his bank remained intact, and the owner pocketed a $1.7 million windfall from taxes he thought were paid and gone several years ago!

IMMEDIATE PROFIT ACTION ITEMS:

- Communicate regularly with your bankers.
- Treat your banker like a customer.
- Develop contingency plans in case your bankers can't or won't work with you on specific needs.
- When seeking financing, match your needs with the bank's wants. Are you their ideal customer; i.e. type of company, size of company, size of loan, type of loan?
- Don't be afraid to offer a restructuring plan for yourself if necessary.

---

87. KEEP YOUR BANKER INFORMED

HOW DOES THIS APPLY TO MY BUSINESS?

_____

_____

_____

_____

_____

Priority   1   2   3   (Circle one)

Action Date_____

Profit Champion _____

Potential Dollar Effect $_____

PICK YOUR INSURANCE AGENTS' BRAINS TO CONTROL INSURANCE PREMIUMS

Sit down with your insurance agents and explore options for reducing the cost of coverage.

One approach that a number of businesses have tried is to freeze the company's contribution toward employee health insurance. If you're paying out, say, $200 per month toward each worker's health coverage, you could agree to continue that same dollar contribution next year. But any premiums above this amount would have to be paid by the employee.

To help workers deal with future increases in premium costs, many employers now offer lower-cost coverage options such as a health maintenance organization or a preferred provider organization.

Some smart businesses emphasize wellness rather than illness for their employees, making contributions towards their employees' expenses for joining a gym or participating in an exercise, weight loss, or smoking program. In other words, employees are rewarded for staying or getting healthy.

Similarly, talk with your agent and profit advisor about ways to reduce the cost of other types of insurance.

Disability coverage, for example, is extremely important — it is the family's safety net if the breadwinner becomes incapacitated. Consider reducing disability premium costs by accepting a longer "elimination period" and self-insuring the short term.

Many disability insurance policies don't begin paying benefits until you've been incapacitated for 30 days. By switching to an elimination period of 60, 90 or even 180 days you can maintain the same dollar coverage and significantly lower your premium costs.

Worker's compensation insurance is a very expensive part of many organizations' budgets. A construction company client decided to set up a safety program in order to reduce these costs. Their program offers incentives — either monetary or otherwise — to those who don't have accidents! These incentives build with the length of time a worker remains without accident. The company also offers bonuses in paid time off for good attendance. There has been a 50 percent drop in sick leave and the company has not had to add additional workers, despite increased workload. On the other hand, any construction worker who comes in late is sent home without a paycheck. Why? Because, their management determines, these workers are late for a reason related to what they were doing the night before. They aren't ready to concentrate on their work and are accident prone.

A commercial glass installer, for example, was encountering steep Worker's compensation premiums due to the heavy number of claims being filed by her employees. It wasn't that the company was out of compliance with workplace safety requirements, or that the employees were particularly accident prone. The high level of claims was a reflection of the nature of our client's business.

But while the installer couldn't cut down on the injury rate, she could take steps to reduce the number of Worker's compensation claims filed by her people. The company contracted with a nearby medical clinic to treat employees with minor bruises, cuts, strains and other injuries for a flat monthly retainer.

Because the clinic arrangement sharply reduced the incidence of Worker's Comp claims by employees, the company's premiums also dropped sharply. After a while she ran a comparative cost analysis and found that for every dollar she paid to this medical clinic, the company saved $2 in insurance premiums.

When you review your company's Worker's Comp costs, it's important to examine the risk categories to which your employees are assigned. The drivers for a trucking company that specializes in delivering explosives would likely be rated high-risk employees. But those high rates should not apply to the company's dispatcher, bookkeeper or secretary.

It's in your interest to work with your insurance agent to place each of your workers in the lowest risk class possible.

Your agent may also be able to help you achieve substantial savings on whole life insurance costs by putting your dividends to work to offset your premiums. That could be the next best thing to "free" life insurance!

Being underinsured can be risky for a business. But by the same token, being overinsured can impose significant unnecessary costs on a company. You would be surprised at the number of businesses that waste considerable sums of money because they have duplicative or unnecessary insurance coverage. Insurance is often the third largest expense for a business.

Take motor vehicle insurance. Some businesses insure vehicles under policies calling for a $200 or $250 deductible. But this often makes no economic sense.

Of course, businesses need insurance as a hedge against major losses—you don't need protection against damages costing you a few hundred dollars. If a company car or truck is damaged in an accident, it isn't likely to be much of a hardship for the business to absorb the first $500 or $1,000 in repairs. So why not raise the deductible on your company's policy to $500 or $1,000?

Sit down with your insurance agent and profit advisor and have them crunch the numbers for you. **You'll be surprised at how much lower your annual premiums will be if you raise deductibles.**

Don't limit your focus to vehicle insurance, however. Ask your agent for suggestions on how to trim other insurance costs as well. There are ways to reduce premiums for all types of coverage—it just takes a little creative brainstorming with your agent and profit advisor.

---

88. PICK YOUR INSURANCE AGENTS' BRAINS TO CONTROL INSURANCE PREMIUMS

HOW DOES THIS APPLY TO MY BUSINESS?

_____

_____

_____

_____

_____

Priority   1   2   3   (Circle one)

Action Date_____

Profit Champion _____

Potential Dollar Effect $_____

TAP OUTSIDE INVESTORS FOR CAPITAL

The first stop for most business owners in need of fresh capital is the local bank. But banks and other financial institutions aren't the only source of funds for businesses, and at times they're not the best source.

From your perspective, there may be little or no risk at all associated with the loan. The extra capital will enable you to add new facilities, expand existing ones, broaden your market share, and pole-vault your company to a new plateau of profitability. But convincing a gun-shy banker of these truths may prove a difficult task.

A successful real estate investor, with a number of valuable properties and a net worth of nearly $20 million, wanted to remodel one of her facilities and sought to borrow $350,000 for this purpose. As collateral, she was willing to put up a piece of real estate appraised at more than $1 million. Clearly, here was a loan proposition safe as Gibraltar. Yet she was turned down flat by the bank!

The investor did what some say businesses should do in the first place, she arranged to finance her remodeling program through outside investors.

Finding private investors willing to bankroll a sound business project isn't as difficult as it may sound. There are plenty of people looking for a safe place to invest their funds at attractive rates. Squirreling money away in a bank or in T-bills will yield them, maybe, 5 to 6 percent. By offering them the equivalent of the interest rates charged by commercial lenders, say 8 to 9 percent or so, you've enabled them to increase their yield by 60 percent—an extremely attractive proposition for any private investor.

397

To be sure, you're not likely to attract any investors if you're seeking capital merely to keep a floundering business afloat for a few more months. But if your company is sound to begin with and an influx of fresh funds would make it even stronger, then you're a prime candidate for outside investors.

One of the most frequently overlooked sources of outside capital is the money sitting around in employee retirement plans. Your company can't borrow from the pension fund set up on behalf of your employees, but other companies can tap into your retirement program for financing. And by the same token, your business can borrow from the pension funds set up by other companies. A corporate retirement fund earning 5 percent on its money would likely be very interested in bankrolling a sound investment in your company that would yield, say, 9 or 10 percent.

Another excellent source of outside capital is your own circle of friends. Assuming the investment truly is rock solid, you'll be doing friends or family a favor by offering them to a high rate of return on their funds. If you do borrow from friends or family, though, keep it as an arms-length transaction. Offer them the same collateral that you would give to a bank — a mortgage on the property, corporate guarantees, personal guarantees, and so on.

And, don't forget the Internet! There are now Web sites which match good ideas to investors. Let your mouse do a little trolling on the Web before you ask anyone else for the money you need to grow.

---

89. TAP OUTSIDE INVESTORS FOR CAPITAL
HOW DOES THIS APPLY TO MY BUSINESS?

_____

_____

_____

_____

_____

Priority   1   2   3 (Circle one)

Action Date_____

Profit Champion _____

Potential Dollar Effect $_____

REVIEW LEASES TO CONTROL COSTS

We represent a law firm. We went to the firm's landlord and mentioned that the firm was interested in renewing its lease only if the firm were treated as a new tenant. The landlord offered several months of free rent and minimal escalations after several years, the normal concession they were giving in a new lease. After we finished that entire negotiation, we said to the landlord, "Look, if we were new tenants, wouldn't you give us a build-out allowance? Build-outs for this law firm would cost about $400,000. Our client signed a new ten-year lease as if they were a new tenant and received a check for $400,000 for build-outs that were unnecessary to construct. It's an upside-down world to think that the tenant receives money instead of paying for it!

Be sure to negotiate a cancellation clause in the lease so that if business takes a turn for the worse, or does so well you need to expand and move to a new location, you will not be obligated to pay the remaining lease payments.

As a general rule, profitable companies lease, rather than own, their properties for two major reasons:

*   Having cash tied up in properties which are, usually, yielding a return less than the cost of capital is not in the shareholders' best interest, and
*   Liquidating these properties over time may be difficult and costly.

For many retail and service organizations, rental costs are structured as the greater of X dollars per year or Y percent of sales. If your business is subject to sales volatility, negotiate your lease, if at all possible, with a lower fixed rental cost plus a higher percentage of sales than normal. In this way, the landlord has a greater vested interest in your sales success and is "encouraged" to help promote your center's business. It means that you pay a lower rent than normal when sales are slow and more when you're doing well and can afford it.

As rent is usually the second largest expense for a retail or service chain, introduce "walk-away" clauses into your rental contract so that you can walk away if sales fall below a certain figure or if a predetermined percentage of your shopping center is vacant for more than three months or if a major tenant moves.

We always encourage our clients to measure their rental space. Just because the lease says you have so many square feet, it may not be so, and you may be paying for too much space. Hire a professional to measure and verify your square footage. We call this a "space audit," and you may want to extend it to your entire building. Canvas some of the other tenants to do a space audit of the common areas you are jointly paying for in your Common Area Maintenance charge. Dig into what is actually included in the operating expenses. Your lease defines this charge. We've found some pretty amazing expenses being included here. Why should you rather than your landlord pay for them?

90. REVIEW LEASES TO CONTROL OCCUPANCY COSTS

HOW DOES THIS APPLY TO MY BUSINESS?

_____

_____

_____

_____

_____

Priority   1   2   3   (Circle one)

Action Date_____

Profit Champion _____

Potential Dollar Effect $_____

SCHEDULE A YEAR-END TAX PLANNING SESSION WITH YOUR CPA

It's never a good time to pay too much in taxes. There are ways for businesses to reduce their tax burden that aren't illegal, immoral or fattening. But it takes some creative planning before the end of the fiscal year. Little, if anything, can be done after the tax year ends.

Meet with your accountant months before the end of the year to do tax planning and prepare an annual tax projection. The idea is to shift income and expenses from one year to another, as well as take advantage of a variety of tax opportunities available to your business to ease the tax bite.

If it turns out you are doing well this year but expect a significant falloff in earnings the following year, your accountant can suggest a number of ways to reduce the overall tax burden by absorbing expenses in the profitable year, or postponing income until the bad year.

Among other things, businesses can pay employee bonuses early; stockpile supplies for the coming year; donate slow-moving merchandise to charity before year end or claim a tax loss by disposing of unused assets early.

If the situation is the opposite—you expect to do even better in the coming months—simply reverse the process and reduce next year's taxable income.

An accountant who adds value to your business can also help you avoid certain kinds of year-end financial transactions that will have severe negative tax implications for your business and your family and create significant tax-saving opportunities.

Let's look at some tax opportunities you may wish to explore with

401

your tax advisor.

- Real estate tax assessments on special use property may be overestimated. Perhaps a successful tax appeal can save thousands to hundreds of thousands of dollars of real estate taxes.

- Personal property tax assessments (in applicable jurisdictions) are based on personal property values—typically machinery and equipment as well as inventory and supplies owned by businesses. We have discovered property that was previously either disposed, sold, scrapped, or donated, but never deleted from financial records. Personal property taxes on non-existent property may have been paid erroneously for years.

- Tax credits for hiring certain targeted groups. Various industries hire people who can qualify for these beneficial tax credits but have not prepared the paperwork to take advantage of this opportunity. Construction, nursing homes, restaurants, moving and storage, hair salons, landscaping, and hotels are but a few of the industries that have employees that may qualify for these tax credits. A client of ours received over $250,000 in the form of these tax credits in a single year. Remember, a dollar of tax credit can save a dollar of tax. A tax deduction only saves taxes at the percentage tax bracket a taxpayer is in.

- Research and development tax credits are available for businesses that have expenditures for "qualified research." These expenditures must be for the purpose of discovering new or improved technological information intended to be useful in the development of new or improved business components of the taxpayer. Is it possible your company has research and development tax credits waiting for you to capture that will significantly reduce your income taxes?

The tax opportunity list is endless. Before signing your business returns, study them and get a feel for what makes sense and what doesn't. Ask your tax advisor to clarify what is and (just as importantly) what is not reflected on your tax returns. Make sure you are seizing the tax opportunities available to your business.

91. SCHEDULE A YEAR-END TAX PLANNING SESSION WITH YOUR CPA

HOW DOES THIS APPLY TO MY BUSINESS?

_____

_____

_____

_____

_____

Priority   1   2   3   (Circle one)

Action Date_____

Profit Champion _____

EVALUATE THE ECONOMIC VIABILITY OF MAJOR EXPENDITURES

Here is our "GUZINTA" method of calculating the economic viability of a proposed fixed asset acquisition. GUZINTA refers to the difference between what goes into the bank ("GUZINTA") and what goes out of ("GUZOUTA") the bank — the net annual cash increase or decrease. Do not compute depreciation for this purpose.

Assume management would like to have a minimum 15 percent return on their investment. Always assume that they are paying cash rather than financing the fixed asset acquisition.

CALCULATION TO DETERMINE THE ECONOMIC VIABILITY OF A PROPOSED FIXED ASSET ACQUISITION*

Year	GUZINTA the Bank (Net Cash Increase)	GUZOUTA the Bank (Net Cash Decrease)	5% Budgeted Rate of Return	Present Value
0	-0-	$100,000	1.000	$(100,000)
1	$ 22,000	X	.870	19,140
2	22,000	X	.756	16,632
3	22,000	X	.658	14,476
4	22,000	X	.572	12,584
5	22,000	X	.497	10,934
6	22,000	X	.432	9,504
7	22,000	X	.376	8,272
8	22,000	X	.327	7,194
9	22,000	X	.284	6,248
10	32,000**	X	.247	7,904

NET PRESENT VALUE   **$ 12,888**

*Computed using present value tables.
**$22,000 cash increase plus $10,000 estimated salvage value.

As you can see, the net present value of this $100,000 expenditure is more than zero, so this investment is producing a rate of return slightly greater than 15 percent. Management has reached its objectives.

To determine the actual rate of return, make the following computations:

$$\frac{\text{Price}}{\text{Annual Cash Saved}} = \text{Years Necessary to Recover Costs}$$

$$\frac{\$100,000}{\$\ 22,000} = 4.5 \text{ Years}$$

Now look at the chart below to determine the annual rate of return from the fixed asset acquisition. You will note that the annual rate of return is 19 percent. Try to spend your money on asset acquisitions that give you the greatest rates of return.

ANNUAL RATE OF RETURN FOR FIXED ASSET ACQUISITIONS

Years of Useful Life	3.00	3.25	3.50	3.75	4.00	4.25	4.50	4.75	5.00	5.50	6.00
3	0										
4	15	11	7	3	0						
5	23	19	15	12	9	6	4	2	0		
6	27	23	20	17	15	12	10	8	6	3	0
7	29	26	23	20	18	15	13	11	10	7	4
8	30	27	25	22	20	18	16	14	13	10	8
9	31	28	26	23	21	19	18	16	15	12	10
10	32	29	27	24	22	21	(19)	18	16	14	11
15	33	30	28	26	25	23	22	20	19	16	15
20	33	30	28	26	25	23	22	20	19	18	16
Over 20	34	31	29	27	26	24	23	21	20	19	17

Make informed fixed-asset-acquisition decisions for your company. As you probably have limited financial resources, spend your money in areas with the potential for the greatest financial returns. The assumptions that are part of the computations necessary to make the fixed asset rate of return analysis are, by their very nature, merely estimates. Disciplining yourself, however, to make these computations will be another way for your business to profit in today's and tomorrow's economy.

92. EVALUATE THE ECONOMIC VIABILITY OF MAJOR EXPENDITURES

HOW DOES THIS APPLY TO MY BUSINESS?

_____

_____

_____

_____

_____

Priority   1   2   3   (Circle one)

Action Date_____

Profit Champion _____

Potential Dollar Effect $_____

CASH IN ON INTEREST-BEARING "SWEEP" ACCOUNTS

If you've never heard of a "sweep" account, you have plenty of company. Some banks don't promote these arrangements and as a result many business owners who maintain healthy checking account balances are unaware of them. As a result, a lot of companies are missing an opportunity for a real financial windfall.

"Sweeps" are essentially interest-bearing checking accounts for which you give the bank permission to invest, or "sweep," certain funds on a day-to-day basis. A typical arrangement could provide that any funds in the account in excess of, say, $25,000, may be invested in overnight paper. You can aggregate accounts for the account balance threshold.

You may not find these kinds of accounts listed among the services offered at your bank. But if the bank does offer these arrangements and you ask about them, you will get the full story.

Take the case of the international mail-order business that routinely keeps large amounts of cash on deposit for short periods. At any given time, this business averages at least $500,000 in its checking account.

When the vice president of the company's bank, with which it had been doing business with for 30 years, was queried about the possibility of securing interest on its deposits, he replied: "A sweeps account? We've been offering those for the past ten years." The mail-order house promptly filled out the paperwork and began earning interest the next day. For thirty years the bank had a free ride on their money — now it was our client's turn to pocket the increase.

A word of caution: "Sweep" accounts are not FDIC-insured. If the bank fails, you may lose your money. Of course, even with a traditional account, FDIC only covers the first $100,000 on deposit. So if you have considerably more than that routinely, sitting in a non-interest bearing checking account, you're not really risking anything by assigning the amount in excess of $100,000 to a "sweep."

---

93. CASH IN ON INTEREST-BEARING "SWEEP" ACCOUNTS

HOW DOES THIS APPLY TO MY BUSINESS?

_____

_____

_____

_____

_____

Priority   1   2   3   (Circle one)

Action Date_____

Profit Champion _____

Potential Dollar Effect $_____

94

100 Ways to Profit
In the New Economy

DETERMINE WHAT TO DO
WITH EXTRA CASH

Without the money to modernize facilities, hire additional employees, and expand into new markets, a company may miss out on opportunities that can ensure the success of the enterprise.

The debt that a business accumulates can eat away at your organization from within. Indeed, this has been the ruin of thousands of companies, from mom-and-pop operations to giant multinational corporations.

If your business is fortunate enough to have some extra cash available, one of the smartest moves you could make might be to reduce the company's debt. At the same time, however, one of the dumbest moves you could make might be to repay debt.

The reason for this apparent contradiction is that not all debt is the same. Let's say your company has the good fortune to have $1 million on hand, and that you've got those funds in certificates of deposit earning you 5-1/2 percent. Suppose, at the same time, that your firm enjoys an open line of credit from a lender, and that you have borrowed several million dollars on that line at 9-1/2 percent interest.

If you were to liquidate your CDs at the first opportunity and use the proceeds to reduce the unpaid balance on your credit line, your company would be money ahead. The difference between the interest you're receiving on your CDs and the rate you're paying on the line of credit is 4 percent. On $1 million, that translates into $40,000 a year on the bottom line!

Suppose, however, that one of your competitors was in the same boat as you—$1 million in 5-1/2 percent CDs and a loan for which the firm is paying 9-1/2 percent. In the case of "Company X," however, let's say that instead of a line of credit obligation, your competitor owes money on some machinery. If Mr. X liquidates his CDs and reduces his equipment loan, his company will also save $40,000 each year. But unlike you, your competitor may have made a fatal mistake.

A line of credit is a renewable cash resource. If you pay it down and discover later that your business needs funds, you can easily re-borrow. Other debt, such as your competitor's equipment loan, is typically not renewable. Paying off this type of loan can be risky business. If you pay off such a debt and subsequently discover that you need to re-borrow funds, you may not be able to do so.

Remember that the time to arrange for a line of credit is when business is good, then forget about it until the crunch hits. That can be a prescription for disaster, however. Trouble is, in a slower economy, bankers are quick to pull in their horns. If your line of credit has been inactive, the bank may terminate your account with little or no warning.

A prominent and very successful physician had a line of credit of $100,000. He secured that line years ago, but never used it. It was an umbrella stored in the closet for a rainy day.

The doctor's collections fell off and his cash flow dried to a trickle. No problem, though. He just wrote himself a check for $20,000 from the credit line, deposited it in his checking account, and used that money to pay all his business and personal bills. Suddenly, however, all of those checks started bouncing!

As it turned out, the credit-line check was no good. Because there had been no activity on the account for several years, the lender terminated the credit line. Supposedly, a notice had been sent to the physician at that time, but he didn't recall seeing it. The damage was done in any event.

This situation could have cascaded into a real catastrophe for the doctor. With the help of a good credit rating and some fancy footwork, however, the physician was able to secure $20,000 of financing from other sources, and all the checks that he wrote were ultimately honored. But it certainly was a very embarrassing episode.

You can avoid similar problems by giving your line of credit a little periodic exercise. Lenders aren't likely to terminate an account that is active and in good standing. Even if you don't need funds, it may be wise to borrow on your credit line occasionally.

Let's say you're able to secure a line of credit of $100,000, and you want to make sure it will remain active and available to you in a crunch. Periodically write yourself a loan for $100,000, place those funds in an interest-bearing account for a month, then pay back the line of credit.

Suppose the spread between the interest charged by the lender and the rate you receive on your deposits is 3 percent. The cost to you of exercising your credit line would then be $250 ($100,000 X 3 percent X 1/12). The cost is less than that after the tax savings. That's a dirt cheap way of ensuring continued access to a $100,000 parachute!

---

94. DETERMINE WHAT TO DO WITH EXTRA CASH

HOW DOES THIS APPLY TO MY BUSINESS?

_____

_____

_____

_____

_____

Priority   1   2   3   (Circle one)

Action Date_____

Profit Champion _____

Potential Dollar Effect $_____

95

100 Ways to Profit In the New Economy

INVEST YOUR ASSETS WISELY

If a business had $100 million invested for 24 years at 6 percent interest, that business would have approximately $400 million at the end of that time. If another business was willing to accept the risk and invested in mutual funds with a 20 percent growth rate, their $100 million for the same 24 year period, including dividends and appreciation, would be worth approximately $7.9 billion. Just as you do with your personal finances, educate yourself on opportunities for investing your business's extra cash. **Remember that if Christopher Columbus had invested $1.00 in 1492 in a 5 percent interest-bearing account, it would be worth $41 billion today. That's the power of compound interest.**

If you find your company with excess cash, establish a company investment policy, then consider the investment options below:

- *Certificates of Deposit.* **Certificates of Deposit (CDs) offer flexible terms of from seven days to over a year, and variable-rate CDs are available. Companies can use staggered maturity dates to meet cash needs. The interest rates can be negotiable based on strength of banking relationship.**

- *Government Securities.* **Treasury Bills (T-bills) are debt obligations of the U.S. Government and are not taxed by states. The minimum investment is $10,000 with maturities from 90 days to one year. Since there is a large secondary market for T-bills, they are very liquid. Treasury notes and bonds are similar to T-bills except that they carry longer maturities (notes - two years or more; bonds - twenty years or more). Interest rates are generally low. Obligations of federal government agencies (such as the Federal National Mortgage**

412

Association) carry higher rates, but are not backed by the full faith and credit of the U.S. Government.

- *Commercial Paper.* Commercial paper represents unsecured promissory notes issued by corporations for short-term financing needs. Maturity ranges from overnight to 270 days. Commercial paper is not generally marketable.

- *Banker's Acceptances.* Banker's acceptances represent drafts issued by corporation and guaranteed by the bank on which they are drawn. Maturities range from 30 days to one year and they can be sold before maturity.

- *Repurchase Agreements.* Repurchase agreements (repos) represent a purchase of securities (generally government obligations) accompanied by agreements to resell them. The difference between the purchase price and the sales price represents the earnings to the investor. The agreements can be arranged for any time period and are often used for overnight and weekend investments. They generally require larger investments.

- *Eurodollar Certificates of Deposit.* Eurodollar Certificates are dollar-denominated negotiable investments that represent a time deposit with a foreign bank or foreign branch of a domestic bank. Maturities are 30 days or more.

These investments provide income that is taxable. The following investment vehicles, which are all relatively low-risk and liquid, offer tax advantages that can provide a higher effective rate of return. Type of entity (partnership, C corporation, or S corporation) may affect the taxability of the investments.

- *Tax-Exempt Funds.* Tax-exempt funds invested in one or more of the varieties of municipal obligations that include municipal bonds, notes, variable rate notes and tax-exempt commercial paper. There are also tax-free money market funds for short-term investments. These are tax-free for C corporations, partners or partnerships, and S corporation shareholders. They may be taxable for state income or franchise tax purposes.

- *Preferred Stock Funds.* These mutual funds hold variable rate and sometimes high-grade, fixed-rate preferred stocks. The dividends may be substantially federal tax exempt. This exclusion is available only to C corporations.

- *Variable-Rate Preferred Stock.* Variable-rate preferred stock is an investment vehicle designed to protect principal (avoiding possible nondeductible capital losses) while taking advantage of the 70- percent dividend exclusion available to C corporations. Investment is in preferred stock of public companies.

For cash that is believed to be available on a long-term basis, these alternatives are appropriate if risk tolerance is low. If you want to be more speculative, there are many other investment choices. These include common stocks (from New York Stock Exchange to over-the-counter markets), corporate bonds, commodities (e.g. gold or silver), options, futures, deeds of trust, limited partnerships, and real estate. The components of the long-term investment mix should be guided by your company investment policy.

---

95. INVEST YOUR ASSETS WISELY

HOW DOES THIS APPLY TO MY BUSINESS?

_____

_____

_____

_____

_____

Priority   1   2   3   (Circle one)

Action Date_____

Profit Champion _____

Potential Dollar Effect $_____

USE A MONTHLY CASH FLOW ANALYSIS TO FORECAST FINANCING NEEDS

The right time to secure financing is when your company is healthy and your financial statements are strong; the worst time to borrow is when your company is in dire straits. The trick is to determine your financing needs at least several months in advance.

Every business should make monthly analyses projecting cash flow for at least the next 12 months. A number of software programs can help you prepare these types of projections for your company. With these analyses, you can predict the lean months, anticipate cash flow crunches, and take corrective action well in advance.

Forewarned by the results of your monthly cash flow analyses, you can discuss your borrowing needs with your banker at a time when you have a variety of options available to you. For their part, lenders are more than willing to work with businesses that display an ability to plan in advance and manage their own destiny.

Indeed, a banker would much rather deal with a business person who expresses a need for financing six months down the road in order to ride out the slow season or replace aging equipment or whatever. In contrast, businesses that wait until the last minute and then call the bank in a panic are risking rejection.

We have accompanied many of our clients to the bank armed with monthly cash flow analyses, and invariably we get a warm reception. These projections eliminate the element of surprise for the banker, and that's half the battle in securing a loan.

96. USE A MONTHLY CASH FLOW ANALYSIS TO FORECAST FINANCING NEEDS

HOW DOES THIS APPLY TO MY BUSINESS?

_____

_____

_____

_____

_____

Priority   1   2   3   (Circle one)

Action Date_____

Profit Champion _____

Potential Dollar Effect $_____

TAP YOUR LIFE INSURANCE FOR FINANCING

In the best of times, if you go to the bank for a loan you might expect to pay at least 7.5 percent to 12 percent for the money. Under less than ideal circumstances, you could count on being hit with somewhat higher interest rates.

Many business owners, however, forget that they're sitting on a cheap and easily accessible source of financing — the cash value of the whole life insurance policies that they've taken out over the years, either personally or through the company. If these policies have been in force for any period of time, you may have accumulated a considerable cash surrender value against which you are able to borrow.

Borrowing against the value of a whole life policy is a lot easier and often cheaper than trying to squeeze money out of a reluctant banker. Typically, you don't need collateral and it doesn't matter what shape your finances are in because the policy is the source for repayment.

Moreover, you can tap into the accumulated value of such a policy at interest rates that would make a miser blush. If you've had your policy for 30 years or so, you may be able to borrow cash on it for as little as four percent. But even if your policy was taken out within the past five years, you might well be able to secure a loan on the policy at somewhere in the neighborhood of eight percent. The icing, however, is that unlike a bank loan, money that you borrow on the cash value of your whole life insurance policy never has to be repaid during your lifetime. It can be repaid at death, with the death benefits.

As attractive as this financing alternative is, consider borrowing on a whole life insurance policy only when all else fails. This should be your last resort — the trump card you play when the chips are down. As long as you are able to line up other sources of financing, keep your life insurance as your ace in the hole.

Talk with your insurance agent about this, and at the same time ask for a rundown of all your current policies, premiums, and cash values.

---

97. TAP YOUR LIFE INSURANCE FOR FINANCING

HOW DOES THIS APPLY TO MY BUSINESS?

_____

_____

_____

_____

_____

Priority   1   2   3   (Circle one)

Action Date_____

Profit Champion _____

Potential Dollar Effect $_____

REFINANCE DEBTS TO TRIM INTEREST COSTS

If interest rates decline, take advantage of reduced credit costs by refinancing existing debts. As a rule of thumb, if you own mortgaged property that you expect to keep for at least two years, consider refinancing when rates drop by two percent. The loan origination fee and other closing costs may work out to a few points — but it could be an amount you're able to recoup in less than a year because of the annual interest rate savings. By refinancing you can reduce your monthly mortgage payments, and over the remaining years of the loan you could end up saving thousands of dollars.

Not bad...but no cigar! If cash flow is not a problem, consider a different arrangement. Instead of reducing your monthly payments, refinance to reduce the term of your mortgage. Because of the lower interest rate, you may pay off your mortgage in fewer years, while keeping the same monthly payments.

The bottom line is that you may be able to eliminate a number of monthly payments on your home mortgage.

In another example, a medical group practice purchased its own office building several years ago. They were able to obtain a $1 million mortgage on the building at 10 percent. When rates dropped below 8.5 percent, they explored refinancing options.

One of the partners in the medical practice, however, owned a home in which he had $1 million in equity. The lender was more than happy to finance the doctor's residence at less interest cost than on the office building. He used the $1 million that he borrowed on his home at

7 percent to pay off the 10 percent loan on the office building. The savings—3 percent of $1 million— equaled $30,000 a year.

The doctor did have a loan origination fee and other closing costs to pay. These fees came to roughly 2-1/2 points, or about $25,000. But the physician more than recouped these charges from his interest savings in the first several years. Indeed, considering the 25-year term of the new mortgage, the effective annual cost of the refinancing was only $1,000 per year.

Look at all of your borrowings, i.e. machinery and equipment, lines of credit, inventory, accounts receivable, working capital, etc., and determine if there can be interest savings by refinancing now.

Be sure to review all loan documents, as well as rates and collateral reported in the footnotes to your financial statements. Perhaps, you can negotiate terms that will reduce the collateral if loan payments are paid promptly for a set period of time. Question the rates your bank is offering you. Many think that prime rates are for prime customers only. This is not the case. Try asking for London Inter Bank Offered Rates (LIBOR), often cheaper than prime rates for a bigger customer with good credit.

98. REFINANCE DEBTS TO TRIM INTEREST COSTS
HOW DOES THIS APPLY TO MY BUSINESS?

Priority   1   2   3   (Circle one)

Action Date_____

Profit Champion _____

Potential Dollar Effect $_____

SHIELD PERSONAL ASSETS FROM CREDITORS

If you learn nothing else from this book, remember this: refuse to use personal assets to secure company debts, and never allow your spouse to sign for a business loan...if at all possible.

When you go to a bank for a loan, the banker will try to get as much collateral as possible from you. As a result, many loans are over-collateralized and businesses that agree to these terms are suffering because of them.

One entrepreneur is in dire straits today because of this very problem. He purchased a piece of raw land with hopes for a substantial gain when the property was sold. The lender was all too willing to provide financing — as long as the investor and his wife agreed to personally guarantee the loan. Unfortunately, the investor accepted those terms.

Now, the unfortunate entrepreneur can't sell the property, and he certainly can't undertake the risk of developing it. Although he has been able to manage the monthly payments on the note, there is a $2.5 million balloon payment coming up, and it may just burst his bubble.

If the lender forecloses on the property, the proceeds from the sale may not be enough to satisfy the loan. In that case, the bank will be able to seize the investor's assets to satisfy the debt. Worse yet, because the investor's wife also signed the note the bank can also go after her property as well, including their home.

The advice we give to our clients is to offer lenders as little collateral as they have to, and treat their family assets as an ace in the hole. The wise ones follow that advice. One business owner applied for a loan of approximately $1 million to modernize her operations. The bank agreed, but asked for a second trust on all of the company's real estate. In addition, the lender demanded that all of the business's other assets be put up as security, and that both the owner and her spouse personally guarantee the note.

If she had agreed to these demands and needed to borrow additional funds at a future date, she would have been out of luck...and possibly out of business. All of her assets—business as well as personal—would have been tied up to secure that note. There would have been no collateral available to obtain additional financing for other business opportunities. With our encouragement, the business owner balked at the bank's demands, and the lender ultimately agreed to take only $1.2 million of collateral on the $1 million loan.

In another example, a law firm applied for a business loan, only to be told by the bank that it would be necessary for the spouses of the partners to personally guarantee the firm's indebtedness. The lawyers told the lender that this was unacceptable, and that they would not do business with the bank under such conditions.

Ultimately, they struck a compromise. Instead of requiring the partners' wives to co-sign the loan, the bank agreed to a plan under which life insurance policies of the partners were assigned to the bank as collateral. If the law firm fails because of the death of one of the partners, the bank is protected from loan default by the proceeds of that partner's life insurance policy. But even if the worst happens, the jointly-held personal wealth of the partners and their families will not be in jeopardy.

Consider establishing limited liability corporations, limited liability partnerships and trusts that not only bring positive tax benefits but truly shield the business's owners.

99. SHIELD PERSONAL ASSETS FROM CREDITORS
HOW DOES THIS APPLY TO MY BUSINESS?

_____

_____

_____

_____

_____

Priority   1   2   3   (Circle one)

Action Date_____

Profit Champion _____

Potential Dollar Effect $_____

100

ANALYZE PRICING
STRUCTURES

A seemingly simple way to improve profits is to raise prices. But let's take a look at what really happens when prices rise. In the following price matrix, first look under the column closest to your organization's gross profit percentage and the row corresponding to your projected price increase or decrease. The percentage computed where the column and the row meet illustrates how much the percentage of sales must decline or increase in order to break even.

		Gross Profit Percentage						
		20%	30%	45%	50%	60%	70%	80%
		Sales can decline by as much as:						
	5%:	-20%	-14%	-10%	- 9%	- 8%	- 7%	- 6%
Price	**10%:**	-33%	-25%	-18%	-17%	-14%	-13%	-11%
Increase	**15%:**	-43%	-33%	-25%	-23%	-20%	-18%	-16%
	20%:	-50%	-40%	-31%	-29%	-25%	-22%	-20%
		Sales must increase by at least:						
	5%:	33%	20%	13%	11%	9%	8%	7%
Price	**10%:**	100%	50%	29%	25%	20%	17%	14%
Decrease	**15%:**	300%	100%	50%	43%	33%	27%	23%
	20%:	n/a	200%	80%	67%	50%	40%	33%

(The -10% value in the 45% column, 5% Price Increase row is circled.)

Now let's look at how we did the computations for this chart so that you can recompute the percentage in ranges specific to your organization.

	Dollar	**Percentages**
Sales	$1,000,000	100%
Cost of Sales	(550,000)	(55%)
Gross profit	$ 450,000	45%

Now assume you want to increase your gross profit to 50 percent. Work the computation in reverse. If your financial goal is a gross profit of $450,000, by increasing your gross profit percentage to 50 percent, cost of sales would be $450,000 (50 percent of sales). Sales would be the sum of Gross Profit ($450,000) + Cost of Sales ($450,000) = $900,000.

Next study this illustration:

Gross Profit	$450,000	50% of sales
Cost of Sales	450,000	50% of sales
Sales Necessary to Achieve Financial Goal	$900,000	100%
Actual Sales Prior to Increase in Gross Profit Percentage	($1,000,000)	
Projected Decrease in Sales to Break Even	($100,000)	
Decrease in Sales to Break Even / Actual Sales Prior to Change in Gross Profit Percentage	(100,000) / $1,000,000	= -10%*

*In the chart, the amount in the 5% Price Increase row under the 45% column.

Therefore if prices increase by 5 percent, sales can decrease by 10 percent and gross profit will remain the same. Now look back at the chart under the 45% column and the row for a 5% price increase, and find the percentage where both intersect. It is -10 percent, the same percentage as computed in the previous example.

Here is a shortcut formula for computing the sales necessary to break even, if the gross profit is changed:

$$\frac{\text{Gross Profit in Dollars}}{\text{Gross Profit as a Percentage}} = \frac{\text{Sales Necessary}}{\text{to Break Even}}$$

Using the previous example: $\dfrac{\$450,000}{50\%} = \$900,000$ (*same as computed above*)

You can prepare a matrix for your own company, illustrating the sensitivity of price changes to sales. **As you begin to analyze it with your profit advisor, you might be surprised at how much additional business you need to break even when you cut prices. The opposite is equally true: When you increase prices you may be more profitable even with a shrinkage in volume.**

---

100. ANALYZE PRICING STRUCTURES
HOW DOES THIS APPLY TO MY BUSINESS?

_____

_____

_____

_____

_____

Priority   1   2   3   (Circle one)

Action Date_____

Profit Champion _____

Potential Dollar Effect $_____

101

POSTSCRIPT — WHO'S WHO IN THE "100 WAYS"

No book entitled "All About Earnings" would be complete without a final acknowledgment of the source of this information and the people behind it.

Indeed, the surest way not to profit in any kind of economy is to fail to recognize the people who make our accomplishments possible.

This book, and the ideas in it, are the fruits of the collective experience and expertise of our staff, clients, and all of the wise business people we have learned from throughout our forty years of collective experience. We continue to learn from each other.

The members of the Institute of Profit Advisors, a North American organization that we co-founded with Practice Development Institute, LLC (PDI) and the Association of Profit Advisors in the United Kingdom (of which we are honorary members), continue to inspire us to dedicate much of our professional careers to adding value to businesses throughout the world.

Kathleen Hughes, our Capital Books publisher, is a joy to work with. She has a unique gift of charm and wit, along with extraordinary writing and marketing skills. She helped us document the many thoughts, systems, and activities that make up this book.

Thanks to our friends and families for their continued support even though precious time was taken from them to write this book. Special thanks to Elinor Schimel, Barry's wife and longtime brainstorming partner, who shared creative ideas and thoughts on how to make this book so meaningful to all readers.

Barry also applauds his own profit team and coach, Gary R. Kravitz, who is so very special in so many ways. Not only has this creation of this book been intellectually fulfilling, but also it has been one of the greatest professional experiences. We wouldn't be teammates if it were not for the Profit Game. Our team has learned how to play and how to win. A special thanks to our master team strategist, Barry J. Friedman, CPA, who is a clear thinker with extraordinary vision.

To our all-star team, David S. Ross, Michael LeMaster, Melissa A. Kamp, Ellen Katz, Jo Anne King, who have always believed in the profit process because they know it's "all about earnings."

We all hope you will take the initiative now to put the Profit Enhancement Process to play in your business. It's a system that will deliver never-ending profits and real value to businesses that manage it effectively. It's your game plan for winning the Profit Game. It's "all about earnings." If you are ready to take your business to a new level of profit*ability,* give us a call at 1-800-WE-PROFIT. Or visit us on our Web site www.weprofit.com.

THE
PROFIT ADVISORS'
Master Action
Profit Plan
for

_____

Name of Your Company

Instructions:
In the following pages, check each of the strategies that you noted in the text as applying to your business and complete the columns as indicated. When you've finished, you'll have a Master Action Profit Plan ready to put to work for your business.

Number & Strategy	Priority 1-2-3	Action Date	Profit Champion	Potential Dollar Effect	Comments
Part 1: Sales & Marketing					
1. Create sales and marketing action plans					
2. Stretch advertising dollars					
3. Survey customers about your business					
4. Increase profits by charging the right price					
5. Broaden markets by bundling products and services					
6. Identify your company's edge in the marketplace					
7. Use trickle marketing for qualified leads					
8. Keep tabs on competitors' prices					
9. Monitor competition to keep on top of the market					
10. Institute the lost sales report to discover what you aren't selling					
11. Establish a sales process					
12. Join the E-Commerce revolution ASAP					
13. Tie sales compensation to meaningful goals					
14. Maintain quality customer relations					
15. Buy something from your company					
16. Put yourself in charge of customer relations					
17. Get your customer to complain					
18. Expand business hours to rope in new customers					

Number & Strategy	Priority 1-2-3	Action Date	Profit Champion	Potential Dollar Effect	Comments
Part 2: Operations					
19. Monitor costs and uses of company vehicles					
20. Eliminate unnecessary utility costs					
21. Sublet unused space					
22. Don't fall in love with your inventory					
23. Guard against losses from theft					
24. Email that's efficient, economical, exciting...					
25. Make sure you are getting value for entertainment and business travel expenses					
26. Slash paper					
27. Cancel insurance on unused vehicles and equipment					
28. Shift to short-term leases to limit exposure					
29. Renegotiate lease terms to mesh with business cycles					
30. Dispose of idle assets					
31. Adopt and monitor credit and collections policies and procedures					
32. Add value to your business: don't buy a job					
33. Use a dunning service to minimize collection agency fees					

Number & Strategy	Priority 1-2-3	Action Date	Profit Champion	Potential Dollar Effect	Comments
34. Use technology to speed sales and collections and trim expenses					
35. Establish cash controls that accelerate deposits					
36. Obtain bids from vendors					
37. Manage supplies as you manage inventory					
38. Scale back orders, but pounce on deals					
39. Avoid costly equipment buying blunders					
40. Pay bills when they're due--but not before					
41. Take advantage of purchase discounts					
42. Use a bank lock box					
43. Control service contract expenditures					
44. Preventing Problems = Recurring Profits					
45. Base Your Prices on Profit Goals, Not Sales' Egos					
46. Make Every Employee a Profit Enhancement Officer (PEO)					

431

Number & Strategy	Priority 1-2-3	Action Date	Profit Champion	Potential Dollar Effect	Comments
Part 3: Organizational Structure					
47. Identify profit centers, keep the winners and lose the losers					
48. Be a hands-on manager					
49. Determine whether managers are managing too little or too much					
50. Make everyone in your business responsible for profit					
51. Establish expense authorization responsibilities					
52. Develop financial flash reports					
53. Systematically increase profits in five easy steps					
54. Draw up contingency plans					
55. Outsourcing provides significant benefits					
56. Form your own team of profit advisors					
57. Protect your company's most valuable asset: yourself					
58. Reshuffle staff duties and cross-train employees to control costs					
59. Eliminate work, not people					
60. Turn your management team into a profit team					

Number & Strategy	Priority 1-2-3	Action Date	Profit Champion	Potential Dollar Effect	Comments
61. Show your employees how a bigger bottomline benefits them as well as the company					
62. Form an internal cost-control committee to trim waste					
63. Use technology to monitor your company's performance					
64. Trim training costs with procedures manuals					
65. Eliminate unproductive meetings					
66. Tap into industry trade and professional associations as well as franchisors					
Part 4: Employees					
67. Link bonuses to performance					
68. Give your employees a raise with the government's money					
69. Reward employees with non-cash compensation					
70. Pay people what they are worth					
71. Farm out payroll chores					
72. Staff with leased employees					

Number & Strategy	Priority 1-2-3	Action Date	Profit Champion	Potential Dollar Effect	Comments
Part 4: Employees *continued*					
73. Make everyone responsible for customer service					
74. Shave labor costs with part-timers					
75. Control employee overtime					
76. Be creative with employees' work schedules					
77. Evaluate staff productivity objectively					
78. Seize opportunities to upgrade your staff					
79. Reward employees for bright ideas					
Part 5: Financial Matters					
80. Take advantage of tax opportunities					
81. Compare increased sales with decreased costs					
82. Budgets may limit financial performance					
83. Negotiate special terms to stretch cash flow					
84. Review spending for publications and membership dues					
85. Develop, understand and monitor key operating statistics					

Number & Strategy	Priority 1-2-3	Action Date	Profit Champion	Potential Dollar Effect	Comments
Part 5: Financial Matters					
86. Measure the effectiveness of your business in key areas					
87. Keep your banker informed					
88. Pick your insurance agents' brains to control insurance premiums					
89. Tap outside investors for capital					
90. Review leases to control costs					
91. Schedule a year-end tax planning session with your CPA					
92. Evaluate the economic viability of major expenditures					
93. Cash in on interest-bearing sweep accounts					
94. Determine what to do with extra cash					
95. Invest your assets wisely					
96. Use a monthly cash flow analysis to forecast financing needs					
97. Tap your life insurance for financing					
98. Refinance debts to trim interest costs					
99. Shield personal assets from creditors					
100. Analyze pricing structures					

Total Potential $ Effect

435

BizActions™
Grow Your Business...
One Message at a Time

BizActions™ is an email communications, business planning, and reminder system that enhances and builds relationships while improving your organization's bottom line.

There are two opportunities for using **BizActions™**:

✔ **BizActions™** for your customers and prospects keeps them thinking of you 52 weeks a year with valuable content that can improve their profitability.

✔ **BizActions™** for you and your employees can increase your business know-how, make you and your team more effective and remind you of the things that need to be done to run your business more successfully.

Effortlessly, customers, prospects, and employees are emailed news and reminders to help them manage their business thus minimizing stress in their lives. In today's competitive world, your customers will appreciate year round business and tax ideas as well as reminders to help them achieve their profit potential. If customers and prospects only think of you periodically, you're missing countless opportunities to propel them and you to the next level of success and profitability.

Your customers, prospects, and employees will receive:

- Messages created by you and about your firm.
- Business tips in areas they choose as determined by their interests. Some representative categories are sales, marketing, finance, management, technology, operations, and human resources.
- Personal tax and financial planning tips. Another feature is a calendar of tax return due dates.
- Personal and business project management annoucing new products, services, and other items you may wish to communicate, as well as action reminders that customers and prospects choose to create.

We do it all for you!

Subscribe to **BizActions™** and we'll do the rest. We'll design your BizActions™ email alerts and co-branded Web sign-up pages, while making sure that your customers and prospects only receive messages from interest categories they select. You will be marketing to customers and prospects 52 weeks a year effortlessly, effectively, and economically.

To learn more about **BizActions™** as a marketing tool for your organization or to sign up for your own free personal use, visit our website. **www.BizActions.com.**

BizActions LLC
1-866-biztips

❏ Yes! Send me information on the following additional opportunities for "Profitability"...

❏ Profit Enhancement Process-100 Ways® and Workshops

The Profit Enhancement Process-100 Ways® and Workshops are designed to coach your organization's decision makers to be more competitive in the profit game—training them in how to play and how to win. Clients are coached to improve their profit*ability*, the skills necessary to recognize financial opportunities and turn ideas into bottom line results. We have been able to identify more than one third of a billion dollars in bottom line opportunities to clients throughout the world.

❏ Speaking Engagements

We are highly sought after speakers for industry meetings and business conferences. We also facilitate profit-generating business workshops, for groups as diverse as the *Success Magazine Conference on Entrepreneurial Leadership*, The American Management Association, The CEO Club, The Executive Committee (TEC), The Young President's Organization, The Young Entrepreneurs Organization, The National Automobile Dealers Association, American Booksellers Association, and the Automotive Parts Rebuilders Association. Our programs are tailored to your organization's needs, presenting a spectrum of ideas that produce dramatic bottom line results.

❏ InfoQuest®

If you looked at your business through your customers' eyes, what would you see? Studies have consistently shown that a "Totally Satisfied" customer is as much as ten times more likely to buy again than a customer who is merely "Somewhat Satisfied." InfoQuest® is a Business Process Review— a one-of-a-kind communication tool that measures and utilizes customer satisfaction to build customer relationships and sales. InfoQuest® surveys have been performed over 31,000 times in 41 countries (and in 16 languages) with an average response rate of 75-80%. InfoQuest® is an extraordinary way to measure your customers' satisfaction and build stronger relationships with your key accounts.

❏ Institute of Profit Advisors

The Profit Advisors, Inc. has teamed with approximately 100 affiliate firms, The Institute of Profit Advisors in the United States and the Association of Profit Advisors in the United Kingdom. We provide, through these internationally recognized affiliates, opportunities to work with your business. If you are interested in hearing more about how our affiliate in your area can help, please check this box.

❏ The Profit Advisors Profit Playbook—

Essential business fundementals for owners, managers, and staff have been incorporated into this unique system, *The Profit Advisors Playbook! The Profit Playbook* is a self-study program that has three components: 1) a comprehensive guidebook of profit-enhancing strategies; 2) a remarkable set of audio-tape interviews; and 3) computer software to help track your profit projects. In *The Profit Playbook*, you will find nearly five hundred proven business profit strategies, many of which can be implemented immediately! In addition, the tapes include interviews with Barry Schimel that dig into and uncover areas of immediate profit improvement. The software provides an easy tracking mechanism that allows your profit team to keep you updated on profit project progress. *The Profit Playbook* comes with a 30-day guarantee. Available in printed version or on CD-ROM.

For more information or to order, fax this sheet or call us with the following:

Don't forget to take a look at our Web site www.weprofit.com

NAME, TITLE, COMPANY _____

ADDRESS_____

CITY_____ STATE_____ ZIP_____

PHONE (*DIRECT DIAL*) _____

FAX _____

E-MAIL _____

# of EMPLOYEES _____

The Profit Advisors, Inc.
Profit Advisors Plaza
932-32B Hungerford Drive
Rockville, MD 20850-1713
Tel: 301-545-0477 "800-WE-PROFIT"
Fax: 301-545-0341

A

accountants, 401
acid test ratio, 387
acquisition, 404-05
advertising, 387
alternatives, 159-60
advertising-to-sales ratio, 387
assets, 62
    current ratio and, 387
    evaluating economic viability of
    acquisitions, 404-05
    idle, 238-39
    most valuable, 309
    shielding from creditors, 421-22
Association of Profit Advisors, 426
associations, trade and professional,
333-34
auditing
    of reports, 231
    of space, 400
    See also Profit Audit, the

B

banker's acceptances, 413
banks, 392-93
    bills and, 267
    cash flow analysis and finance fore
    casting and, 415
    deposits, 252-53
    deposits, lock boxes, 269-70
    "sweep" accounts, 407-08
billing, 242
    See also collections; payments (due)
bills, 265-66, 267-68
BizActions, 227, 436
bonuses, 337-39
brainstorming, 103-04, 319-20
budgeting
    financial performance and, 378-80
    traditional, 29, 31-32
business evaluation. *See* measuring; rating; surveying
business hours, 56-57
business plans, 50
business protection, 309-11
business success
    employees and, 20
    engines of, 80-81
    essentials of, 79
    fundamentals of, 99

business travel, 228-29
business value, 246-47
buy/sell agreement checklist for business partners, 309-11

C

cafeteria plan (Section 125), 340-41
capital, 321, 397-98
cash
    acid test ratio and, 387
    deposits and, 252-53, 252-53
    life insurance and, 417-18
    reducing debt and, 409-11
cash flow, 321
    analyzing to forecast financing
    needs, 415
    contingency planning and, 303-04
    stretching, 381-82
CEO Pledge, 96-98
Certificates of Deposit (CDs), 409-10,
412
    Eurodollar, 413
Certified Purchasing Managers (CPMs),
296
    collections, 241-44
collection agencies v. dunning services, 248-49
commercial paper, 413
compatibility, 168
compensation plans, 52, 155-56, 193-94
    Employee Stock Ownership Plan, 343
    phantom stock, 342-43
    Section 125 cafeteria plan, 340-41
competition, 168
    monitoring, 182-83
    pricing and, 179-80
complaints, 204-05
consumers. See customers
contingency plans (cash flow), 303
    developing, 304
cost control
    employee overtime, 354-55
    employee training, 313-14
    insurance premiums, 394-96
    leasing, 399-400
    service contracts, 271-72
    training and, 313-14
    waste, 324-25
cost-control committee, 324-25
cost cutting, 142-43, 146, 147-48

increasing sales and, 376-77
insurance, 232-33
labor, 352-53
leasing, 234-37
paper, 230-31
refinancing debt, 419-20
training, 328-29
utilities, 216-17
costs, 87, 144
customers and, 30
inventory and, 220
layoffs and, 316
most expensive, 92
pricing and, 167
travel and, 228-29
See also expenditures
CPAs (Certified Public Accountants), 401-02
credit, 410-11, 419-20
credit and collections, 241-44
creditors, 421-22
cross-selling, 143-44
cross-training, 313-14
current ratio, 387
customer expectation, 196-97
customer loyalty, 205-06, 350
discounting and, 276
customer relations, 202
maintaining quality with Customer Relations Index, 196-97
measuring (checklist), 390
customers, 49, 52, 53, 56, 144, 149-50, 168
complaints and, 204-05
credit and collections, 241-44
factors influencing buying decisions, 277
overhead and, 30
retention of, 196-97
surveying, 27-28, 162-63
survey sample, 164-66
Web sites and, 160, 191
customer satisfaction, 162, 205, 351
measuring (checklist), 390
customer service, 62, 321
making employees responsible for, 350-51
monitoring, 201
questionnaire, 198-99

D

daily sales to receivables ratio, 387
debt, 409-11
refinancing, 419-20
departmentalism, 120-21, 151, 300
deposits, 252-53, 407-08
lock boxes, 269-70
discounting, 243
customer confidence and, 276
payments and, 267-68
distribution channels, 168
document imaging, 230-31
dunning services, 248-49

E

e-commerce, 250
email, 226-27, 250, 436
employees, 2, 61, 65, 118, 122, 151
bonuses and, 337-39
business plans and, 50
business success and, 20
compensation plans, 52, 340-41, 342-43
exit questionnaire, 136-38
idle, 313
interviewing as consultants, 26-27
interviewing for profit opportunities, 58-59
job security and, 321
layoffs and, 316
Master Action Profit Plan, 433-34
as most valuable business resource, 322
motivation and, 105
outsourcing, 305-06
part-time, 352-53
performance checklist, 390
and personnel manuals of, 48
as Profit Enhancement Officers, 71-72
profit strategies and, 149-50
rating company standing with, 55
rewarding, 73, 105, 149, 368
surveying as consultants, 26-27
as team members, 19, 20
theft and, 224-25
training and, 313-14, 328-29
turnover and, 53, 135
See also management